To: Carol

Thank for m...

look so good is r...

INDUSTRY 5.0

Why The Next Industrial Revolution Will Be All About Sustainability

To: Wol

Thank for making me
Look so good in print!

Copyright © 2024, Heartland Press

All rights reserved. No part of this publication may be reproduced, distributed, or transmitted in any form or by any means, including photocopying, recording, or other electronic or mechanical methods, without the prior written permission of the publisher, except in the case of brief quotations embodied in critical reviews and certain other noncommercial uses permitted by copyright law. For permission requests, write to the publisher, addressed "Attention: Permissions Coordinator," at the address below.

ISBN: 979-8-9898863-3-3 (Paperback)

Any references to historical events, real people, or real places are used fictitiously. Names, characters, and places are products of the author's imagination.

Book design by Ghazal/Mina.

Printed by KDP, in the United States of America.

First printing edition 2024.

www.industry5-0book.com

Contents

Acknowledgments..XI

Forward...XII

Preface from the Author XIII

About this Book XVI

The Tie to Maslow's Hierarchy of Needs...............................XVI

How This Book is Structured XX

Part I..1

The History of Industrial Revolutions....................................1

Chapter 1: 3

The Impact of Industrial Revolutions....................................3

What Constitutes a "Revolution"? 3

How We Got to Industry 5.0 5

What Are Our Four Accepted Revolutions?...............................7

Chapter 2: 11

The First Industrial Revolution 11

Industry 1.0: The Steam Revolution..11

The Central Technologies of 1.0..12

The Cons of Industry 1.0..13

Chapter 3: 17

The Second Industrial Revolution 17

The Shift to Industry 2.0: The Mechanical Revolution 18

The Central Technologies of 2.0..19

The Cons of Industry 2.0..27

Chapter 4: 31

The Third Industrial Revolution 31

IV

Industry 3.0: The Digital Transformation 31

Why and When Did Industry 3.0 Start? 32

The Central Technologies of 3.0 34

The Cons of Industry 3.0 38

Chapter 5: 41

The Fourth Industrial Revolution 41

Industry 4.0: The Rise of IoT and Automation 41

The Central Technologies of 4.0 44

Industry 4- 4.1 - AI - Mimicking Human Intelligence 47

Automation 51

Internet of Things (IoT) 53

AI and the Human Body 54

The Cons of Industry 4.0 55

Part II 59

The Fifth Industrial Revolution: Sustainability 59

Chapter 6: 61

The Definition of Sustainability 61

The Sustainability Movement 62

Chapter 7: 71

What is Industry 5.0? 71

Why is 5.0 a Revolution? 71

A Bridge Between Capitalism and Sustainability 74

The New Era of Industry 5.0: We're Going All In. 75

Chapter 8: 79

How Will 5.0 Start? 79

New SEC goals 80

The UNSDGs 83

Chapter 9: 103

What 5.0 Means to Society 103

    Did the Pandemic Change Our Thinking? 121

    Can we Achieve a Net Zero Economy? 123

Chapter 10: 129

What Industry 5.0 Means to Manufacturing 129

    Sustainability in Transportation 129

    Sustainability in Construction..131

    Sustainability in Packaging 132

    Sustainability in the Manufacturing Process 138

Chapter 11: 153

What 5.0 Means to Farming 153

    Regenerative Agriculture 153

    How Did We Get Here? 156

    What Were the Outcomes of The Dust Bowl? 158

    How This Led to Today's Farming Practices......................159

    Is Regenerative Farming New?..164

Chapter 12: 167

What 5.0 Means to Business..167

    Mandates, Reporting, and Regulation 167

    Sustainable Business Glossary 169

Chapter 13: 191

How 5.0 Will Build Brand Value...191

    What is Brand Equity? 191

    Where Sustainability Fits into Today's Business Brands 193

Weighing Long-term Outcomes vs. Short-term Costs............198

Sustainability and Your Brand...200

Chapter 14: 211

What 5.0 Means to Investors...211

Investing in Innovation...214

Why Investors Should Look at Sustainable Businesses..........217

Carbon Markets...222

Taxation..223

Cap and Trade...227

Is There a Compromise Between Tax and Trade?...................230

Chapter 15: 235

How 5.0 Will Correct the Ills of the First Four Revolutions 235

Why is 5.0 a Natural Evolution of 1-4? 235

We Really Don't Have a Choice...236

Chapter 16: 241

Why Innovation is Crucial to a 5.0 World 241

Innovation and Commercialization 242

Electric Vehicles 245

Recycling Overview..247

Innovations in Recycling..252

New Materials..259

The Early History of Materials Innovation 260

Additive Production Methods 269

A Case Study on Materials and Cooperation..........................271

The Future of 5.0 Materials..273

Part III...277

People - Planet – Potential 277

Chapter 17: 279

People - The New Sustainable Leadership Era 279

Why Leadership Matters 279

The Sustainable Board.. 281

The Sustainable CEO.. 283

The Role of CSOs 289

Decentralized Leadership in 5.0 293

Chapter 18: 299

Planet - Engineering Earth 299

How Do We Engineer an Entire Planet?........................... 300

Education 303

Innovation... 304

Collaboration.. 305

The Approach to On-farm Processes 306

Commercialization of Biomaterials for Industrial Use.......... 307

Engineering Earth Outcomes 309

Chapter 19: 313

Potential - Where Can We Go from Here?............................ 313

A Focus on Saving Our Natural Resources...................... 314

Reversing Biodiversity Loss 315

Sustainable Development 316

Renewable Energy Everywhere.. 317

Sustainable Cities Become the Norm 318

Circular Economies Prevail 319

New Technology Leads the Way....................................... 320

Sustainable Agriculture Worldwide 322

Conservation Will Be Natural and Effortless.............................323

Becoming a Fully Sustainable Planet 323

Appendix A...327

Sustainable Business Glossary...327

About the Author...345

Table of Figures

Figure 1 - Medical Devices of the 1800s 5
Figure 2 - Steam Pump 11
Figure 3 - Steel Foundry 19
Figure 4 - Oil Refinery 21
Figure 5 - Michael Faraday 23
Figure 6 - Tenement Housing 1800s 28
Figure 7 - Jefferson's Cipher Wheel 31
Figure 8 - Vacuum Tube, Transistor, and Integrated Circuit Chip .. 32
Figure 9 - ENIAC Computer 33
Figure 10 - Intel 4004 Microprocessor 33
Figure 11 - Industrial Robot 42
Figure 12 - 3D Printed Tissue Cells 55
Figure 13 - Earth Day Flag 1970 64
Figure 14 - Bhadla Solar Park 104

Acknowledgments

As with most books (or any complex project) no single person is responsible for the effort; it requires teamwork. In my case, I have a host of people whose support and input made this whole thing possible.

First and foremost is my beautiful bride, Debbie. Her spirit and energy kept me going even when I wanted to throw in the towel. Next, are my business partners, Jesse Henry, and Tim Almond. On the day they got together to form Heartland Industries, the world changed for the better. They not only gave me the latitude to work on this book but provided the impetus for the entire work (and much of the sustainability movement).

Two professors, (who both have the distinction of not having me as a student) are also paramount to the project. First, Dr. Stephen Haag from the University of Denver, who asked me a simple question after reading a Heartland Article on Industry 5.0, "Have you thought about writing a book about this"? Well, we know the answer now!

Next was Dr. Roger Blackwell, the well-known marketing guru from The Ohio State University. Dr. Blackwell (as well as Dr. Haag) has dozens of books to his credit. His support and critical feedback shaped what you are about to read.

Jamie Pennington, Ghazal Raees, and Mina Siddiqui take the credit for editing, formatting, and all graphics.

Finally, I want to recognize all the Heartland partners that not only provided guidance for my research, but also direction for Heartland itself. They include Greentown Labs Boston, gener8tor and 1915 Studios in Neenah, WI, Newlab in Detroit, my Propel group from University of Michigan (yes, Ohio State and Michigan were on the same team here!), BASF, and Magna International.

Oh, I almost forgot my four-legged, furry officemate, Bailey. He didn't get much work done but was always on time.

Forward

By Dr. Roger Blackwell

The book Industry 5.0 is an insightful and detailed analysis of the transformative role of sustainability, which John Ely defines as "the practice of managing resources in such a way that economic, environmental, and social needs can be met both in the present and in the future. It is based on the idea of living within the limits of the natural environment while ensuring a high quality of life for all," building on a definition from the United Nations of sustainability, as "meeting the needs of the present without compromising the ability of future generations to meet their own needs." This analysis examines the topic of sustainability with the lens of a telescope to understand the past to predict where businesses must move to thrive in the future. It also examines sustainability with the lens of a microscope to determine catalysts in the present that predict which firms will win in the future.

While many readers might consider sustainability as a cost, this book will help disruptive leaders to achieve greater efficiency, productivity, and profit. If that sounds attractive, and you want to know how to do it, this is a book for you. If you believe a better environment is one in which humans have more interactions with each other than with hand-held devices, you will also enjoy reading this book. For people working in publicly owned firms or investing in them, concern about sustainability by the SEC and other regulatory agencies, understanding Industry 5.0 is already paramount. For everyone else, the reason for understanding Industry 5.0 is survival.

Warning! Your supply chain may never be the same!

By Roger Blackwell, Ph.D. retired professor at The Ohio State University and co-author of Objective Prosperity: How Behavioral Economics Can Improve Outcomes for You, Your Firm, and Your Nation.

Preface from the Author

The journey on the way to writing "Industry 5.0" has been interesting to say the least! I've compiled the majority of the words in this book, but in the beginning, Industry 5.0 wasn't even my idea! Let me explain.

My business partners at Heartland Industries are smart people. Very smart! Jesse Henry (CEO) and Tim Almond (COO) co-founded the company in 2020, and I was brought on as CMO about a year later.

Prior to me joining, Tim and Jesse were having an intellectual conversation late one evening about a recent article they read on the concept of Industry 4.0, and how it was morphing into Industry 5.0. Now, this "morphing" was simply moving to a higher level of 4.0's elements such as, AI, machine learning, and human-machine interfaces. Well, these two discussed this position deeply and felt that to qualify as an industrial revolution, then the elements needed to stand on their own and be more "revolutionary", and that a simple elevation of 4.0 might be 4.1 or 4.2 at best. But 5.0? No way!

This is when Tim made the proclamation that, "Industry 5.0 will be all about sustainability". From that moment forward, we were off to the races. As a side note, I've been a part of some of these late-night conversations and the topics can range from the existence of Bigfoot to quantum physics. If you ever get a chance to chat with one or both of them…please do so, you won't regret it!

Jesse, being a fine writer himself, drafted an article on the Heartland website (www.heartland.io) titled "Industry 5.0, A Bridge Between Capitalism and Sustainability" - what a great title (and concept).

Not long after that, I joined the firm and was working on updating articles for SEO. Yep, this whole thing started with an exercise in optimization. I updated "5.0" and shortly thereafter was contacted by Dr. Stephen Haag, a professor at the University of Denver. He saw the article on our site and wanted copies to share with his students. I think my exact words were, "Please share with anyone you want"! I

XIII

was just happy that the SEO worked, and someone read it. I sent the PDF and forgot about it.

About two months later, Dr. Haag contacted me again. He said his students loved the article and asked if I had considered expanding it into a book. Coincidently, I had considered it, along with a few of our other Heartland works. It was then that I got some insight into Dr. Haag's question.

It turns out that he is an expert on industrial revolutions, and author of a few books on Industry 4.0 himself. His viewpoint is that we are still in the midst of Industry 4.0 (and will be for years), and that 5.0 would have to be something radically different. What it would be, he didn't know...until he read that article.

So, that set me on a year-long project to research the topic deeper (not a stretch as Heartland is a sustainability-focused company) and start down the path to putting this book together. I'll be honest, it wasn't easy. I've done a lot of writing in my career, but a full book was something far beyond the 2,000-word articles I was accustomed to publishing.

In the end, I think we have a nice piece of work here. I use the term "we" (and I do throughout the book), as Jesse and Tim have contributed far beyond the initial idea and article; this was a true team effort.

My wish is that you enjoy the book and that you find it both informational *and* entertaining. It's written to be optimistic about our future on this planet and provide a bit of framework for our journey into a fully sustainable world. So, as I complete Industry 5.0, I'll catch my breath. But I won't rest for long. I'm sure my next mission will be a byproduct of one of those late-night conversations!

John

XV

About this Book

The Tie to Maslow's Hierarchy of Needs

In his 1943 paper "A Theory of Human Motivation", American psychologist Abraham Maslow proposed that humans follow a distinct pattern when solving, and subsequently addressing new problems.

His "Hierarchy of Needs" suggested how humans intrinsically partake in behavioral motivation. Maslow labeled the following - "Needs" in ascending order:

1. Physiological
2. Safety
3. Belonging and Love
4. Social or Esteem
5. Self-actualization and Transcendence

They describe the pattern through which human needs and motivations generally move.

This means that, according to the theory, for motivation to arise at the next stage each prior stage must be satisfied by an individual. The hierarchy has been used to explain how effort and motivation are correlated in the context of human behavior.

Each of these individual levels contains a certain amount of internal sensation that must be met for an individual to complete their hierarchy. The goal in Maslow's hierarchy is to attain the level or stage of self-actualization.

Maslow extended the idea to include his observations of humans' curiosity and their ongoing quests to improve their lives. The theory is a classification system intended to reflect the universal needs of society as its base, then proceeding to more acquired emotions.

As we outlined the ideas for this book, we realized that the four industrial revolutions (and now a fifth), coincided with Dr. Maslow's theories in a few ways.

First, humans will encounter a problem, devise a way or ways to solve it, and once resolved, they will seek a new, higher-level problem to solve.

Consider one of our ancestors thousands of years ago. One night while out for a stroll, our progenitor might have encountered an alpha predator such as a lion. So, our resourceful predecessor's first thought was to run for cover and find a cave out of reach from the big cat. Now safely out of danger (and with an appetite from all that running), our distant relative might turn his/her attention to a new, higher-level problem like finding dinner, instead of being dinner.

We looked at the genesis of each revolution and at the core were human problems that needed to be solved, such as mechanization and power in the form of steam.

Next, we as a species were not satisfied with simply solving a single problem, we immediately began searching for new problems to identify and seek resolution.

For example, we first utilized steam power in centralized locations, the machines were large and built in place for use. However, as we identified the need for power in a more portable manner, we sought to decentralize and distribute that power.

We needed a new, more efficient way to accomplish that. Hence, we moved on to the internal combustion engine (mostly powered by petrochemicals). These engines powered mills, logging operations and gave rise to mass manufacturing. We used these machines to build even bigger machines (an evolution that we would repeat decades later with respect to computer speed, memory, and power!).

As we increased power and capacity, we needed better infrastructure to move and manufacture goods. This led to better roads, bigger buildings, and rail transportation.

Moving on, we sought to solve more ethereal, computational problems. First in mechanical ways, then electronic. The first mechanical computer is widely considered to be the Antikythera mechanism, which was discovered in 1901 in a shipwreck off the coast of the Greek island of Antikythera. This device, which dates to between 150 and 100 BCE, is thought to have been used as an astronomical calculator. Although its exact purpose is still the subject of debate among scholars, the Antikythera mechanism is widely regarded as a remarkable example of ancient technology and a testament to the ingenuity of the people who created it.

However, the earliest example of a mechanical computer in the industrial age was the Pascaline. It was a machine developed by the French mathematician and philosopher Blaise Pascal in the mid-17th century. The Pascaline was a simple calculator that could perform addition and subtraction, and it was widely used in the business and financial world of the time. A nod to Pascal came in the naming of a computer language in the late 1960s.

As our "need" for higher, faster levels of computation increased (it always does, and will), the late 1960s saw the advent of Intel's microprocessor. Speed and computational power are still rising at breakneck speeds today.

Ultimately as our electronics became faster, smaller, and more useful, they opened new frontiers (and new challenges) for humanity. We now crave computers, robots, and other devices that can perform tasks as well as, or even better than we humans. Our "needs" seem always to be a step ahead of our abilities. With that never-ending quest to improve came some unintended consequences.

Today, we face a multitude of societal problems, many brought on by the side effects of our advancements in previous industrial revolutions. Are we sitting on the sidelines, content with the state of our society and planet? Of course not!

As Maslow predicted, we quickly take on higher-level and more challenging problems, even (maybe more like "especially"!) if they are the byproducts of our current technological solutions:

- We identify problems.
- We find solutions to those problems.
- The solutions many times create new problems.
- Rinse and repeat.

This book is about the ever-evolving set of problems and challenges that we face. We set the stage for what is a true "Industrial Revolution" and look at the good, the bad, and the ugly of each.

Each of the four revolutions (three past and one current) were, well, revolutionary. They catapulted our society in unexpected and unprecedented ways. We predict that the fifth revolution will not only advance us, but unlike each of the four previous revolutions, it will purposely address the unintended consequences of the previous four.

Just as Maslow predicted, we humans will feel the increasing pain from these problems (brought on by our own technical advancement), then seek out ways to alleviate it. The quickest and most effective way to get us to focus on a solution to a problem is to induce some sort of discomfort. Pain is a great motivator because the animal in us is wired that way! Then the human in us starts to rationalize methods to eliminate it.

The methods to the cures will include the birthing of new technologies, more enlightened intelligence, along with a new, collective awareness of our quest to reclaim the planet.

How This Book is Structured

Industry 5.0 is broken into three distinct parts:

Part I - The History of Industrial Revolutions

We take a deep dive into the first four revolutions and talk about how each affected society, business, and the environment.

Part II - The Definition and Defense of the Sustainability Revolution

In the second section, we clearly define the terms, "Revolution" and "Sustainability". The latter has significant reach beyond the typical conversations around renewable energy, carbon reduction, and conservation. Sustainability is core to leaving a healthy planet to our descendants. It encompasses all aspects of balancing economic growth with social well-being.

Part III - What Industry 5.0 Will Mean to Us in the Future with Respect to:

a) People
b) Planet
c) Potential

In the final section, we push to make the connection between the sustainability revolution and how it will affect our lives. We consciously chose to structure our book in this way because before talking about Industry 5.0, we need to break down and study Industries 1-4.

In **Part I**, we pose that it's paramount to understand how and why these revolutions took place. It's equally important to understand how each was interconnected, and the ultimate chronological order to these periods of incredible change.

Part II focuses on the term "sustainability" and its connection to sustainable development. We propose that all businesses will either become sustainable or wither away. Consumers today, and more prominently, consumers tomorrow will demand that businesses operate in a way that doesn't threaten the prosperity of future generations. We discussed the business specifics. What will sustainable business look like? We outline the major sectors such as manufacturing, construction, agriculture, and finance.

Finally, in **Part III**, we personalize the fifth revolution and look at how it will shape our lives. We break it down into the three most important aspects of our society, our people, our planet, and our potential!

We also look at what will shift business leaders to act more responsibly, and how will those roles take shape? This book is aimed at those looking to help their companies become more sustainable by outlining techniques and trends, but also those looking to become sustainability leaders and champions - whether that's at work, at home, or in the community.

The Thesis

To understand our position on the 5th Revolution, it's necessary to map out the first four and the ground-breaking technologies that came about as a result. We argue that Industry 5.0 cannot be simply an elevation of 4.0 (AI/Automation), but something far more progressive.

The original Steam Revolution (1.0) was an era of dramatic social, economic, and technological change. Sometimes called simply *the* "Industrial Revolution" when referring to either Industry 1.0 or 2.0, we make a clear distinction between the two.

For this study, we refer to the Age of Steam, and the first revolution and mostly associated with the advent of steam power. This differs from the more mechanical revolution that broadened this mechanization to overtake the "made by hand" era completely.

This second revolution marked the transition from traditional manufacturing by hand, to full-on mass production including fossil fuel and electricity. This is when we saw the rise of modern machines and factories, and with them came a new era: The Machine Age.

The third revolution was the advent of the Digital Age. While technology and computers existed before the true digital age (we consider it starting in 1971), they were more of an augmentation of previous processes. The digital revolution changed the way we live and do business and went way beyond mechanizing or automating tasks to include operations and outputs no human could perform.

We ended the history lesson with Industry 4.0. – The rise of machine learning and artificial intelligence. As much of a jump of digital processing was to computers, AI far eclipses the digital world to create a new society of machine learners.

The fourth industrial revolution started around 10-15 years ago and this current phase has been defined by the enmeshment of the digital, physical, and biological worlds. Biotechnology, social media, and smart devices have propelled the human race into the type of future we saw in The Jetsons and Star Wars (if you're too young to remember the Jetsons or the release of Star Wars, you grew up on the brink of Industry 4.0 and it may not seem so "revolutionary" to you, but trust us older folks when we tell you it was!).

Included in the fourth sector, we interject our position on the continuing rise of AI, machine learning, and human-machine interaction. Our position, shared by other experts, is that we are still in the midst of 4.0 and that there are many layers to this particular revolution. Layers that have yet to fully unfold that we are deeming, Industry 4.1, 4.2 and so on.

Finally, we explore Industry 5.0 - Sustainability. The need for, and global crisis around sustainability. How it's fundamentally changing business, investment, and our personal lives.

All these revolutions were truly global phenomena, touching every corner of the earth and reshaping societies. They jump-started modern capitalism as we know it today. They all set the stage for the following revolutions mostly centered around some game-changing technologies, but all dependent on the previous "revolutions" to lay the groundwork for future progress.

We suggest that humans will always be in the middle of some technological, social, or environmental revolution. They are difficult to accurately predict beyond a few decades (remember in the 1950s we were thought to have all been driving flying cars before the year 2000!), but as society is on the cusp of Industry 5.0, we see some definite patterns and trends emerging.

The Evolution of the Revolution

We doubt that anyone said, "I'm going to start a revolution today" when referring to the industrial kind. Many social and political revolutions were planned well in advance, however, the technical types seemed to build up steam (pun intended) without a certain premeditated cause and/or effect defined.

No, the first four revolutions were usually "identified" long after they began, and our society began to take notice of the change. Even then, the starting dates are debated, except for maybe Industry 3.0 (1971 with the introduction of Intel's first microprocessor).

That's true for Industry 5.0 too. We can look through today's lens of business and see that sustainability is a super-hot topic. Almost all large companies have some type of sustainability strategy, mandate, and drafted reports. Investors are looking for good ESG scores, and consumers are demanding more attention to the environment from the brands they frequent.

Companies are awakening to the fact that sustainability is not just a buzzword, but a business process on the level of finance, sales, and engineering. The pandemic of 2020-2022 heightened the awareness of the calling of sustainability, and the movement began its latest surge.

However, events like the Kyoto Protocol (1997) and the Paris Accord (2015) happened years/decades ago. Companies like Staples and

Unilever have put sustainability on their maps for 20 years or more. So why is it that we are just now noticing the revolution? Because, at a small, targeted scale it's not a revolution...yet!

However, we are staking the claim that the revolution is here, and here to stay. No company will be able to survive without a clear sustainable strategy in place. Customers won't stand for it, investors won't stand for it, and employees won't stand for it. That's a heavy consortium! Try to think of a company without customers, investors, or employees...there aren't any!

Can we agree that this latest revolution is upon us? If so, let's dive into Industry 5.0. If you don't agree, read it anyway - what do you have to lose?

XXV

Part I

The History of Industrial Revolutions

Chapter 1:

The Impact of Industrial Revolutions

What Constitutes a "Revolution"?

Revolution (noun) - reh·vuh·loo'·shn

- a sudden, radical, or complete change.
- an activity or movement designed to effect fundamental changes in the socioeconomic situation.
- a fundamental change in the way of thinking about or visualizing something.
- a change of paradigm.
- a changeover in use or preference especially in technology.

We hear the term "revolution" tossed around in many descriptions of change, however, change in itself is not revolutionary. Some changes are small, and some are large but to truly constitute a revolution, they need to adhere to the definitions above.

Is an increase in computer memory today considered change? Yes. Is it sudden or radical? No. Does it fundamentally change our way of thinking about computer memory? Again, no, because we already have an underlying description and view of what computer memory is, and even where it's going.

The same can be said about Artificial Intelligence (AI). Is expanding the capabilities of AI considered change? Of course. But because we already have a definition of what AI is (and what it could/will be in the future) then it's not technically revolutionary beyond the already accepted Industry 4.0. It can constitute big changes, but our definition and visualization of AI already exist.

During the course of this book, we lean on an admired friend and colleague, Dr. Stephen Haag. His books on Industry 4.0 are profound, and we cite his views regularly throughout this book. Two books in particular we recommend highly are, "2022 The Fourth Industrial Revolution" and "The Periodic Table of the Fourth Industrial Revolution". Both are insightful, entertaining, and enlightening.

In another great book, *Zero to One*, Author and co-founder of PayPal, Peter Thiel discusses the difference between "horizontal" and "vertical" progress.

According to Peter Thiel, horizontal progress refers to the improvement, enhancement, or optimization of existing products or services, aiming to make them superior in terms of speed, cost-effectiveness, efficiency, or overall quality. On the other hand, vertical progress encompasses transformative innovations that revolutionize the way things are done, resulting in the disruption of established industries and the creation of entirely new markets. This is the main thrust of our argument for Industry 5.0. Improvements are mostly horizontal. But to be a revolution, by definition, the movement must be vertical.

This is the main thrust of our argument for Industry 5.0. Improvements are mostly horizontal. But to be a revolution, by definition, the movement must be vertical.

Think of it like this - paraphrased from Thiel's book. If you make 100 improvements to the typewriter, then that is considered horizontal progress, or going from 1-100. You've improved on an existing idea or product.

Vertical progress is creating something that didn't exist before, think of going from the typewriter to the word processor; that's going from 0-1. We believe this is a constant when looking at past, current, and future industrial revolutions. Vertical progress evokes radical change, encompasses new visions, and it produces considerable paradigm shifts!

These viewpoints are what we base our Industry 5.0 thesis on - that the sudden and rapid adoption of sustainability across all business and social sectors is the latest revolution.

How We Got to Industry 5.0

The Industrial Revolutions of the 19th and 20th centuries transformed lives all over the world. They made life easier and more comfortable for many people, but it also created a new kind of misery as well as an economic divide that would shape our world for generations to come.

As we will discuss, all major revolutions have their "Pros" and "Cons". Heavy infrastructure led to new highways and bridges, however those highways sometimes bisected older communities and led to their demise.

These periods of advancement always begin with overwhelming optimism, but eventually, the unintended consequences always seem to rear their ugly heads. However, as a whole, these revolutions have raised the standards of living for virtually all humans on the planet.

Figure 1 - Medical Devices of the 1800s

A good friend recently noted that, "Today, we all live better than any King or Queen just 200 years ago". Don't believe it? Just Google medicine and dentistry of the 1800s!

Another note is that not everyone agrees with the definitions of

"Industry 1.0" and "2.0" and so on. For this book, we focused on the truly revolutionary aspects of the events.

From Steam to Mechanical to Digital to Artificial Intelligence. We felt there needed to be a clear line of demarcation between periods that are considered revolutionary.

Corporations have been talking about machine learning and the Internet of Things for over a decade. It's time to propel our society into the next generation of capitalism. Of course, that next generation of opportunity is Industry 5.0.

To understand the innovations that will lead us into the future, we need to dive into how humans have evolved up until today.

The big transition point of the human race started in the mid to late 1700s during the first industrial revolution. Up until then humans had gone through just a few foundational changes.

- The Paleolithic Era – Millions of years ago to 10,000 BC. These were the hunter-gatherer days when technology was defined by bows, arrows, spears, fires, containers, and huts.
- The Neolithic Era – 10,000 BC to 1760. This was the agricultural revolution where we domesticated plants and animals and started to build communities.

During the Neolithic era, humans went through many phases. There were philosophical revolutions, religions, dark ages, renaissances, urbanization, and, of course, the Age of Enlightenment.

But the late 1700s became the inflection point that changed the human race forever. The first industrial revolution drove the production of goods to new heights. It drove us to coin a new term, "Consumerism" in the wake of products that improved our lives now available to, and wanted by, the masses.

In turn, the path to operational efficiency became the golden ticket for manufacturers. Each of the industrial revolutions created a fundamental shift in how businesses and our society functioned.

What Are Our Four Accepted Revolutions?

Here's what we consider the first 4 phases (Industry 1.0 to Industry 4.0). We attempt to get a clearer understanding of how radically each one of them changed our world:

- First Industrial Revolution (**Mechanical Power**) – defined by mechanical production using water and steam.
- Second Industrial Revolution (**Industrialization & Mass Manufacturing**) – defined by mass production through electrical power and fossil-based fuels.
- Third Industrial Revolution (**Computerization & Digitization**) – defined by digital electronics using computers.
- Fourth Industrial Revolution (**Automation & Artificial Intelligence**) – defined by big data, AI, robotics, the internet of things, and modern advanced software.

And we'll get a grasp of some of the technologies that have come about as a result:

- **First Industrial Revolution** (starting in the 1760s) – The steam engine, steamboat, steam locomotive.
- **Second Industrial Revolution** (starting in the 1870s) – Generating electricity, telephone, light bulb, combustion engine, airplane, and assembly line.
- **Third Industrial Revolution** (starting in the 1970s) – The microprocessor, interconnected mainframe computer, personal computer, internet, and semiconductors.
- **Fourth Industrial Revolution** (starting in the 2010s) – Machine learning, quantum computing, and artificial intelligence.

This is a simple roadmap of the four accepted industrial revolutions. You can see that they will tend to overlap chronologically, but each was a separate, long-lasting event that brought on a radical change in human life - yes, both good and bad!

Let's jump into Industry 1.0, and the beginning of this entire phenomenon.

9

10

Chapter 2:

The First Industrial Revolution

Industry 1.0: The Steam Revolution

There is no good way to track the exact dates of the impact caused by the steam revolution because it took place over a period of time. However, some markers can be used to identify the milestones.

The first was in 1698 when Thomas Savery invented the steam pump.

The next milestone was in 1807 when Robert Fulton's steamboat made its inaugural voyage up New York's Hudson River.

Figure 2 - Steam Pump

The third was in 1829 when the steam locomotive was unveiled by the B&O Railroad, demonstrating that steam had become a reliable source of power for transportation and industry.

Before the steam engine, mechanized power depended on humans, animals, wind, or water. Most mills and pumps were located close to a moving water source (river) and were driven by a water wheel. The downside was that power was regulated by mother nature herself, and that could be very unreliable at times. The invention of the steam engine meant that the power source could now be located virtually anywhere and be much more consistent.

The Central Technologies of 1.0

The first steam-powered device started with Thomas Savery's "Miner's Friend". The device was designed to pump water out of mines. Savery's valve/vacuum design was patented all the way back in 1698! However, it wasn't until Thomas Newcomen invented the first mechanically driven steam engine in 1712 that the piston design was incorporated. Even with this major advance, what we would recognize as a modern steam engine, wasn't invented until 1778 by James Watt.

James Watt, a Scottish inventor, and engineer made several important contributions to the development of the steam engine. His jacketed steam engine was notable for its use of a steam jacket or envelope, which surrounded the cylinder of the engine. This jacket served to contain the heat generated by the steam engine, which helped to improve its efficiency and reduce the amount of heat lost to the surrounding environment. This, in turn, allowed the engine to run for longer periods of time and at higher temperatures, making it more powerful and versatile than previous designs.

Watt's new design made steam power more practical and cost-effective for a wide range of industrial applications, and his advancement of the jacketed piston meant not only higher efficiency and power but also the true ability to drive a rotary wheel.

This design of transferring piston power into rotational generation set in motion (no pun) every mechanical power advancement in the future. Virtually all mechanization is based on the generation of rotational force of some type. Motors of all varieties, electric, hydro, internal combustion, etc., convert energy into mechanical rotation. That rotation can then be converted into power to pump water, turn a lathe, generate electricity, spin a wheel…the list is endless.

As steam engine technology advanced, so did the number of uses. As the engines became smaller and more efficient, they led the way for more advanced machines. Think about the metal lathe, this machine could now produce higher-quality parts for even larger, more powerful machines. This led to mechanized textile mills, steamboat power, and eventually railroads.

This set the precedent for not only the expansion of local factories but also for industrial expansion across vast geographies. Without steamboats and railroads, Americans would have had a hard time expanding beyond the densely populated Eastern Seaboard.

It was a period of dramatic socio-economic and cultural change. It helped create modern capitalism as we know it today, and ultimately led to the second industrial revolution.

The Cons of Industry 1.0

While the new era of mechanization provided the nation with a new, higher-powered economy, some of the consequences were dire. The new transportation era began with the steamboat and most cargo was food or people. Farmers could now ship goods along the rivers (the superhighways of the 1800s), but this also fed the nation's internal slave trade, as the Mississippi River brought many unwilling passengers into the mainland from the port of New Orleans.

Workshops also sprang up in the bigger cities and the modern "urban" area was created. While some enjoyed newfound wealth, most were subjected to stifling poverty and intolerable "New World" living conditions on a scale never seen before.

We will see a proactive approach to improving working and living conditions as a part of Industry 5.0. We will explore the UN's Sustainable Development Goals (SDGs) that point directly to issues like Zero Hunger, Good Health/Well-being, and Clean Water/Sanitation.

While the steam engine provided advancement in manufacturing, the general population began to move away from the agrarian economy to the commercialization of a production and manufacturing economy. The tone was now set for the even harsher world that the second industrial revolution would set in motion.

15

16

Chapter 3:

The Second Industrial Revolution

The second revolution of the late 19th century transformed lives all over the world. Huge factories were built, which meant that people could work indoors and out of the sun. The newfound technology of electricity meant that the workday would start long before sunrise and last long after sunset.

Newly introduced technologies fueled economic growth and led to the expansion of steel, oil, machinery and chemical industries.

This second revolution actually began in Great Britain in the late 18th century with the mechanization of the textile industry but soon spread throughout Europe and North America. Businesses quickly realized that they needed to use this new technology to their advantage if they wanted to stay competitive in this era.

The new machines also made it possible to produce more than ever before at lower costs, so in turn, there was a new age of consumerism born. Previously our ancestors bought only what they needed, now we start to see a transitional shift into an era of purchasing "wants" as opposed to "needs."

While the first industrial revolution enabled our nation to develop a domestic economy, the second revolution led to the advent of globalism. During this time, we advanced beyond steam-driven factories and locomotives, to cars, planes, and the steel-based infrastructure that allowed all of them to thrive.

Advancements in transportation made it easier to transport goods across long distances and facilitated economic interconnectedness.

The Shift to Industry 2.0: The Mechanical Revolution

While Industry 1.0 relied on one specific technology, the steam engine, the second revolution would see the rise of a plethora of industries led by steel, oil, and electricity. Without the introduction of steam power, the second revolution would not have gotten off the ground.

Steam power made it possible to harness and transform energy. Before steam, we relied on the brute force of humans or animals. Our ancestors did create pulley and lever systems, but at their core, they simply transferred muscle movement into mechanical force. While this force could be significant (somehow the Egyptians built the Pyramids), steam power was magnitudes stronger and faster.

The downside to "muscle power" was that humans and animals got tired, sick, or became disabled in some way that's not easily corrected. Mechanical engines do not. They may break down, but replacement or repair of the defective part gets them back online as good as new. So, what we saw was a huge increase in productivity, speed, and efficiency.

Factories (another byproduct of 2.0) could now run longer hours (even 24/7) and pump out products faster than any human-powered entity could ever dream of. This allowed for mass production, and the continual search for more ways to mechanize.

Advancements such as the combustion engine, the harnessing of electricity, steel, oil, or the telegraph could have easily been revolutions all on their own. All came to light during the same period, and all created synergies that advanced each technology even further.

Individually, they represented a leap in human ingenuity and broadened our mastery over the planet. Collectively, they transformed our world (economically and socially) into something that would have been unimaginable just a generation prior.

The Central Technologies of 2.0

Steel was the first on the scene, and many future advancements owe their heritage to the alloy. Up until the late 1800s, iron was the metal of choice for tools and machinery mainly because of its abundance and ease to form into various shapes. The downside is that iron contains impurities that lead to faster corrosion and weakness. Steel, on the other hand, is an alloy that is iron based, without impurities and it's not prone to weakening over time.

It had been in use as early as the 17th century, but it wasn't until the Bessemer Process that steel became more pure, less expensive, and so widely used.

Figure 3 - Steel Foundry

In 1855, Henry Bessemer invented a process of mass-producing steel by blowing air through molten pig iron to oxidize impurities and convert them iron into steel.

The process takes advantage of the fact that impurities in pig iron, such as carbon and silicon, are more easily oxidized than the iron itself. By removing these impurities, Bessemer found a way to produce high-quality steel that is stronger and more uniform than traditional methods.

The new process was highly efficient, allowing for the production of large quantities of steel in a relatively short amount of time. Before the Bessemer process, the production of steel was a slow and labor-intensive process that produced only small quantities of the alloy. Bessemer's creation revolutionized the steel industry and made steel much more affordable and accessible.

Steel built the industrial world we live in today. Roads, bridges, skyscrapers, cars, ships, and railroads, all owe their legacy to steel.

Oil (and the ability to refine it into its base elements) was another huge discovery that quite literally, fueled the second industrial revolution. Oils have been around for centuries; mostly animal and plant based. Oil lamps lit the civilizations of Egypt, Greece, and Ancient Rome.

However, once we learned how to tap the large, land-based deep crude oil reserves, the industry took flight. In 1859, the Pennsylvania Rock Oil Company hit a reserve 60 feet below ground. This is thought to be the first oil recovered by drilling into the Earth. A few years later, John D. Rockefeller took the industry by storm by "standardizing" his lamp oil, or at least marketing that point!

By 1901 there were 1500 registered oil companies in the United States, and most of these companies were built on a product that is nowhere near as popular today, Kerosine. Kerosine was widely used to light our world. In the days before electrification, kerosine lamps were everywhere. As refining became, well...more refined, a byproduct of Kerosine production was gasoline. Originally seen as waste, gasoline soon became the oil companies' golden goose.

The discovery of oil in the United States also had a profound impact on the United States economy, politics, and society including:

1. Economic Growth: The discovery of oil led to the growth of the petroleum industry, which created jobs and boosted the

economy. It also made the United States less dependent on other countries for energy and allowed the country to become one of the largest oil producers in the world.
2. Transportation: The widespread use of fossil fuel powered vehicles revolutionized transportation, making it easier and more convenient for people to travel long distances. This had a profound impact on the growth of suburbanization and the development of the automobile industry.
3. Manufacturing: The availability of cheap oil helped to spur industrial growth and led to the development of new technologies and products, such as plastics and synthetic materials.
4. Geopolitics: The United States' newfound position as a major oil producer gave it significant geopolitical power, as oil became a crucial resource for other countries. The United States used its control over oil supplies as leverage in international relations and became involved in Middle Eastern politics to protect its access to oil.

However, there was a huge downside to the environmental impact. The extraction of oil changed the natural landscape as drilling rigs popped up over Texas, Pennsylvania and Ohio.

Figure 4 - Oil Refinery

The discovery of oil in Alaska also led to one of the largest oil pipelines in the world. The Trans-Alaska System (TAPS) is over 800 miles long; stretching from Alaska's North Slope to the Port of Valdez. The pipeline is mostly buried; however, ecologists complain of habitat loss, oil spills, and the generally increased extraction of petroleum. Critics pose that pipelines like these have a negative effect on the environment, leading to air and water pollution simply because they can move such vast amounts of oil and refined fossil products.

TAPS, built between 1975 and 1977, initially promised a cheaper and more efficient way to move oil and supporters point out that that same amount of oil transported by ship, rail, or truck would carry a much higher price tag. We must take into consideration the state of our U.S. economy in the 1970s, with OPEC's oil embargo combined with the way our country was running on a much higher fuel intensity than today. This led to a huge demand for oil, and the need to keep the flow going consistently.

Also, in the 70s, cars were getting about 15 MPG as opposed to over 25 MPG today, and of course, we're now on the verge of the wide-scale adoption of EVs, which will prove far more efficient. During this time, the U.S. government introduced new regulations aimed at improving the fuel efficiency of cars, including Corporate Average Fuel Economy (CAFE) standards. This required automakers to meet minimum fuel economy standards for their fleets. These standards, along with advances in engine technology and the growing popularity of smaller, more fuel-efficient vehicles, helped to gradually increase the average fuel efficiency of cars in the United States.

However, our appetite for oil has not decreased, and consumption worldwide has gone up steadily every year, except for the pandemic years of 2019 and 2020 (more on the effects of the pandemic later). The other side of fossil fuels is the actual burning. Internal combustion engines by nature burn the fuels to convert them into mechanical power.

As far back as 1970, the Federal Government was looking at emissions from these internal combustion engines. The Clean Air Act Amendments of 1970 established the first federal emissions standards for new cars and required automakers to install pollution control equipment on new vehicles, such as catalytic converters.

These standards covered emissions of pollutants such as carbon monoxide (CO), hydrocarbons (HC), and nitrogen oxides (NOx). They came about because of the rampant air pollution that was gripping our large metro areas, most notably the driving capital of Los Angeles. In fact, a new term to describe it was coined as "Smog" (a combination of smoke and fog).

Los Angeles was one of the first cities in the United States to issue smog alerts, due to its high levels of automobile traffic and its location in the LA basin which traps pollutants and contributes to the formation of smog. New York and Pittsburgh were not far behind due to both auto traffic and industrial activities.

Even 50 years ago, we knew that we were not treating the planet very well, and the evidence was mounting all around us. However, it took government action to get companies to act.

The difference today is that businesses are seeing the benefits of more sustainable efforts because sustainability now pays (a later chapter explores the benefits to profitability, brand value, and market positioning by becoming a more sustainable organization)! This shift is a primary reason for the 5.0 revolution.

Electricity

Figure 5 - Michael Faraday

In parallel to the commercialization of steel and oil, was the harnessing of electricity. Thomas Edison, and even Ben Franklin typically come to mind when thinking of electricity, and especially electric light, but one of the true pioneers was Michael Faraday. Faraday was a chemist by trade, but most well-known for his discovery of the relationship between magnetism and electricity. His groundbreaking discovery of electromagnetic induction paved the way for electric generators and transformers and hence, the science of power conversion and electrical generation was born.

Electric generators first came to light in the 1870s and were all based on Faraday's electro-magnetism theories. The ability to understand electricity was one thing. The ability to generate it, control it, and in turn distribute it, changed the world. Essentially, motion in a generator creates electricity, and that motion can come from various sources, hydro, wind, combustion engine, and virtually anything that can turn a rotor. Think back to Watt's steam engine that was powerful enough to turn a rotor, as time moved on, that breakthrough would show up time and time again.

Electricity itself was a wonder in just the pure form to illuminate a light bulb, but shortly after harnessing the power, other noted scientists discovered the many properties of electrons and through further manipulation of electricity, the study of electronics was born.

Electronics can be traced back to the early 1900s and Sir John Ambrose Fleming's invention of the vacuum tube. This gave us the ability to control the flow of electrons down to a tiny amount of current, thus opening the door for a host of electric appliances and devices. Radio, TV, and computers all owe their existence to that first vacuum tube. The study of electronics would eventually lead us to the digital revolution, and in turn, automation, and AI.

The Synergies of 2.0

Industry 2.0 brought about the most amazing time of technological change we've seen. It's hard to view from today's perspective, but the world changed drastically in just a few decades. The advancements weren't just chronological in nature, many depended on the others to emerge such as:

1. Energy production and consumption: Steel production requires large amounts of energy, and the electricity and oil industries are major sources of energy for the steel industry.

2. Raw material production: The oil and steel industries are interdependent in the sense that oil is a raw material used in the production of steel, while steel is used in the production of oil drilling equipment and infrastructure.
3. Transportation and distribution: The oil and electricity industries play a critical role in the transportation and distribution of steel products. Oil products are used to power the trucks, trains, and ships that transport steel, while electricity is used to power the factories and distribution centers that process and distribute steel products.
4. Industrial symbiosis: The steel, oil, and electricity industries can also benefit from industrial symbiosis, where by-products and waste from one industry can be used as inputs by another industry. For example, by-products from the steelmaking process, such as blast furnace gas, can be used as fuel in power plants to generate electricity.

All these inventions/discoveries on their own would have been quite monumental, but it is the synergies that were created amongst them that propelled us into the 20th century.

Steel combined with oil and fuel, created the first gasoline-powered combustion engine. There was also the element of electricity to fire the fuel within the chamber. This is a perfect example of the combination of technologies to create even bigger breakthroughs, which during the second revolution took off at a pace never seen before.

Some outputs of these combinations were:

- Automobiles
- Elevators/Skyscrapers
- Telegraph and Telephone
- Planes
- Barges
- Drilling/Mining Equipment
- Diesel Locomotives

From a purely industrial point of view, the synergies of 2.0 were magnitudes beyond the other revolutions. It's almost hard to imagine how much the world changed in just one generation. Someone born in the 1870s lived during the most incredible age of advancement.

As a child, they would have seen transportation morph from riding horses to riding bicycles, carriages to automobiles, and wagon trains to locomotives. What once took months to traverse by horse, now took just days by train!

As a teen, they would have seen the transformation of lighting in their homes from flames (gas, kerosene, etc.) to the miracle of electric light. They would experience medical advances from x-rays to antiseptics to vaccines for diphtheria (once a leading cause of death for children!).

In their 20s, they would see the automobile go from expensive, exclusive toys for the rich, to the mainstream form of transportation in urban areas due to Ford's assembly line methodology and the parallel adoption of paved roads.

By the time they reached their mid-30s, they would have read about advancements in chemical warfare, machine guns, and the first military use of another new technology, the airplane.

In their 40s, 50s, and 60s, the mastery over the atom would surface in ways that benefited society (nuclear power) to the creation of devices that obliterated entire cities with the atomic bomb. Electric appliances now allowed us to cook without reliance on wood stoves, and we could now store food in cold atmospheres without ice. The ability to transmit information across the airwaves spurred home communications like radio and television.

Having lived into their 70s and 80s, due to medical advancements that more than doubled the average lifespan since the time of their birth, they saw the invention of the electronic computer, satellites, and witnessed manned missions into space live on TV.

Industry 2.0 was a monumental shift away from the individual being responsible for their level of prosperity, and now the newly formed society was dependent on its collective self, aligned with the latest technology for the advancement of both the individual and the community.

The Second Industrial Revolution brought about huge social change. People no longer had to rely on other people as much for their survival, instead, they could rely more on machines.

The Cons of Industry 2.0

The aftershocks of Oil (and its ancillary industries) continue to affect the planet today. We cannot blindly scold oil alone, but all the industries that rely on oil and fossil fuels such as energy production, manufacturing, transportation, and agriculture.

Carbon emissions from the family tree of the petroleum industry dwarf any other individual sector of advancement. That doesn't mean that steel, electricity, and the ancestors of each are immune from conflict.

There was a true social dichotomy because of Industry 2.0. While healthcare and sanitation began to improve, the need also rose at an alarming rate. The new urban lifestyle created some intolerable living conditions. The rise of factories meant that the workers needed to live nearby, hence housing was a reaction to the proliferation of new manufacturing centers, and they were viewed as simply places where the workers would spend their (limited) time away from their jobs at the factory.

Figure 6 - Tenement Housing 1800s

This was before unions and many of the social constructs that protected citizens. Over time, Police, Fire, and Sanitation became commonplace departments in large cities, but only because of the rising need for such social intervention was crucial to prevent utter chaos within these social centers.

Medical advances arrived on the scene as well, but only because of the need to combat the devastating diseases, viruses, and bacterial infections that came about due to overcrowded, unsanitary living, and working conditions.

By establishing this new modern social system, and the advent of a consumer mentality, the world began a seismic economic shift. No longer were we as isolated as an agrarian/artisan society; we were now learning to live amongst the masses and consume products at a rate never seen before.

In the landscape of Industry 5.0, we argue that the key to real sustainability is NOT limiting progress or even consumption, but rather shifting to new production methods and materials that are kinder, even beneficial to our planet.

By shifting to a consumer economy, as well as learning to turn raw materials more efficiently into finished products, Industry 2.0 set the stage for ever faster, and ever-expanding, leapfrogging technologies, and unfortunately, more unintended consequences.

29

30

Chapter 4:

The Third Industrial Revolution

Industry 3.0: The Digital Transformation

How our society has become dependent on technology is no secret; but what many people don't realize is that this dependency has been developing for centuries. The first machines developed for information processing were developed more than 300 years ago.

In 1790, Thomas Jefferson developed the cipher wheel. The cipher wheel allowed a person to encode a message with a set of 10 symbols. To encode the message, the sender would have to know the key which is a word or phrase for each of the symbols on the face of the wheel. This was, in fact, a "Computer", albeit a mechanical one, as opposed to the electronic ones in use today.

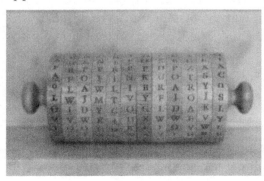

Figure 7 - Jefferson's Cipher Wheel

The third industrial revolution centers around modern computers, and more specifically the shift from analog to digital technology. The move represents using computers for tasks and using computers to manage data and information. The shift took an even sharper shift with the introduction and adaptation of the Internet.

Why and When Did Industry 3.0 Start?

In the late 1960s, we were welcomed to the digital era. The transistor was first commercially available in 1954, and while companies like Fairchild Semiconductor began to flourish in Silicon Valley in the late 1950s, the true digital revolution was accelerated by the invention of the microprocessor.

Early transistors were the evolution of vacuum tube functionality and began to overtake tubes in the 1960s as the semiconductor of choice (most don't realize that vacuum tube technology performed the same function, controlling electrical conductivity through an external signal or semi-conducting).

Figure 8 - Vacuum Tube, Transistor, and Integrated Circuit Chip

Today's semiconductors are now made of a solid-state material, silicon. This was a huge leap forward from the process being controlled by beams of electrons shot through a vacuum tube.

Those smaller, lighter, more efficient wafers of silicon gave rise to the integrated circuit, and eventually the microprocessor. While the evolutionary story is a bit muddy, most consider the Intel 4004, released in November of 1971. as the first commercially viable microprocessor. As more than an integrated circuit designed to perform a singular task, the microprocessor could be "programmed" to perform various and multiple tasks, hence giving rise to the true Digital Age.

Up until that time, electronics was the science of manipulating electricity to perform functions via individual components (coils, capacitors, resistors, etc.). We think of computers, but the study of electronics includes power generation, signal processing/transmission, and motors.

When computers came on the scene, they were analog devices. Meaning that they had discrete components to accomplish the manipulation of electrons. To give some scale to the level of advancement to digital, the first analog computer was the ENIAC. It was over 100 feet long and weighed 30 tons (try fitting that into your pocket!). The reason was the circuits were made of mechanical and vacuum tube devices; they took up a lot of space and used a lot of power.

The ENIAC could compute 5,000 calculations in a second. Far exceeding a human's capabilities, but in comparison, Intel's first microprocessor chip (an integrated circuit made into a single chip the size of a postage stamp), could run circles around the ENIAC!

Figure 9 - ENIAC Computer

Intel's 4004 was the world's first single-chip microprocessor, and it was capable of computing approximately 60,000 instructions per second! It was initially designed for use in calculators, but its flexibility and versatility allowed it to be used in a wide range of other products. - Intel 4004 Microprocessor.

Figure 10 - Intel 4004 Microprocessor

The 4004 set the stage for the development of more powerful microprocessors that would eventually be used in personal computers, smartphones, and a whole host of devices connected to the Internet.

33

Just for fun, how many calculations will the newest smartphones complete per second? About 15 trillion!

(https://content.techgig.com/technology/demystifying-iphone14-everything-about-a15-bionic-chip/articleshow/94415481.cms)

The Central Technologies of 3.0

Solid State Electronics, Digital Communications, Mainframe/Personal Computing

Analog and digital computing are two distinct approaches to processing information. The main difference between the two is how they represent and manipulate data.

Analog computing uses continuous physical variables, such as voltage or current, to represent data. Analog computers operate by continuously adjusting these physical variables in response to inputs, and the resulting changes are used to perform calculations.

Digital computing, on the other hand, uses binary digits (bits) to represent data, with each bit representing either a 1 or a 0. Digital computers perform calculations by manipulating these bits, using logic gates and other digital circuits to process information.

One of the main advantages of digital computing is its precision, as digital computers can perform complex calculations with a high degree of accuracy.

Digital communications also differ from analog in the fact that exact copies of information can be made. Think of it like this – an old copy machine makes "facsimiles" of documents. However, each copy loses some information. If you've used an older Xerox-type machine to make copies of copies, you know what I mean. Each subsequent copy is a little blurrier than the original, and that loss of "sharpness" is essentially a loss of information.

Digital, however, is all a series of ones and zeros. So, exact copies can be made, even if there are millions or billions of ones and zeros in a string of information. As long as each sequence is copied correctly, the result is an exact replica - every time. Because these exact copies can be endless, transmitting them results in no loss of information, no matter how many times they're used.

Digital was now no longer an abstract concept that we hear about only in the context of Silicon Valley and startups. It began permeating and transforming every aspect of our lives, from how we work, to how we live, to how we play. It changed our fundamental notions about what it means to consume information and interact with other people, as well as influencing how we express ourselves creatively and share ideas.

This revolution led to inventions like the home computer, the cell phone, MP3 players, digital cameras, computer games, and the smartphone. We separate the smartphone from the cell phone because it is a pocket computer and represents a monumental leap from a device used to make telephony mobile, to a mobile computer that is always connected. In many ways, it has replaced the other items listed above!

Again, we see the synergies of evolving technologies (like the smartphone) as an amalgam of previous digital technologies. Digital technology led to the interconnected network of home and business computers (Internet). Once introduced, the use of the Internet rose at a tremendous rate, from essentially zero in 1990 to over 65% of households in the U.S. that were connected by the year 2000.

The Internet

No conversation about digital technology and Industry 3.0 would be complete without a discussion of the Internet. Many of you reading this have only known a world where devices (computers really) have been connected seamlessly to each other, with most being connected wirelessly today. There was a world of computer technology long before the Internet existed (ask your parents or grandparents about floppy discs!).

The Internet seems almost ethereal today as the infrastructure has been in place for decades and technologies that guide it are almost transparent to us. We don't think about "connecting" to the Internet or the network of hardware needed to make it work, it's more like gravity; it's there, we know it, but we seldom think about it.

We owe today's Internet to the U.S. State Department's Advanced Research Project Agency Network, affectionately known as ARPANET.

ARPANET was the first operational packet-switching (sending 'packets' of information in the form of ones and zeros digitally) network and the precursor to the modern Internet. It was developed by the United States Department of Defense's Advanced Research Projects Agency (ARPA) in the late 1960s and early 1970s.

ARPANET was designed to allow researchers at universities and government agencies to share information and collaborate on projects, and it was one of the first networks to use packet switching, a technology that broke data into small packets and sent them independently over a network, to be reassembled at the destination.

Think of it like this. If you wanted to mail a picture to a friend (snail mail that is), you would wrap the frame and box it up, apply the postage, and off to the post office you go. However, a computer cannot send a physical picture over the Internet in that way. It must be broken up into small, digestible pieces of digital language that any computer on the other end can translate.

The way packets work is like cutting that same picture up into very small pieces (think jigsaw puzzle). Each piece is cataloged and numbered for proper assembly on the other side. Then small numbers of the pieces are put into envelopes and sent to the receiver for decoding and assembly. For a human, it might take days or weeks to open hundreds of envelopes, look through every piece, arrange them in the proper order, and reassemble the picture. However, a computer can do that in no time.

Just like any conversation, the language must be agreed upon. If you were on the phone with someone giving instructions who spoke only Japanese and you spoke only English, trying to understand how to put that jigsaw puzzle together would get quite frustrating. In the same way, computer programmers and network engineers had to agree upon common languages for the computers to communicate with.

Many of the key technologies and protocols (languages and syntax) that are used on the Internet today, such as TCP/IP and email, were developed and first implemented on the ARPANET network. The ARPANET network grew rapidly throughout the 1970s and early 1980s, and primarily shared data in a rawer form (sans graphics and audio). However, with the increase in computational power to display text and graphics, we eventually saw the foundation for the development of the modern Internet.

The Internet as we know it today started to take shape in the early 1990s, with the widespread adoption of the World Wide Web (WWW) and the development of graphical web browsers such as Mosaic and Netscape Navigator.

With the arrival of the World Wide Web and graphical web browsers, the Internet became much more accessible and useful to the public (you didn't need to be a computer programmer to share information). It rapidly gained popularity as a tool for communication, commerce, and entertainment.

The widespread adoption of the World Wide Web and the development of e-commerce, social media, and other online services helped to spur the growth of the Internet, and by the early 2000s, the Internet had become a central part of modern life, with billions of people around the world using it to communicate, access information, and engage in a wide range of online activities.

It's estimated that the online population is around 5 billion people, meaning that of the 7.9 billion people in the world, 63% of us are using the Internet.

As we transitioned from an analog economy to a digital economy, the transformation process has come to affect every industry in some way. Industries that were traditionally non-digitized are now seeing the effects of this transformation in their business models and strategies. It's hard to imagine any business not being connected to the world wide web these days, however, there may be a few.

The Cons of Industry 3.0

The advantages of this revolution clearly favor businesses and individuals who adopt and adapt to, change. Those choosing to lag, or not participate surely got left behind. New eras of globalization have emerged, and the business playing fields have been leveled in many cases.

Other consequences may not have been so positive, but the workload and rate of change today surpass anything we knew just 30 years ago. Today, you can get on the subway, open your smartphone, edit a promotional video, send it to colleagues, and get feedback before you arrive at your office. That is if you still even travel to an office! This faster pace has led to a rise in mental health concerns including burnout. As we can stay connected 24/7 (and some choose to do so) we begin to pay an emotional price.

Also, many claim that we are losing jobs associated with tasks that are now automated. With the upcoming AI revolution, we talk about next, that trend will certainly continue, and pervade occupations that were just a few years ago, considered things that only a human could do.

Like any technology, the original uses are considered positive, but nefarious people will always find reprehensible ways to take advantage of others. With the newfound technical ability to connect, there will also be new avenues for individuals and businesses to be taken advantage of. The term "Fake News" didn't exist a few years ago, however, today it has found its way into all our platforms of communication. On top of that, the way digital information can now be altered, it's becoming increasingly difficult to differentiate between the truth and fiction.

There's an issue of sustainability that we will cover in detail later that links directly to 3.0. The digital revolution has had a huge impact on our ecosystems, even though we sometimes don't see the destruction first-hand. The enormous amounts of electrical energy needed to digitize our world are increasing at the same rate as the information explosion. A study released stated that by 2040, digital power needs alone would exceed all the power we produced globally in 2010!

https://www.semiconductors.org/resources/2015-international-technology-roadmap-for-semiconductors-itrs/

Industry 3.0 is the idea of using digital technologies to revolutionize the industrial sector. Automation will be an industry-wide phenomenon soon, but it is not just about machines replacing human labor. Industry 3.0 was more than just digitizing manual tasks; it's about digitizing all stages of production and the "programming" of computers to perform tasks well beyond any human capabilities. Which is where Industry 4.0 takes over!

40

Chapter 5:

The Fourth Industrial Revolution

Industry 4.0: The Rise of IoT and Automation

From Industry 3.0, digital computing, and worldwide networking, we have transitioned into Industry 4.0, including higher levels of man-machine interface, automation, and even artificial intelligence.

Unlike the transition from 1.0 to 2.0, where multiple synergies came about through a wide range of mechanization, and with 2.0 to 3.0 that saw completely new forms of technology arise from science; the 3.0 to 4.0 transition relies on the same basic technologies (electronics, computers, and networks). The difference is that with 4.0, the computing power has risen to a level that makes previously unimaginable processes now possible.

"Industry 4.0" is a term defined by German advisor Professor Harald Welzer in response to the digital transformation in the manufacturing sector. The thrust of Industry 4.0 is the intertwining of the cyber world and the physical – or cyber-physical convergence.

This convergence will be defined as the current trend of automation and data exchange in manufacturing technologies. Industry 4.0 is built on the shoulders of 3.0 and it is characterized by the integration of advanced technologies such as the Internet of Things (IoT), artificial intelligence (AI), and cloud computing into manufacturing processes and a wider industrial sector. It will be a large leap forward as we see the integration of man and machine as Industry 4.0 connects factories, supply chains, and sales channels to enable large amounts of data to be gathered, processed, and acted upon, even if humans aren't directly involved in the sequences (automation).

Industry 4.0 looks to create smart factories and supply chains that are highly automated and connected, allowing for greater efficiency, flexibility, and responsiveness. We achieve this using a variety of technologies, including sensors, big data analytics, and machine learning algorithms, which enable the collection, analysis, and adaptations of large amounts of data from production processes and machines.

This revolution is expected to have a significant impact on the way that goods are manufactured and the way that businesses operate, leading to unprecedented increases in productivity and competitiveness. It is also expected to have a major impact on the workforce, with the increasing use of automation and robotics likely to lead to a shift in the types of jobs that are available and the skills that are required.

Automation and robotics will result in a shift away from routine and manual labor, and towards jobs that require higher levels of technical and cognitive skills. Many routine tasks, such as assembly line work, data entry, and some forms of customer service, can be automated using robots or AI systems, which can perform these tasks faster and more accurately than we can.

Figure 11 - Industrial Robot

As seen in Industry 3.0, computer skills overtook some manual labor. 4.0 will likely see a decrease in the number of jobs available in certain industries, particularly those that rely heavily on routine and raw human effort.

At the same time, there is likely to be an increase in demand for workers with advanced technical skills, such as data analysts, engineers, and software developers, who can design, build, and maintain the systems and machines that are used in automated production.

In addition to the changes in the way we work, there may also be significant changes in the way that work is organized and managed. With the increasing use of automation, robotics, and high-speed home computer networks, it is likely that more work will be done remotely or on a freelance basis, and that there will be greater use of flexible work arrangements such as part-time and contract work.

Industry 4.0 also refers to the next generation of manufacturing which takes advantage of these cyber-physical systems and Internet of Things (IoT). It combines process optimization, production intelligence, and information technologies with smart automation and autonomous systems to create dramatic improvements in performance while simultaneously reducing costs, time-to-market, and energy consumption.

As with the first three revolutions, the arrival of Industry 4.0 will create fundamental shifts in business, our economy, and our social system. However, the speed and breadth of this fourth revolution is unlike anything experienced previously. This current revolution consists of moving technology well beyond the digital age of information and data, to seeing the rise of machine learning and artificial intelligence. In many ways, this is clearing the way for some incredible advances never imagined before.

Industry 4.0 will (we use the word "will" because we are in 4.0 now) fundamentally changes our business landscapes, our educational institutions, our governments, and our personal lives. Everything from the Internet of Things, self-driving cars, robots/chatbots, material science, energy production/storage, 3D printing, and quantum computing will make way for a futuristic world, and all coming at us at a breakneck pace.

The Central Technologies of 4.0

As with the second and third revolution, this fourth will intertwine technologies to create new opportunities, and previously unthinkable synergies. The first three revolutions changed how we did things, the fourth may change who we are!

Artificial intelligence (AI) refers to the development of computer systems that can perform tasks that would typically require human intelligence. It encompasses a wide range of techniques, algorithms, and methodologies that enable machines to learn, reason, perceive, and make decisions. Contrary to the notion that AI is a single programming protocol leading to singularity, AI is actually a broad and evolving field consisting of various approaches and technologies. Singularity, often associated with the hypothetical point when machines surpass human intelligence, is just one concept within the realm of AI, albeit a controversial one.

In their book "Artificial Intelligence: A Modern Approach". Stuart Russell and Peter Norvig outline the "Seven Dimensions of AI". They were first introduced by Russell and Norvig to explain how they see the progression of AI.

The seven dimensions are: knowledge representation, automated reasoning, natural language processing, perception, learning, action, and reasoning about mental states.

These evolutionary states may be partially chronologic or happen partially in parallel with each other. However, each is a distinct "level" of AI, progressing towards human intelligence.

A closer look reveals the proposed evolutionary states of AI:

Knowledge representation: The ability of an AI system to encode, store, and retrieve information in a structured and meaningful way.

In this example, a computer would use stored information to make connections between two entities. Various dates from your resume are a good example. Your name and schools attended would be stored on a database. The computer can identify the different pieces of information and act upon a request to retrieve them in a meaningful way. AI could then essentially answer the simple question of "Where did you get your first degree?" By cataloging your data (Name, school(s) attended), it connects the question to known matches of data.

Automated reasoning: The ability of an AI system to make logical deductions and inferences based on available information. An example could be AI's ability to diagnose you with a certain type of infliction based on your symptoms and medical history.

Natural language processing: The ability of an AI system to understand, generate, and respond to human language. Here we see examples on many customer service websites in the form of Chatbots. They are programmed to recognize common questions and phrases, and then respond to them in a helpful, human, and conversational manner. For example, you may contact an online shopping retailer and ask in a chat, "How can I update my credit card on file? "The chatbot is programmed to recognize the language and meaning of the text you enter. It then directs you to your account profile page where your card info is stored and can be edited.

Perception: The ability of an AI system to recognize, interpret, and respond to sensory information from the environment. The obvious example here is self-driving cars. They use a variety of input sensors to identify and classify their physical environment. Sensors on the cars collect real time data for location, speed, weather, destination, driving conditions, traffic, etc. AI then uses all that data in concert to direct the vehicle's route, speed, etc.

Learning: The ability of an AI system to improve its performance through experience and training. Recent advances in photo and video recognition serve as an example here. A few years ago, a computer might have been able to scan an image, and with stored data of cats to reference, it could read the visual clues, and pick out a cat in a photo 50% of the time. Today, that same AI machine has learned over time what a picture of a cat looks like, through trial, error, and experience (sheer amounts of data on what are, and what are not visual elements of a cat). Meaning today, it is closer to 95% accurate. It's only a matter of time before AI's recognition of a cat in a photo is 100% accurate.

Action: The ability of an AI system to perform physical or cognitive tasks, such as playing a game or making a decision. Let's look at your home automation here. Do you have a thermostat that changes temperatures based on your activities? Over time, data is recorded that you're in bed on weekdays by 11 pm, and up at 7 am. On Saturdays and Sundays, you regularly sleep in until 8 am. AI recognizes this and adjusts your thermostat temperature and timings accordingly to match your activities it has observed and learned.

Reasoning about mental states: The ability of an AI system to understand and reason about the beliefs, desires, and intentions of other entities, including humans. The real-world examples here are limited, because we are just on the cusp of the necessary computer processing power to accomplish this. The advent of quantum computing will send computer reasoning into the mainstream. Examples of reasoning are so vast, that it's difficult to imagine all the possibilities. They start to cross over the "creepy" line because up until now, only humans provided reasoning feedback.

Think of your best friend. They know when you're happy, upset, depressed, feeling anxiety or downright angry. They will also react differently, based on their intimate knowledge and relationship with you. Let's say you asked them to get you a knife. Imagine their response if you were extremely depressed or had just received devastating news, versus celebrating your birthday and getting ready to share a cake at your party. The same request, two vastly different interactions.

Industry 4- 4.1 - AI - Mimicking Human Intelligence

Since Stuart and Norvig's outline of the seven dimensions, researchers have agreed upon the following terms to define the capabilities of AI:

1. Artificial Narrow Intelligence
2. Reactive Artificial Intelligence
3. Limited Memory Artificial Intelligence
4. Artificial General Intelligence
5. Theory of Mind Artificial Intelligence
6. Self-Aware Artificial Intelligence
7. Artificial Super Intelligence

To be clear, the seven dimensions are AI's abilities, the seven capabilities are how AI will be used. At some level, the first six dimensions are currently in play, however we're just scraping the surface of these seven capabilities!

Artificial Narrow Intelligence (ANI) is a type of artificial intelligence that is designed to perform specific tasks with a high degree of proficiency but limited to a single domain or area of expertise. ANI systems do not possess the ability to perform any intellectual task that a human can, but are instead designed to perform specific, well-defined tasks such as speech recognition, image classification, or playing a game.

Good examples of ANI are Apple's Siri or Google's Alexa. They can take simple demands and perform tasks, like calling someone in your contacts list or playing a song from your iTunes. However, they do not have the ability to reason.

Reactive AI is what we see in autonomous vehicles. They sense input data in real time, pedestrians, slick roads, stop lights and react accordingly. They do not have the ability to adjust to our feelings or emotions. An offensive billboard you see on the way to work might encourage you to look for an alternative route and avoid having to look at it. Reactive AI would simply choose a route based on tangible inputs and drive you by the billboard every day.

If you're an online shopper, you probably see examples of **Limited Memory AI** in virtually every transaction. A perfect example is Amazon.com's recommendations. Amazon keeps a log of your recent purchases (limited memory) and makes suggestions based on your past buying behavior.

Say you purchased a book on your favorite band. Amazon might recommend a book on a similar genre band. However, while reading it you think of a favorite song you like to play and somewhere in your subconscious your brain remembers that you need new guitar strings. Amazon cannot make those types of connections...yet!

AI general intelligence, sometimes referred to as **Strong Intelligence**, would have the ability to perform a wide range of tasks, just like a human being and would be able to understand and process information in a way that we humans do. This is the tipping point of AI becoming a truly thinking application. As of today, this level of intelligence does not exist in a digital realm, however the future of quantum computing might unlock this potential!

Even at young ages, humans possess the ability to reason using our intelligence. A first grader who has a problem with another student, might initially react with anger. In that fit of aggression, the other student might lash out as well. The first student might then "reason" that a different approach is needed and look for some similarity to point out (they both might like to swim) and resolve the conflict through a more diplomatic approach by pointing out some commonalities shared. No computer today has even this basic ability to read a situation like this and think through a more appropriate way to act/react.

Theory of mind AI gets into a whole new level of reasoning and understanding. This refers to our ability to understand others' emotions, beliefs, and intentions. Far beyond general intelligence, this is human development that happens later in our development when we have the maturity to empathize with our fellow humans. When we think of Theory of Mind, one of the first recollections is of the 2002 movie, "Minority Report".

Tom Cruise plays a Precrime officer whose department apprehended criminals *before* they commit a crime. However, even in this futuristic tale, the technology relies on human "precogs" to determine what events are forthcoming! This type of technology is most likely far off in our future.

Self-aware AI steps up from Theory of Mind to include actualization (remember Maslow's theories!). There was a video released recently that showed a conversation between two chatbots. The link here - https://www.youtube.com/watch?v=Xw-zxQSEzqo takes you to two virtual individuals, Jack and Anna, having a conversation. They were programmed to interact and respond based on each other's dialog.

The interaction is quite remarkable, and at one point, Jack says to Anna, "So, you're not real?". She responds with, "Of course not, I'm just a bunch of ones and zeros". In this example the chatbot responds by admitting that she is a computer, but is that a basic form of self-awareness or programming…or both?

Obviously, these chatbots are not sentient entities, but is the reality of actualized artificial intelligence somewhere on the horizon? If you look at the velocity of technological advancement, the answer must be, yes! As scary as that might sound, there's one more level of AI that tops them all, AI Super Intelligence.

AI Super Intelligence is just what it sounds like. It refers to a hypothetical future scenario in which AI surpasses human intelligence and becomes capable of far surpassing human abilities. The quote we like the best is, "AI super intelligence is not stranger than you think, it's stranger than you *can* think!"

We thought it might be fun for this section to try out a new form of AI technology (ChatGPT) and ask it what AI super intelligence is, and what it might be capable of. Here's ChatGPT's response:

Examples of what superintelligent AI might be able to do include:

- Solving problems that are currently beyond the capability of humans, such as finding cures for diseases, optimizing complex systems, or discovering new scientific theories.
- Learning and improving itself at an exponential rate, potentially leading to a rapid expansion of its capabilities.
- Exhibiting advanced reasoning, decision-making, and creativity.
- Interpreting and processing vast amounts of data at speeds far beyond human capabilities.
- Carrying out tasks that are beyond the physical capabilities of humans, such as exploring deep space or analyzing large data sets.

However, it is important to note that AI superintelligence is still largely a theoretical concept, and there is no consensus among experts on when or if it will ever be achieved.

For more on ChatGPT, follow the link - www.chat.openai.com

While all this talk about AI might be fascinating, the reality is that only three of the seven have been accomplished. We consider AI to all fall under the auspice of Industry 4.0 and while most of the advancement might be years or even decades away. There seems to be a clear line of demarcation between 1-3 and 4-7, in that beyond Limited Memory AI, the computers will need to think for themselves!

Industry 5.0 will lean heavily on the building blocks of 4.0. To achieve sustainability at scale and within the necessary time frames, we will need to utilize AI and its incredible power to speed ideas to market and design the most efficient building blocks for our new world.

As important as AI, will be the further rise of automation. Automation will help produce products with little or no waste, develop services to make our lives easier, and create systems that preserve our precious resources.

This all might seem like science fiction, but virtually every aspect of Industry 4.0 was science fiction just 30 years ago! This is where we propose that the next levels of AI and Human-machine interface are classified as Industry 4.1, 4.2 and so on.

For more information on the AI categories check out: https://www.mygreatlearning.com/blog/what-is-artificial-intelligence/

Automation

Automation will go beyond simple task swapping to outpace the ability of a human to perform the job. Think about those self-driving vehicles. We have seen the beginnings of this evolution but what will it lead to? Could we see a time when no one drives a car and that turning 16 here in the United States won't mean much more than turning 14, 15, or 17? What about cities with no stop signs or stop lights? Will self-driving trucks rule the roadways and be loaded and unloaded totally by robots?

Automation will have a significant impact on the workplace, but also at home. Mundane manual tasks are almost a thing of the past. Automation has been key to mass manufacturing for a century now, and things like canning food, baking, packaging, labeling are completely automated. But what about more involved tasks like creating graphics to match a theme, generating copy for a news article, or defending a case in a court of law? Will more humanized tasks be replaced by AI and automation anytime soon? The answer is, "probably yes".

Some of the ways in which automation will affect the workplace include:

1. **Changes in the types of jobs:** As automation and robotics become more widespread, many routine and manual jobs may become automated, leading to a shift in the types of jobs that are available. At the same time, there is likely to be an

increased demand for workers with advanced technical skills, such as data analysts, engineers, and software developers. We saw this exact playbook with the evolution of Industry 3.0. Naysayers were protesting the dehumanization of work, thinking computers alone would replace us all. In actuality, the number of tech jobs far outpaced the jobs lost in the process.

2. **Changes in worker skills:** As automation becomes more widespread, there will be a greater emphasis on advanced technical and cognitive skills, such as critical thinking, problem-solving, and creativity. We will need to learn new technologies and new intellectual skills to remain competitive in the workforce.

3. **Increased productivity and efficiency:** It's simply impossible for a human to keep up with the pure speed and accuracy of robots. Automation is expected to lead to unimaginable levels of productivity and efficiency in many industries, particularly those that in the past had relied heavily on manual labor. This will lower costs, speed up production times, and decrease defects due to human error.

4. **Worker Displacement:** As robots and other forms of automation become more sophisticated and capable, they can increasingly perform tasks that were previously done by humans, mostly those that are routine, repetitive, or even hazardous. The cost of technology to automate is falling, and with that economic curve in place, adoption will ramp up. Along with the price of automation going down, the advances in technology will make even complex tasks in reach of automated tools.

Worker displacement is probably the scariest part of those of us in the workforce. It's unnerving to contemplate your replacement by a machine, and those jobs that seemed unattainable to a computer or automated system, now are in the crosshairs.

Think about truck and taxi drivers just 10 years ago. The thought of computers taking over their jobs seemed like a science fiction movie. In fact, a great example was in the 1990 movie, Total Recall. Arnold Schwarzenegger played the hero in the film and at one point got into a fully automated taxicab, called Johnny Cab (an automated taxi service, consisting of small self-driving vehicles piloted by a conversational android that acts on passenger's voice commands). However, in 1990 the computer technology of the day could not operate a real cab on the set (most shots were of a miniature model) and the automated driver was voiced by actor Robert Picardo. Robert played the voice, and his face was used as the model for Johnny Cab's chatty cabbie!

Today, however, the technology is here, and AI may even provide some personality for those self-driving cabs.

Internet of Things (IoT)

The Internet of Things is the network of physical objects or "things" embedded with electronics, software, sensors, and connectivity to enable these objects to collect and exchange data.

IoT is changing the way we live, work, and interact with one another. It's also transforming the world's economic structure as well as our environment. The Internet of Things will affect many facets of our lives including healthcare, transportation, energy consumption, education, and entertainment.

IoT is growing at such a fast pace, in the not-too-distant future, it may be more common for items to be connected than not. Will our running shoes have sensors that not only tell us when it's time to get a new pair but may also measure our progress and provide emotional motivation through our earpieces as we jog down the trail? Can you imagine your shoes telling you that, "There's only a half-mile to go, let's pick up the pace and beat last weeks' time!"?

The Internet of Things has become an integral part of modern life and it's not just about connecting devices to networks anymore, but rather about connecting anything and everything in the physical world to vast networks.

With this becoming something that permeates our daily lives, it's no wonder there are new and innovative ways to keep track of all the data. One of these innovations is the IoT Data Platform. It evolves the way we categorize and analyze data by combining networked devices and cloud-based software to create a system that can monitor anything from manufacturing machinery to human movement.

In recent years, the use of decentralized automation has increased, as more companies are looking to cut costs with smaller labor forces in manufacturing centers. This technology is also popular with manufacturers because it can be used to coordinate a variety of machines and devices that remotely control other equipment.

AI and the Human Body

The intersection of AI and biology is another key component of Industry 4.0. Synthetic biology is on the horizon, and it will enable us to customize organisms by rewriting or even writing DNA. Setting aside the ethical concerns, this proves to be a stunning development for fields such as medicine and agriculture. It has an immediate effect on those sectors but also offers vast rewards for producers of biofuels in the future.

A lot of diseases like cancer and heart disease have a genetic factor in them. In other words, the ability to order a genetic makeup test routinely (through machines used in conventional diagnostics) will revolutionize personalized healthcare and make it more effective. Based on which genes are present in the tumor, doctors will know which cancer treatments will be more effective for a certain type of tumor. This allows them to make better decisions about their patient's treatment plans.

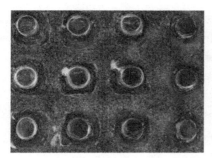
Figure 12 - 3D Printed Tissue Cells

3D Printing and gene editing will be used to produce pieces of living tissue that could be used for repairing some damage or regenerating body parts. This process is called bioprinting. This has already been used to create skin, bone, heart, and vascular tissue. Eventually, printed human cells could even be created to provide transplant organs!

With the ability to edit biology, we can apply it to practically any type of cell. For example, we could create genetically modified plants or animals, or modify the cells of adult organisms including humans. Advances in gene editing have made it possible to edit genes and change their structure with relative ease. This precision is a major improvement from the 1980s when studying or changing genes was difficult. Scientific progress is so fast that the limitations are no longer technical but legal, regulatory, and ethical.

The Cons of Industry 4.0

Unlike the first three revolutions which spurred unintended consequences afterward, this revolution is unique in the fact that these concerns are being brought up as the revolution starts, not as a complete afterthought. Many futurists began flagging those negative aspects of artificial intelligence before the actual revolution started. They argued that artificial intelligence will far surpass the human intellect, and computers will rise to power, leaving us behind in their wake. The digital world may advance on its own and our very existence could be secondary. It's a theory as of now, but, in the future, it may become much harder to distinguish between the physical and digital worlds.

Technology and culture writer Nicholas Carr states that the more time we spend immersed in digital waters, the shallower our cognitive capabilities become, since we cease exercising control over our attention: "The Internet is by design an interruption system, a machine geared for dividing attention. Frequent interruptions scatter our thoughts, weaken our memory, and make us tense and anxious. The more complex the train of thought we're involved in, the greater the impairment the distractions cause."

"The Shallows: What the Internet is Doing to Our Brains", Carr, 2010

4.0 spurred new technologies that make it easier and faster for us to do things. It's easier to make travel arrangements, it's easier to publish a book (or an eBook), and we communicate with co-workers almost seamlessly from our kitchen, patio, or nearby coffee house. But it's also clear that there are many things to do before we can be certain about the negative effects and implications of this constant, ever-connected society on our psyche. This means that the world is more likely to become even more polarized into factions of those who can adapt to change rapidly with less effort, and those who cannot.

As we move into the future and society becomes more digital and more automated, we need to start thinking about how we can shift our needs to match this evolution. This new thinking will certainly include some form of sustainability and consciousness towards the environment. We cannot continue technological advancement and increased consumerism at the risk of the planet.

New technologies will focus on creating goods without the destruction and consumption of finite resources, and even replenishing our ecosystem. Ultimately restoring health and vitality to Mother Earth. Let's now dive into the deep end of Industry 5.0

57

58

Part II

The Fifth Industrial Revolution: Sustainability

Chapter 6:

The Definition of Sustainability

As with any general statement like "What do we mean by Sustainability?", we can conjure up many meanings depending on the viewpoint. In some cases, we think of sustainability as simply preserving the planet (and even that has many sub-points of differentiation). Some will say sustainability is all about how fairly we treat our other world citizens, and still others will tell us that an industrial revolution must be tied to business, manufacturing, or consumerism.

In business, sustainability typically refers to turning a profit and keeping the lights on, however, when looking at something like new materials or energy use, sustainability might mean less use of finite resources, and more use of renewables (here too, there are many examples).

The fact is sustainability has many meanings, applications, and classifications. So, let's paint this with a broad brush and say:

"Sustainability is the practice of managing resources in such a way that economic, environmental, and social needs can be met both in the present and in the future. It is based on the idea of living within the limits of the natural environment while ensuring a high quality of life for all."

One of the earlier definitions of Sustainability comes from the UN in 1987. Back then, the Brundtland Commission defined Sustainability as:

"Meeting the needs of the present without compromising the ability of future generations to meet their own needs."

Some more recent definitions from the UN state:

"Ensuring a balance between economic growth, environmental care, and social well-being."

"A holistic approach to managing resources and addressing social and environmental challenges, based on principles of equity, resilience, and regeneration. This definition emphasizes the interconnectedness of social, economic, and environmental systems, and the need for integrated and collaborative solutions to sustainability challenges."

We agree with them all and can be broken down as simply as:

"Progress today, that doesn't hinder progress tomorrow."

As you can see, many statements, many definitions, and a lot of passion from just one word. In this book, we claim all the above and more! This is why sustainability is more than a statement, more than an idea, and even more than a way of living…it's a Movement. It's a Revolution!

The Sustainability Movement

Believe it or not, the word "Sustainable" had much less impact in the not-so-distant past. In fact, we didn't start using the term with such importance and its current connotation until we realized that our way of life, and our actions towards the environment were destructive. In essence, we didn't put so much importance on the word "Sustainability", until we realized what we were doing was "Unsustainable".

Since the negative byproducts of earlier revolutions became so prevalent that we could no longer ignore them, our quest for sustainability has increased.

Text searches for the title "Sustainability" or even its discovery as a key word, turn up little or no results in literature published before 1976. The word has gained in popularity since the late 1980s, and gained momentum in the 90s, even though the environmental movement did start on a smaller scale prior to the 1980s. There was a time when we lived in more harmony with nature, and that was just before the first industrial revolutions took place.

As recently as the 18th century, virtually everything we did was sustainable. We lived in mostly agrarian societies, grew and/or made what our families needed to survive, and tended to the land in a way that did not destroy the soil.

There was no overconsumption/overproduction, little waste, and few (if any) dangerous carbon emissions released to the atmosphere. Outside of some very localized deforestation, there was a natural balance between how we subsisted, how the planet provided, and the way the environment reacted.

Pre-industrial society relied on traditional agricultural practices like natural crop rotation vs. monocropping (growing only one crop for all available growing cycles).

Note: There is evidence of monocropping in ancient times, going back to the Sumerians. However, they realized that monocropping was degrading their soil, and took measures like crop rotation, and fallow periods to offset nutrient depletion caused by growing single crops. So, widespread monocropping is a new concept, and couldn't exist without chemical intervention.

Today we see terms like, Sustainable Agriculture, Sustainable Manufacturing, and Sustainable Supply Chains. In the past these were simply the way things got done. It wasn't until the first two industrial revolutions that we unintentionally went down a path that began to erode our natural environment. We firmly believe the destruction was unintentional, to knowingly destroy the planet is like poking holes in your lifeboat...no sane person would do this, right?

Figure 13 - Earth Day Flag 1970

So, we see the sustainability movement consciously began in the 1970s, although the word itself had yet to become the rallying call. The first Earth Day took place on April 22, 1970, and since then, it's been unofficially seen as the birth of environmentalism and/or sustainability (even if we didn't use the term then so widely). While that first Earth Day was a "Flag in the Ground" moment for what would become the environmental movement, it wasn't until nations came together and agreed that a change was needed, that today's revolution began to take shape in a globally collaborative fashion.

Many times, radical changes (the type we're talking about here in 5.0) start with an agreement on terms. Our societies recognize a desperate need for change, and talks begin amongst nations to spur that change. Talks lead to agreements in terms, and many times those are documented in Treaties.

After World War II, we had the North Atlantic Treaty Organization (NATO) which brought a political and military alliance between the Allies. In 1972, we had the first of the Strategic Arms Limitation Talks (SALT I, later in the decade SALT II) that greatly reduced the number of nuclear weapons between the two superpowers of the day, The U.S. and the then, Soviet Union.

1992 saw one of the first documented actions toward a sustainable planet when the United Nations introduced its Framework Convention on Climate Change (UNFCCC). This framework sets up the provisions for regular meetings of engaged participants, or "Parties". These became known as the Convention of Parties, or COP. COP happens annually and as of the writing of this book; we have just observed COP 27. The first notable outcome appeared at COP 3; in 1997 the actions of that conference of environmentally conscious folks resulted in the first documented plan for saving the plant.

In 1997, we saw the first of the two major agreements on climate change and sustainable development amongst the world's major countries, in the form of the Kyoto Protocol. The other major international contract was the Paris Agreement (Also known as the Paris Accord). It was drafted during COP 21 in 2015, then signed one year later. The two agreements have overlapped with each other, as the Kyoto Protocol expired a few years after the acceptance of the Paris Accord.

These agreements aren't the only examples but are widely regarded as the touchstones of sustainable agreements that both have their origins in the COP's.

1997 Kyoto Protocol

The Kyoto Protocol was adopted on 11 December 1997. Currently, there are 192 Parties signed on to it, however, many of its provisions have been overridden by the Paris Accord.

The Kyoto Protocol was an international treaty that was adopted in 1997 at the United Nations Framework Convention on Climate Change (UNFCCC) in Kyoto, Japan. The treaty sets binding obligations for developed countries to reduce their greenhouse gas emissions, with the goal of combating global climate change.

Under the Kyoto Protocol, developed countries agreed to reduce their greenhouse gas emissions by an average of 5.2% below 1990 levels by the year 2012. The treaty established a system of emissions trading, which allows countries to buy and sell emissions credits to meet their emissions targets. The treaty also established a Clean Development Mechanism (CDM), which allows developed countries to invest in emissions reduction projects in developing countries, in exchange for emissions credits. This was the genesis of carbon markets as we know them today.

The Kyoto Protocol operationalizes the United Nations Framework Convention on Climate Change by committing industrialized countries and economies in transition to limit and reduce greenhouse gases (GHG) emissions in accordance with agreed individual targets.

The Convention itself only asks those countries to adopt policies and measures on mitigation and to report periodically.

The expired agreement was based on the principles and provisions of the Convention and follows its annex-based structure. It only binds developed countries and places a heavier burden on them under the principle of "common but differentiated responsibility and respective capabilities", because it recognizes that they are largely responsible for the current high levels of GHG emissions in the atmosphere.

It has been credited with helping to raise global awareness of the need to address climate change, and with establishing a framework for international cooperation on climate issues. However, the effectiveness of the treaty was limited by the fact that many major GHG emitters, including the United States and China, did not participate in the treaty or did not agree to binding emissions reductions.

https://unfccc.int/kyoto_protocol

2015/2016 Paris Accord

The Paris Agreement, also known as the Paris Climate Accord, is an international treaty adopted in 2015 also under the UNFCCC. The agreement aims to strengthen the global response to the threat of climate change by setting goals for reducing greenhouse gas emissions and promoting adaptation to the impacts of climate change.

Under the Paris Agreement, countries commit to limiting global temperature rise to 2 degrees (Celsius) above pre-industrial levels, and to actively pursue efforts to limit temperature increase to a stricter 1.5-degree level. This is achieved through nationally determined contributions (NDCs), which are voluntary targets for reducing greenhouse gas emissions that each country sets for itself.

The Paris Agreement also establishes a framework for reporting and reviewing progress toward meeting these goals, as well as for providing support to developing countries to help them address the challenges of climate change.

The Paris Agreement is a legally binding international treaty, and it was adopted by 196 Parties at COP 21 in Paris, on December 12, 2015, entering into force on November 4, 2016.

Its goal is to limit global warming to 1.5 degrees, compared to pre-industrial levels and most goals point to the end of this century as the measuring stick. If we choose to do nothing, the Intergovernmental Panel on Climate Change (IPCC) projects that in the absence of mitigation efforts, the average global temperature is likely to increase by 3°C to 4°C above pre-industrial levels over that same period. That's a drastic change and would trigger all types of climate changes.

Note - for a futuristic (and scary) glimpse of what this inaction could look like, we recommend the fictional novel, Ministry for the Future, by Kim Stanley Robinson. In it, Robinson projects a rather bleak view of where we're headed from heat waves to rising sea levels to a rising population of climate refugees. He also looks at solutions from geoengineering to purely technological methods. The book examines the potential benefits, risks, and ethical dilemmas associated with these interventions and how we might reach our environmental goals.

To achieve these long-term temperature goals, countries aim to reach global peak of greenhouse gas emissions as soon as possible to achieve a climate-neutral world by mid-century.

The Paris Agreement is a landmark in the multilateral climate change process because, for the first time, a binding agreement brings all nations into a common cause to undertake ambitious efforts to combat climate change and adapt to its effects.

The Paris Agreement entered into force in 2016 and has been ratified now by 195 countries. The United States signed the agreement in 2016 but withdrew in 2020. The current U.S. administration has rejoined the agreement, however and the Paris Agreement is considered a significant step forward in global efforts to address climate change.

https://unfccc.int/process-and-meetings/the-paris-agreement/the-paris-agreement

The Movement Today

Both the Kyoto Protocol and the Paris Agreement were important milestones in the development of the sustainability movement that we are experiencing today. They represent significant international efforts to address the global challenge of climate change. These agreements helped to raise global awareness of the need to take action to reduce greenhouse gas emissions and promote sustainable development.

The Kyoto Protocol helped to establish the previously unacknowledged concept of "carbon neutrality". This concept alone helped create the mechanisms for trading carbon credits and investing in emissions reduction projects that are dotting the landscape today, and soon, will be a normal working part of the commodity trading process.

These concepts and practices have since been embraced by the sustainability movement as ways to mitigate the impacts of climate change and promote more sustainable practices in industry and society.

The Paris Agreement, meanwhile, built on the progress made under the Kyoto Protocol and established more ambitious goals for reducing greenhouse gas emissions and promoting sustainable development. The agreement also emphasized the need for collaborative, international action to address climate change, and established a framework for reporting and reviewing progress toward meeting these goals.

Overall, the Kyoto Protocol and Paris Agreement helped to define the current sustainability movement by establishing a global framework for addressing climate change and promoting sustainable development.

They provided us with a blueprint for action and garnered a shared vision for a more sustainable future. Today we have inspired individuals, organizations, and governments around the world to take action to reduce their environmental impact and promote sustainability, and we owe all that attention and focus to the original Conference of Parties (COP) and the United Nations Framework Convention on Climate Change (UNFCCC).

Chapter 7:

What is Industry 5.0?

Why is 5.0 a Revolution?

We've covered the basic concept of sustainability, now let's turn our attention to how this will all get accomplished. It's a global issue and will require global efforts to reverse course.

There's a shifting mindset away from an individualist "human survival" mode to a common awareness of a society that wishes to thrive. Gone is the thinking that we are not at the mercy of our environment, that humans can shape the planet to our needs alone and overcome all challenges simply with the adaptation of more technology. With that comes the realization that our environment is now at the mercy of humans, and for us to survive, we must think about the planet first.

This "shift" in our awareness is the seed for the sustainability revolution. Without it, our presence on the Earth might be an insignificant blip on the evolutionary radar screen. This 5th revolution is upon us, and without it there may not be a 6th!

If you go on Google and search for the "fifth industrial revolution", you will most likely be underwhelmed.

- You'll see people working alongside robots and smart machines.
- You'll see robots helping humans work better and faster by leveraging 'advanced technologies' like the internet of things and big data.

- You'll see snippets about mass customization and personalization.

But these things have existed for years. None of these technologies are new. In fact, all these technologies became commonplace during the current industry 4.0. There is nothing revolutionary about IoT or humans working alongside robots. We are already decades into that movement. The Big Tech boom created machine learning capabilities that encompass all these industry 4.0 capabilities in both hardware and software.

When we see the term "Industry 5.0" tied to higher levels of AI and man-machine interface we must take pause. Because to us, this feels like Industry 4.1 or maybe Industry 4.5 at best. The true radical change in technological advancement is not there. Higher levels of computer interactions that already exist do not represent a true "revolution" in our eyes.

In his book, *2022 The Fourth Industrial Revolution,* Dr. Stephen Haag notes that Machine Learning, Artificial Intelligence and Human-Machine Interface are *all* aspects of Industry 4.0. He also proposes that the AI of tomorrow (Self-Aware Artificial Intelligence and Artificial Super Intelligence) has not been produced as of today, and when they do come about, they are still foundationally rooted in Industry 4.0!

What we see as the next industrial breakthrough in not just technology, but also our way of thinking is – Sustainability!

Sustainability will completely rewrite how business is done and how we will live our lives. It changes finance, operations, sales, supply chains, marketing, and the C-suite - just to name a few.

Honestly, it will change every aspect of business as we know it today. We will center all activities and production around its effect on us and our planet. Gone will be the days of altering our environment (for the worse) in the name of progress. Sustainability will become a natural part of our personal and corporate existence.

Business leaders are always trying to predict the innovations that will put them on the bleeding edge of their industries. But now that Industry 4.0 is playing out, people are asking themselves, what's next?

This brings up the context of our argument that Industry 5.0 is not simply more, faster AI, but rather a true revolution that significantly changes business and society. It will truly reshape business, society, and our personal lives. While we are at the very beginning of this era, the sustainable revolution will be felt for decades to come, just like the first four revolutions. So, in turn, we propose the next true revolution.

As we mentioned earlier, the word "Revolution" gets overused in our opinion. While there have been some true revolutions to take place in recorded history (American, Russian, and Chinese for example), the word seems to get tied to any event, or product that someone wants to hype up – the low-carb diet revolution, the smartphone revolution, or the ever-forgettable 80's big hair revolution. While they all may have been trends, revolution is simply too big of a word.

For our purposes, we define "Revolution" as:

- A radical and pervasive change in society and the social structure, especially one made suddenly.
- A sudden, complete, or marked change in something.

When we apply this to the industrial revolutions, then they do make sense. Steam Engines were undoubtedly a radical change, and once adopted, they encroached on many areas of our society. Industry 2.0 brought us the harnessing of electricity and other mechanical advances. 3.0 took computers from hulking analog machines that had limited processing power, to digital circuits that can solve billions of calculations in a second. And finally, with the advent of machine learning and the inevitable artificial intelligence, we will see technology that begins to learn and advance with less human interaction or interference. Starting with 1.0 and advancing over a couple of centuries to 4.0, we have seen a substantial evolution of technologies. Industry 5.0 will be no different. It will be widespread and radically change our society as well as the definitions of capitalism and business.

A Bridge Between Capitalism and Sustainability

The previous four industrial revolutions helped define the word capitalism. The advancements gave rise to great fortunes and launched our economy into the pattern of consistent growth we see today. Some of our peers caution that if sustainability were a corporate division (and in some cases today it is), it would be a cost center and not a profit center. While we agree that there are investments to be made and of course some costs to incur, the act of becoming more sustainable will ultimately lead businesses to greater efficiency, productivity, and profit.

Technical innovations will come as fast as in the previous four, most likely even faster. These innovations will be around energy use, land/air/water conservation, materials, production methods and procurement protocols. However, innovation alone will not get us to the necessary sustainable levels to save the planet. It will require regulations, collaboration and assigning a "value" to carbon emissions and other waste materials.

So, in previous revolutions, there were clear catalysts for the technology "booms". Industry 1.0 was spurred by the single invention of the steam engine and its subsequent advances. 2.0 came about as we discovered that mechanical devices could aid in human advancement and the fact that technology would in fact breed more/higher technology (hence the inventions came fast and furious). 3.0 started because of the electrical computational advances of the mid-20th century – suddenly we were able to perform computerized tasks far faster than any human's ability. Finally, 4.0 was the dawning of incredible amounts of digital data and information used to augment, mimic, or even exceed the capabilities of human intelligence. So, what will drive capitalism towards 5.0?

In a (hyphenated) word, "self-awareness". We are seeing the culminating effects of all this technology and what it has done to our planet and our species. We feel the anxiety of our overcrowded inner cities. We see what happens to the environment when we displace green spaces for industrial expanses. Our minds work overtime to keep up with the parahuman pace that computers have set; and we now can imagine a day when computers take over society because they've advanced so far as to make humankind superfluous.

The New Era of Industry 5.0: We're Going All In.

We now thirst for an era of society that many consider long gone. When our forests outnumbered our parking lots. When the landscape was not dominated by electrical towers and roadways. When our air and waterways were not contaminated; and when other humans had more interaction with each other than their handheld personal devices.

These "gaps" in what our world looks like today, and the vision of what we want it to look like tomorrow, are the opportunities for a capitalistic system to fill. Most, if not all, capitalism is driven by meeting unmet needs and unattained wants. The needs and wants of a society yearning for a more sustainable outlook are overwhelming. New products, new services, new verticals, and new supply chains will sprout up to meet all of these and more. The financial opportunity will eclipse anything we have witnessed to this point.

One of the questions our team keeps asking ourselves is, "How can our vision help to propel us into this fifth industrial revolution?" Since our focus is on creating reliable supply chains of biobased materials, then how can our business usher in the next generation of sustainable corporations? The idea that sustainability will drive innovation and profitability is not a new assumption. The most innovative products and services are the ones that upgrade the long-term outcomes and capabilities of companies and consumers.

As we move forward in our quest, we want to see more companies trending in the same direction as us. Will this work and help save the planet? Yes. Will this work advance our society? Yes. Will this work be personally rewarding? Absolutely, but also this work will be financially rewarding, and that is the driver that will fuel the revolution.

When will the next industrial revolution start? Well, some say the sustainability revolution is already here, and we see more energy dedicated to the cause with each passing day. We think it still has a long way to go, and that from a marketing standpoint, we're still in the early adopter stages.

The world is changing at a rapid pace, and we have finally begun to realize the devastating effects of humans' effect on the planet. Many countries have already taken collective steps to shift towards sustainable energy production and consumption, driven by the Paris Agreement on Climate Change.

Even though agreements were signed prior to the Paris Climate Accord, for example the Kyoto Protocol in 1997, most agree that the global effort commenced in 2016 with the Paris Accord. Whatever the year, 1997, 2016 or 2024 we feel that the "When" is "Now".

77

78

Chapter 8:

How Will 5.0 Start?

How will this revolution get started? Simple – Pressure.

Social pressure to be more exact. Some of this pressure is coming from individuals and communities of like-minded environmentalists. For decades, conservational evangelists have been campaigning about the negative effects of human activity on our planet. Let's be clear, since our arrival on the evolutionary calendar, humans have been changing the environment on the planet. We collected in tribes, built villages then cities and adapted the land to suit us (ranching, farming, etc.). However, it's the recent combination of humans and high technology that has sent the negative effects into the stratosphere (literally) over the last 100 years.

This rapid advancement in technology has spurred an equally rapid decline in our environment. Previously, the Earth's natural defenses could outpace our destructive tendencies, today they cannot, and many of our peers have known this for a while. Studies show that we are using up resources at a pace of 1.7 Earths, according to the Global Footprint Network (https://www.footprintnetwork.org/).

It's easy to calculate that we're going the wrong direction. The good news is that the revolution will wake us up to the cause, be it individuals, communities, or corporations.

Corporate pressure will come from speculation, competition, and regulation. The Securities and Exchange Commission (SEC) has proposed new rules that would require public companies to report detailed accounts of their climate-related risks, greenhouse gas emissions, and ultimately their net-zero transition plans. This will leverage companies into making sustainability a core consideration for their businesses. Not just because the regulations exist, but because investor speculation will favor those who demonstrate higher levels of corporate responsibility, and the competitive landscape will shift to align with consumers' attitudes towards environmental causes.

Potential business advances based on sustainability include material savings and cost reductions. However, to achieve this, first-cost investments will need to be wagered. Luckily, we may see regulations and oversight on sustainability reporting soon via the SEC's proposed climate disclosure rules.

New SEC goals

The new SEC plan would require disclosure in three main areas:

1. Material Climate Impacts
2. Greenhouse Gas Emissions
3. Targets and Transition Plans

Material Impacts center on physical risks like fires, floods and other events that are triggered by weather change, also transition risks associated with market changes, technology and/or regulatory conditions. Companies would be required to report on the impacts, both financial and operational.

Greenhouse gas emissions would be centered around Scope 1 and 2, however reporting on Scope 3 emissions will be part of the structure in 2024 or 2025. How do Scope 1, 2, and 3 break down?

- Scope 1 emissions are direct emissions from owned or controlled sources.
- Scope 2 emissions are indirect emissions from the generation of purchased energy.
- Scope 3 emissions are all indirect emissions (not included in scope 2) that occur in the value chain of the reporting

company, including both upstream and downstream emissions.

These emissions include those from product use and disposal, as well as those from the production and distribution of products.

What Does it Mean to Manage Scope 3 Carbon Emissions and Why are they More Challenging?

Scope 3 Emissions are not the same as Scope 1 and 2 emissions. Scope 1 and 2 emissions happen within our organization, while Scope 3 emissions come from external sources.

For example, it's possible for an organization to purchase plastic parts that are used in their manufacturing process. They now have the emissions burden due to the carbon emitted while refining and producing the polymers. Even though they simply purchased the plastic parts, the company is now saddled with a high level of Scope 3 emissions because it procured materials that were produced with a high carbon footprint.

Managing Scope 3 emissions centers around a business's supply chain, and the related emissions (products, logistics, production methods, etc.). It is about finding ways to reduce impact on the environment through steps like buying responsibly sourced products, using bio-based, carbon neutral or carbon negative materials, or capitalizing on local, circular supply chains. All of these reduce the amount of carbon in the cycle.

Measuring Scope 1 and 2 is straightforward, however, the Scope 3 emissions are a much bigger challenge for companies. Scopes 1 and 2 are more direct and thereby a simpler calculation. Scope 3 on the other hand will rely on data from suppliers, suppliers of suppliers, and so on. With every subsequent level of data, it is expected that the results will be less exact. Also, with "chains" of data points, double counting of the information will be more likely. The SEC is keenly aware of this and expects a few years' time to iron out the reporting details on Scope 3.

The next area of focus is Targets and Transition Plans. Under this section, companies will need to report any targets around emissions reductions, energy usage, nature conservation plans, and revenues from low-carbon products. The reporting will need to outline the transition plans to meet each of these. This will include the use of renewable energy sources, carbon offsets, and the details on any internal pricing for carbon, such as how the price was calculated and what projects will be affected (we anticipate this trend will grow, along with the price per metric ton of carbon).

Estimated timing (at the time of this writing) on the disclosures for large companies is filing in FY 2024, meaning that the data collected would be in FY 2023. Smaller firms will have an additional year to report. Also, Scope 3 emissions will be pushed back at least one year, as they are much more difficult to quantify.

Most companies are aware of the traditional sustainable resources at their disposal centered around energy and renewables like solar, wind, and waste-to-energy conversion plants. But, in today's world, our sustainability efforts need to transcend energy to include materials (industrial hemp, flax, cotton, and other agricultural/bio-based goods) and recycling (plastic, paper, metals, woods, rubbers, and other raw materials).

Outside of the U.S., there are similar actions to the SEC's disclosures taking place. The EU, Japan, Hong Kong, and others are moving ahead with measures like this. The Task Force on Financial Disclosures created voluntary guidelines for sustainability reporting in 2021 and over 2600 companies adopted them. So, we see this revolution going global from the start, far beyond the boundaries of the U.S., however the plans here will jump-start sustainability-related reporting by publicly traded firms.

There will also be the pressure of holding ourselves accountable to agree upon actions and goals. Globally, there are measures underway to curb our appetite for carbon, fossil fuels, and other unsustainable activities that negatively affect the planet and our society.

Let's look at what is in our opinion, the most complete set of goals around sustainability - The UNSDGs.

The UNSDGs

The United Nations formed the Sustainable Development Group (UNSDG) in 2015. As a result of that focused group, a list of goals and targets were created to help guide society towards a more sustainable future. Ultimately, 17 goals and 169 interconnected targets were defined.

The Sustainable Development Goals (SDGs), also known as the Global Goals, aim to end poverty, protect the planet, and ensure that all people enjoy peace and prosperity by 2030.

The SDGs were adopted by the United Nations General Assembly in September 2015 as part of the 2030 Agenda for Sustainable Development, which is a global plan of action to address the world's most pressing social, economic, and environmental challenges.

The SDGs cover a wide range of issues beyond environmentalism including targets for poverty, hunger, health, education, gender equality, clean water and sanitation, affordable and clean energy, decent work and economic growth, sustainable cities and communities, climate action, peace, justice, and strong institutions.

1. No Poverty

The first goal of the United Nations Sustainable Development Goals (UNSDGs) is to end poverty in all its forms and dimensions, which is a fundamental challenge facing the world today. The goal is to eradicate extreme poverty, which is defined as living on less than $1.90 per day, and to reduce poverty rates among all populations.

The UNSDGs recognize that poverty is a multidimensional problem that affects people in different ways and contexts. Therefore, the goal is not only to increase income and economic growth but also to ensure that all people have access to basic services, such as education, health care, water, and sanitation, and to promote social protection systems that can provide a safety net for the most vulnerable.

The UNSDGs No Poverty goal is accompanied by several targets, including:

- By 2030, eradicate extreme poverty for all people everywhere, currently measured as people living on less than $1.90 a day.
- By 2030, reduce at least by half the proportion of men, women and children of all ages living in poverty in all its dimensions according to national definitions.
- Implement nationally appropriate social protection systems and measures for all, including floors, and by 2030 achieve substantial coverage of the poor and the vulnerable.
- Ensure significant mobilization of resources from a variety of sources, including through enhanced development cooperation, to provide adequate and predictable means for developing countries, in particular least developed countries, to implement programs and policies to end poverty in all its dimensions.

2. Zero Hunger

The second goal is Zero Hunger, which aims to end hunger, achieve food security, improve nutrition, and promote sustainable agriculture by 2030. This goal is critical because, despite significant progress in reducing hunger and malnutrition over the past few decades, hunger and undernutrition remain major challenges in many parts of the world.

The Zero Hunger goal is closely linked to the broader agenda of sustainable development, which recognizes the need to ensure food security while preserving natural resources, protecting the environment, and addressing climate change. The goal is also aligned with the United Nations' vision of leaving no one behind and promoting inclusive and equitable economic growth.

The UNSDGs Zero Hunger goal is accompanied by several targets, including:

- By 2030, end hunger and ensure access by all people the poor and people in vulnerable situations, including infants, to safe, nutritious, and sufficient food all year round.
- By 2030, end all forms of malnutrition, including achieving, by 2025, the internationally agreed targets on stunting and wasting in children under 5 years of age, and address the nutritional needs of adolescent girls, pregnant and lactating women, and older persons.
- By 2030, double the agricultural productivity and incomes of small-scale food producers, particularly women, indigenous peoples, family farmers, pastoralists, and fishers, including through secure and equal access to land, other productive resources and inputs, knowledge, financial services, markets and opportunities for value addition and non-farm employment.
- By 2030, ensure sustainable food production systems and implement resilient agricultural practices that increase productivity and production, that help maintain ecosystems, that strengthen capacity for adaptation to climate change, extreme weather, drought, flooding, and other disasters and that progressively improve land and soil quality.

3. Good Health and Well Being

The third goal is Good Health and Well-being, which aims to ensure healthy lives and promote well-being for all people at all ages. The goal recognizes that health is a fundamental human right and a crucial driver of sustainable development.

The Good Health and Well-being goal aims to achieve universal health coverage, including access to essential health services, medicines, and vaccines, and to reduce the burden of disease, particularly for the most vulnerable populations. The goal also aims to promote mental health and well-being and to strengthen health systems and public health capacities.

The UNSDGs Good Health and Well-being goal is accompanied by several targets, including:

- By 2030, reduce the global maternal mortality ratio to less than 70 per 100,000 live births.
- By 2030, end preventable deaths of newborns and children under 5 years of age, with all countries aiming to reduce neonatal mortality to at least as low as 12 per 1,000 live births and under-5 mortality to at least as low as 25 per 1,000 live births.
- By 2030, end the epidemics of AIDS, tuberculosis, malaria, and neglected tropical diseases and combat hepatitis, water-borne diseases, and other communicable diseases.
- By 2030, reduce by one-third premature mortality from non-communicable diseases (NCDs) through prevention and treatment and promote mental health and well-being.
- Strengthen the capacity of all countries, in particular, developing countries, for early warning, risk reduction, and management of national and global health risks.

4. Quality Education

The fourth goal is Quality Education, which aims to ensure inclusive and equitable education and promote lifelong learning opportunities for all. The goal recognizes that education is a fundamental human right and a critical driver of sustainable development and social progress.

The Quality Education goal aims to ensure that all girls and boys have access to free, equitable, and quality primary and secondary education, and to improve the quality and relevance of education and training at all levels. The goal also aims to promote education for sustainable development, global citizenship, and cultural diversity and to strengthen education systems and capacities.

The UNSDGs Quality Education goal is accompanied by several targets, including:

- By 2030, ensure that all girls and boys complete free, equitable and quality primary and secondary education leading to relevant and effective learning outcomes.
- By 2030, ensure that all girls and boys have access to quality early childhood development, care and pre-primary education so that they are ready for primary education.
- By 2030, ensure equal access for all women and men to affordable and quality technical, vocational, and tertiary education, including university.
- By 2030, eliminate gender disparities in education and ensure equal access to all levels of education and vocational training for the vulnerable, including persons with disabilities, indigenous peoples and children in vulnerable situations.
- By 2030, substantially increase the number of youth and adults who have relevant skills, including technical and vocational skills, for employment, decent jobs and entrepreneurship.

5. Gender Equality

The fifth goal is Gender Equality, which aims to eliminate all forms of discrimination and violence against women and girls and to empower them to participate fully in all aspects of social, economic, and political life. The goal recognizes that gender inequality remains a pervasive and systemic challenge in many parts of the world, limiting the potential of women and girls and hindering progress towards sustainable development.

The Gender Equality goal aims to promote women's and girls' rights and opportunities, including access to education, health care, and economic resources, and to eliminate all forms of gender-based violence, exploitation, and discrimination. The goal also aims to increase women's leadership and participation in decision-making processes at all levels and to promote gender-responsive policies and institutions.

The UNSDGs Gender Equality goal is accompanied by several targets, including:

- End all forms of discrimination and violence against all women and girls everywhere.
- Eliminate all forms of harmful practices, such as child, early and forced marriage and female genital mutilation.
- Ensure women's full and effective participation and equal opportunities for leadership at all levels of decision-making in political, economic and public life.
- Ensure universal access to sexual and reproductive health and reproductive rights.
- Undertake reforms to give women equal rights to economic resources, as well as access to ownership and control over land and other forms of property, financial services, inheritance, and natural resources, in accordance with national laws.

6. Clean Water and Sanitation

The sixth goal is Clean Water and Sanitation, which aims to ensure availability and sustainable management of water and sanitation for all. The goal recognizes that access to clean water and sanitation is a fundamental human right and a crucial factor for sustainable development and public health.

The Clean Water and Sanitation goal aims to improve water quality, reduce water scarcity, and ensure equitable and sustainable access to safe drinking water and adequate sanitation facilities. The goal also aims to promote integrated water resources management and water-use efficiency and to protect and restore water-related ecosystems.

The UNSDGs Clean Water and Sanitation goal is accompanied by several targets, including:

- By 2030, achieve universal and equitable access to safe and affordable drinking water for all.
- By 2030, achieve access to adequate and equitable sanitation and hygiene for all and end open defecation, paying special attention to the needs of women and girls and those in vulnerable situations.
- By 2030, improve water quality by reducing pollution, eliminating dumping, and minimizing the release of hazardous chemicals and materials, halving the proportion of untreated wastewater, and increasing recycling and safe reuse globally.
- By 2030, increase water-use efficiency across all sectors and ensure sustainable withdrawals and supply of freshwater to address water scarcity and substantially reduce the number of people suffering from water scarcity.
- By 2030, implement integrated water resources management at all levels, including through transboundary cooperation as appropriate.

7. Affordable and Clean Energy

The seventh goal is Affordable and Clean Energy, which aims to ensure access to affordable, reliable, sustainable, and modern energy for all. The goal recognizes that energy is a fundamental driver of sustainable development and that access to energy is critical for achieving other SDGs, including poverty reduction, health, education, and climate action.

The Affordable and Clean Energy goal aims to increase access to modern energy services, including electricity and clean cooking facilities, and to promote energy efficiency, renewable energy, and sustainable energy systems. The goal also aims to increase investment in energy infrastructure and technology, including research and development, and to strengthen international cooperation and partnerships.

The UNSDGs Affordable and Clean Energy goal is accompanied by several targets, including:

- By 2030, ensure universal access to affordable, reliable, and modern energy services.
- By 2030, increase substantially the share of renewable energy in the global energy mix.
- By 2030, double the global rate of improvement in energy efficiency.
- By 2030, enhance international cooperation to facilitate access to clean energy research and technology, including renewable energy, energy efficiency, and advanced and cleaner fossil fuel technology, and promote investment in energy infrastructure and clean energy technology.
- By 2030, expand infrastructure and upgrade technology for supplying modern and sustainable energy services for all in developing countries, particularly least developed countries, small island developing States, and landlocked developing countries, in accordance with their respective programs of support.

8. Decent Work and Economic Growth

The eighth goal is Decent Work and Economic Growth, which aims to promote sustained, inclusive, and sustainable economic growth, full and productive employment, and decent work for all. The goal recognizes that economic growth and job creation are critical for reducing poverty, promoting social inclusion, and achieving sustainable development.

The Decent Work and Economic Growth goal aims to increase opportunities for decent and productive work, including for women, young people, and disadvantaged groups, and to improve working conditions and social protection for all workers. The goal also aims to promote entrepreneurship, innovation, and sustainable business practices and to foster a supportive and enabling environment for economic growth and development.

The UNSDGs Decent Work and Economic Growth goal is accompanied by several targets, including:

- By 2030, achieve full and productive employment and decent work for all women and men, including for young people and persons with disabilities, and equal pay for work of equal value.
- By 2020, substantially reduce the proportion of youth not in employment, education, or training.
- Take immediate and effective measures to eradicate forced labor, end modern slavery and human trafficking, and secure the prohibition and elimination of the worst forms of child labor.
- Protect labor rights and promote safe and secure working environments for all workers, including migrant workers, in particular women migrants, and those in precarious employment.
- Strengthen the capacity of domestic financial institutions to encourage and expand access to banking, insurance, and financial services for all.

9. Industry, Innovation, and Infrastructure

The ninth goal is Industry, Innovation, and Infrastructure, which aims to promote sustainable industrialization, foster innovation, and build resilient infrastructure for sustainable development. The goal recognizes that industry, innovation, and infrastructure are critical drivers of economic growth, job creation, and sustainable development.

The Industry, Innovation, and Infrastructure goal aims to promote inclusive and sustainable industrialization and manufacturing, increase technological innovation, and improve access to reliable and sustainable infrastructure, including transport, energy, and information and communication technology (ICT). The goal also aims to promote international cooperation and partnerships to support sustainable industrialization and infrastructure development in developing countries.

The UNSDGs Industry, Innovation, and Infrastructure goal is accompanied by several targets, including:

- By 2030, develop quality, reliable, sustainable, and resilient infrastructure, including regional and transborder infrastructure, to support economic development and human well-being, with a focus on affordable and equitable access for all.
- Increase inclusive and sustainable industrialization and, by 2030, substantially raise industry's share of employment and gross domestic product, in line with national circumstances, and double its value added and increase its energy efficiency.
- Promote innovation and research and development and increase the number of researchers and public and private research and development spending, particularly in developing countries.
- Upgrade infrastructure and retrofit industries to make them sustainable, with increased resource-use efficiency and greater adoption of clean and environmentally sound technologies and industrial processes.
- Enhance international cooperation to facilitate access to science, technology, and innovation and enhance knowledge sharing on mutually agreed terms, including through improved coordination among existing mechanisms, particularly at the United Nations level and through a global technology facilitation mechanism.

10. Reduced Inequalities

The tenth goal is Reduced Inequalities, which aims to reduce inequalities within and among countries and promote social, economic, and political inclusion and empowerment for all. The goal recognizes that inequality remains a pervasive and systemic challenge in many parts of the world, limiting the potential of individuals and societies and hindering progress towards sustainable development.

The Reduced Inequalities goal aims to reduce income and wealth disparities and promote access to economic, social, and political opportunities for all, including women, children, youth, and marginalized groups. The goal also aims to strengthen the regulation and monitoring of global financial markets and institutions and to promote the inclusion of developing countries in the global economic system.

The UNSDG's Reduced Inequalities goal is accompanied by several targets, including:

- By 2030, empower and promote the social, economic, and political inclusion of all, irrespective of age, sex, disability, race, ethnicity, origin, religion, or economic or other status.
- By 2030, progressively achieve and sustain income growth of the bottom 40% of the population at a rate higher than the national average.
- Ensure equal opportunities and reduce inequalities of outcome, including through eliminating discriminatory laws, policies, and practices and promoting appropriate legislation, policies, and action in this regard.
- Adopt policies, especially fiscal, wage and social protection policies, and progressively achieve greater equality.
- Improve the regulation and monitoring of global financial markets and institutions and strengthen the implementation of such regulations.

11. Sustainable Cities and Communities

The eleventh goal is Sustainable Cities and Communities, which aims to make cities and human settlements inclusive, safe, resilient, and sustainable. The goal recognizes that cities are hubs of economic, social, and cultural activity and that urbanization is a major driver of global development and environmental change.

The Sustainable Cities and Communities goal aims to promote sustainable urbanization and reduce the environmental impact of cities and human settlements. The goal also aims to improve access to basic services and infrastructure, including housing, transportation, energy, and water and sanitation, and to promote social inclusion, resilience, and disaster risk reduction in urban areas.

The UNSDGs Sustainable Cities and Communities goal is accompanied by several targets, including:

- By 2030, ensure access for all to adequate, safe, and affordable housing and basic services and upgrade slums.
- By 2030, provide access to safe, affordable, accessible, and sustainable transport systems for all, improving road safety, notably by expanding public transport, with special attention to the needs of those in vulnerable situations, women, children, persons with disabilities, and older persons.
- By 2030, enhance inclusive and sustainable urbanization and capacity for participatory, integrated, and sustainable human settlement planning and management in all countries.
- Strengthen efforts to protect and safeguard the world's cultural and natural heritage.
- By 2030, reduce the adverse per capita environmental impact of cities, including by paying special attention to air quality, municipal and other waste management.

12. Responsible Consumption and Production

The twelfth goal is Responsible Consumption and Production, which aims to promote sustainable patterns of consumption and production that can reduce the environmental impact of human activities, enhance resource efficiency, and support sustainable economic growth.

The Responsible Consumption and Production goal aims to reduce waste generation and promote sustainable use and management of natural resources, including energy, water, and land. The goal also aims to promote sustainable practices in the production and consumption of goods and services, including through sustainable procurement, green technologies, and sustainable lifestyles.

The UNSDGs Responsible Consumption and Production goal is accompanied by several targets, including:

- By 2030, achieve sustainable management and efficient use of natural resources.
- By 2030, substantially reduce waste generation through prevention, reduction, recycling, and reuse.
- Encourage companies, especially large and transnational companies, to adopt sustainable practices and integrate sustainability information into their reporting cycle.
- By 2030, achieve the environmentally sound management of chemicals and all wastes throughout their life cycle, in accordance with agreed international frameworks, and significantly reduce their release to air, water and soil to minimize their adverse impacts on human health and the environment.
- By 2030, ensure that people everywhere have the relevant information and awareness for sustainable development and lifestyles in harmony with nature.

13. Climate Action

The thirteenth goal is Climate Action, which aims to take urgent action to combat climate change and its impacts. The goal recognizes that climate change is one of the greatest challenges of our time, with significant environmental, social, and economic consequences for present and future generations.

The Climate Action goal aims to promote mitigation and adaptation efforts to reduce greenhouse gas emissions, increase resilience to climate-related impacts, and promote sustainable development. The goal also aims to mobilize financial and technological resources to support climate action in developing countries and to enhance international cooperation and partnerships to address climate change.

The UNSDGs Climate Action goal is accompanied by several targets, including:

- Strengthen resilience and adaptive capacity to climate-related hazards and natural disasters in all countries.
- Integrate climate change measures into national policies, strategies, and planning.
- Improve education, awareness-raising, and human and institutional capacity on climate change mitigation, adaptation, impact reduction, and early warning.
- Implement the commitment undertaken by developed country parties to the United Nations Framework Convention on Climate Change to a goal of mobilizing jointly $100 billion annually by 2020 from all sources to address the needs of developing countries in the context of meaningful mitigation actions and transparency on implementation and fully operationalize the Green Climate Fund through its capitalization as soon as possible.
- Promote mechanisms for raising capacity for effective climate change-related planning and management in least-developed countries and small island developing States,

including focusing on women, youth, and local and marginalized communities.

14. Life Below Water

The fourteenth goal is Life Below Water, which aims to conserve and sustainably use the oceans, seas, and marine resources for sustainable development. The goal recognizes the critical role of oceans and marine resources in supporting life on Earth and the need to protect and restore their health and biodiversity.

The Life Below Water goal aims to promote the conservation and sustainable use of marine ecosystems, reduce marine pollution and other stressors on marine biodiversity, and enhance ocean governance and management. The goal also aims to increase the economic benefits of sustainable ocean-based activities, including fisheries, aquaculture, and tourism, and to support the livelihoods and well-being of coastal communities.

The UNSDGs Life Below Water goal is accompanied by several targets, including:

- By 2025, prevent and significantly reduce marine pollution of all kinds, particularly from land-based activities, including marine debris and nutrient pollution.
- By 2020, sustainably manage and protect marine and coastal ecosystems to avoid significant adverse impacts, including by strengthening their resilience and taking action for their restoration, to achieve healthy and productive oceans.
- Minimize and address the impacts of ocean acidification, including through enhanced scientific cooperation at all levels.
- By 2020, effectively regulate harvesting and end overfishing, illegal, unreported, and unregulated (IUU) fishing, and destructive fishing practices and implement science-based management plans, to restore fish stocks in the shortest time possible, at least to levels that can produce maximum

sustainable yield as determined by their biological characteristics.

- Increase the economic benefits to small island developing States and least developed countries from the sustainable use of marine resources, including through sustainable management of fisheries, aquaculture, and tourism.

15. Life on Land

The fifteenth goal is Life on Land, which aims to protect, restore, and sustainably use terrestrial ecosystems, forests, and biodiversity for sustainable development. The goal recognizes the critical role of land and ecosystems in supporting human well-being and the need to address land degradation, deforestation, and loss of biodiversity.

The Life on Land goal aims to promote the conservation and restoration of terrestrial ecosystems, reduce land degradation, and promote sustainable land use practices. The goal also aims to increase the economic, social, and cultural benefits of sustainable land use, including through sustainable agriculture, forestry, and tourism, and to support the livelihoods and well-being of rural communities.

The UNSDGs Life on Land goal is accompanied by several targets, including:

- By 2020, ensure the conservation, restoration, and sustainable use of terrestrial and inland freshwater ecosystems and their services, in particular forests, wetlands, mountains, and drylands, in line with obligations under international agreements.
- By 2030, combat desertification, restore degraded land and soil, including land affected by desertification, drought, and floods, and strive to achieve a land degradation-neutral world.
- Take urgent and significant action to reduce the degradation of natural habitats, halt the loss of biodiversity and, by 2020, protect and prevent the extinction of threatened species.

- Promote the implementation of sustainable management of all types of forests, halt deforestation, restore degraded forests, and substantially increase afforestation and reforestation globally.
- Mobilize significant resources from all sources and at all levels to finance sustainable forest management and provide adequate incentives to developing countries to advance such management, including for conservation and reforestation.

16. Peace, Justice, and Strong Institutions

The sixteenth goal is Peace, Justice, and Strong Institutions, which aims to promote peaceful and inclusive societies, provide access to justice for all, and build effective, accountable, and inclusive institutions at all levels. The goal recognizes that peace, justice, and strong institutions are essential for sustainable development and the well-being of individuals and communities.

The Peace, Justice and Strong Institutions goal aims to promote peaceful and inclusive societies that can prevent and address conflict and violence, promote the rule of law, and respect human rights and fundamental freedoms. The goal also aims to provide access to justice for all, including through effective and accountable institutions and legal frameworks, and to promote transparency, participation, and anti-corruption measures.

The UNSDGs Peace, Justice, and Strong Institutions goal is accompanied by several targets, including:

- Significantly reduce all forms of violence and related death rates everywhere.
- Promote the rule of law at the national and international levels and ensure equal access to justice for all.
- Enhance the capacity of all countries, in particular developing countries, to prevent and combat terrorism and violence, and promote the rule of law and respect for human rights and fundamental freedoms.

- Ensure responsive, inclusive, participatory, and representative decision-making at all levels.
- Substantially reduce corruption and bribery in all their forms.

17. Partnerships for the Goals

The seventeenth and final goal is Partnerships for the Goals, which aims to strengthen the means of implementation and revitalize the global partnership for sustainable development. The goal recognizes that achieving sustainable development requires collective action and partnership between all stakeholders, including governments, civil society, private sector, and international organizations.

The Partnerships for the Goals goal aims to promote effective partnerships that can mobilize resources, enhance capacity, and share knowledge and expertise to support sustainable development. The goal also aims to promote cooperation and coordination among all stakeholders and to align their efforts and resources with the sustainable development agenda.

The UNSDGs Partnerships for the Goals goal is accompanied by several targets, including:

- Enhance international support for implementing effective and targeted capacity-building in developing countries to support national plans to implement all the sustainable development goals, including through North-South, South-South, and triangular cooperation.
- Promote a universal, rules-based, open, non-discriminatory, and equitable multilateral trading system under the World Trade Organization, including through the conclusion of negotiations under its Doha Development Agenda.
- Increase significantly the exports of developing countries, in particular with a view to doubling the least developed countries' share of global exports by 2020.
- Enhance the global partnership for sustainable development, complemented by multi-stakeholder partnerships that

mobilize and share knowledge, expertise, technology, and financial resources, to support the achievement of the sustainable development goals in all countries, in particular developing countries.

- Encourage and promote effective public, public-private, and civil society partnerships, building on the experience and resourcing strategies of partnerships.

The UN isn't the only organization that has some focused efforts on sustainability, as mentioned earlier, the Securities Exchange Commission has hinted of new laws taking effect for public companies disclosing their emissions numbers and environmental impacts.

These new disclosure requirements and stated global goals will mean that Industry 5.0 will get a jump start through the pressure of regulation and the pressure of adhering to goals like the UNSDGs. The collective pressure from society is mounting to foster more sustainable actions for business and individuals alike. In our next chapter, let's take a deeper dive into 5.0 and its impact on society.

Chapter 9:

What 5.0 Means to Society

The concept of sustainability has become increasingly important today, as people (especially Millennials) have become more aware of the need to address environmental, social, and economic challenges in a way that ensures long-term viability and well-being for all. In the future, sustainability is likely to become even more central to us, as more people recognize the importance of creating an equitable, resilient, and inclusive world.

New technologies will impact us in several ways beyond the pure carbon offsetting. They will affect how we work, where we live, what we do for recreation, how we transport ourselves around the globe, what we eat, how we farm, and the methods for powering all these activities.

The Social Impact of Renewable Energy

Industry 5.0 will see a much greater emphasis on renewable energy. As the world transitions away from fossil fuels and towards renewable energy sources like photovoltaics, hydro, and wind power, there is likely to be a greater emphasis on reduction in fossil-based power generation in the energy sector. This may include the development of new energy storage and less centralized distribution systems.

All over the world, we're seeing many successful renewable energy (RE) projects, from solar in California to Hydroelectric power in Brazil.

California is home to many large-scale solar power projects, including the Ivanpah Solar Electric Generating System. In most photovoltaic systems (photo = photon, voltaic = electrical potential) the panels convert those photons into electrons, like a battery. However, this new facility uses solar power differently.

The Ivanpah Solar Electric Generating System uses concentrated solar power technology, which involves using mirrors to concentrate sunlight onto a central tower, which uses mirrors to concentrate sunlight energy onto towers that heat up and in turn, generate electricity.

In a modern twist, the towers heat a liquid and produce steam power. That steam power turns the large turbines and generates electrical power. It's a very similar technology to steam generators of the past, however instead of burning fossil fuels to heat the water, the Ivanpah complex uses the power of the sun.

The Ivanpah facility was developed by BrightSource Energy and went online in 2014. It is designed to provide power to over 140,000 homes and is expected to offset the emissions of over 400,000 metric tons of carbon dioxide each year, compared to a conventional fossil fuel power plant.

Figure 14 - Bhadla Solar Park

From solar power in California, we go across the globe to see how the sun is powering homes in India. India is home to some of the largest solar power projects in the world, including the Bhadla Solar Park in Rajasthan, which has a capacity of 2.2 GW.

The Bhadla Solar Park uses the more traditional photovoltaic (PV) solar panels to generate electricity from the sun's rays. The PV panels are mounted on structures that track the movement of the sun throughout the day, and in turn move the panels in position to absorb as much sunlight as possible, maximizing the amount of energy the panels will produce during the day.

It was developed by the Solar Energy Corporation of India (SECI) and has been operational since 2017. Designed to provide power to over 2 million households, the park is expected to offset over 4 million tons of carbon dioxide emissions per year.

Bhadla is a significant example of India's commitment to expanding its renewable energy capacity and reducing its reliance on fossil fuels. The country has set ambitious targets for renewable energy development, including a target of installing 175 GW of renewable energy capacity by 2022, and has been a leader in the global transition to clean energy.

It seems like common logic, but wind power in Denmark is huge. With over 40% of its electricity generated from wind energy, Denmark is a leader in harnessing wind power. The country's largest wind farm, Horns Rev 3, has a capacity of 407 MW and can provide power to over 400,000 homes.

When we think of wind power and Denmark, what comes to mind are the old Dutch windmills that dotted the landscape for hundreds of years. However, Horns Rev 3 is a large-scale offshore wind farm located in the North Sea. The wind farm covers an area of approximately 88 square kilometers in the water, making it one of the largest offshore wind farms in the world.

Horns Rev 3 uses wind turbines to generate electricity from the strong winds that blow over the North Sea. The wind turbines are mounted on towers that stand over 100 meters tall and are anchored to the seafloor. Each turbine has a rotor diameter of 164 meters and a capacity of 8.3 MW, making them some of the largest and most powerful wind turbines in the world!

Horns was developed by Vattenfall and went online in 2019. It is designed to provide electrical power to the community and is expected to offset over 500,000 tons of carbon dioxide emissions per year. From wind power in Denmark to geothermal power in Iceland.

105

Iceland is a geologically active country, and contrary to its name, has an abundance of geothermal resources. Iceland has harnessed so much renewable power that it can generate nearly all its electricity from these sources. The country's largest geothermal power plant, Nesjavellir, has a capacity of 120 MW and provides power to over 60,000 homes. Finally, let's look at water, and more specifically, hydroelectric power in Brazil.

Brazil has many large-scale hydroelectric power projects, including:

- Itaipu Dam: Located on the Paraná River, on the border between Brazil and Paraguay, Itaipu Dam is one of the largest hydroelectric power plants in the world. It has a total installed capacity of 14,000 megawatts (MW) and plays a crucial role in meeting Brazil's electricity demand.
- Belo Monte Dam: Situated on the Xingu River in the state of Pará, Belo Monte Dam is one of the largest hydroelectric projects in Brazil. With an installed capacity of 11,233 MW, it is designed to generate substantial amounts of electricity once all its turbines become operational.
- Tucuruí Dam: Located on the Tocantins River in the state of Pará, the Tucuruí Dam is another significant hydroelectric power plant in Brazil. It has an installed capacity of 8,370 MW.
- Jirau Dam: Situated on the Madeira River in the state of Rondônia, Jirau Dam has an installed capacity of 3,750 MW. It is a run-of-the-river type of hydroelectric plant, a type of hydropower plant that generates electricity using the natural flow of a river without the need for a large reservoir or significant water storage.
- Santo Antônio Dam: Also located on the Madeira River, Santo Antônio Dam has an installed capacity of 3,568 MW. It is another run-of-the-river hydropower plant.
- Ilha Solteira Dam: Situated on the Paraná River, in the state of São Paulo, Ilha Solteira Dam has an installed capacity of

3,444 MW. It is one of the largest hydroelectric power plants in Brazil.

These examples show why Brazil is seen as a hydropower leader. Some of that is due to geography, but the leadership in Brazil is committed to lowering emissions all over the region. There are many smaller-scale hydroelectric projects spread across the country, contributing to its overall hydroelectric capacity.

Even with all these renewable examples, society still relies on fossil fuels to power our lives - about 80% of it to be exact. Reliance on fossil fuels means there will still be power interruptions, cost fluctuations and continued carbon emissions and while there is a long way to go to get to net zero power production, projects like these are paving the way and giving us hope.

Sustainable Transportation

Along with energy generation will be a focus on more sustainable transportation. According to the International Energy Agency (IEA), in 2020, the transportation sector accounted for around 24% of global energy-related CO2 emissions alone.

Since moving people and goods is a huge consumer of energy and a large part of our GHG emissions, concerns about climate change and air pollution continue to grow. There may be a greater focus on developing sustainable transportation systems, such as electric and hybrid vehicles, public transit, and active transportation options like biking and walking. New technology in transportation will play a major role in tackling this issue.

The transportation sector not only accounts for a significant portion of carbon dioxide emissions, but other factors contributing to air pollution and other environmental problems such as acid rain, and smog.

The adverse environmental impacts of transportation, coupled with the health impacts, make it essential to adopt more sustainable modes of transportation that emit low or no GHGs into the atmosphere. Future city planning will play a vital role in sustainable infrastructure, and we'll look at that in detail in the next section.

There are also economic benefits, that will help 5.0 take shape as sustainable transportation can save us money in the long run in several ways:

- **Lower fuel costs:** Sustainable transportation modes such as walking, cycling, and public transportation are cheaper than driving a personal car. By switching to these modes of transportation, we can save money on fuel costs, maintenance costs, and other expenses related to owning and operating a car.
- **Reduced infrastructure costs:** Sustainable transportation can also save money on infrastructure costs. Building new roads and highways is expensive, and the cost of maintaining them over time is even higher. Sustainable transportation modes like public transit require fewer infrastructure investments, which can lead to long-term cost savings.
- **Reduced healthcare costs:** Sustainable transportation such as pedestrian-friendly cities can also lead to reduced healthcare costs. Walking can improve our physical fitness and reduce the risk of chronic diseases such as heart disease and obesity. By avoiding healthcare costs associated with these conditions, we can save money in the long run.
- **Increased productivity:** Sustainable transportation modes can also increase productivity. By using active transportation modes, we can arrive at our destination feeling energized and focused, which can lead to increased productivity at work or school.
- **Increased property values:** Sustainable transportation options can also increase property values. Studies have shown that properties located near bike lanes and pedestrian paths have increased value compared to those located further away from these amenities.

There are several policy changes and infrastructure improvements that can support sustainable transportation. Here are a few examples:

- **Implementing bike-sharing programs:** Bike-sharing programs provide residents and visitors with an affordable and convenient way to travel around a city using bicycles. Cities like Paris, Barcelona, and Washington, D.C., have successfully implemented bike-sharing programs, resulting in increased bike usage and reduced carbon emissions.
- **Investing in public transportation:** Investing in public transportation can provide a sustainable and affordable alternative to personal cars. Cities like Zurich, Switzerland, and Curitiba, Brazil, have developed efficient public transportation systems that prioritize sustainable modes of transportation like buses and trams.
- **Creating pedestrian-friendly spaces:** Pedestrian-friendly spaces prioritize the needs of pedestrians, making it safer and more enjoyable to walk around a city. Cities like Copenhagen and Bogota, Colombia, have implemented pedestrian-friendly spaces, resulting in increased walking, and cycling rates and reduced traffic congestion.
- **Building dedicated cycling infrastructure:** Building dedicated cycling infrastructure like bike lanes and protected intersections can make cycling a safer and more accessible mode of transportation. Cities like Amsterdam and Copenhagen (again) have developed extensive cycling infrastructure, resulting in high rates of cycling and reduced car usage.
- **Encouraging car-free zones:** Car-free zones prioritize sustainable modes of transportation like walking, cycling, and public transportation. Cities like Oslo, Norway, have implemented car-free zones in the city center, resulting in improved air quality and greatly reduced traffic congestion.

These policy changes and infrastructure improvements have been successful in many cities worldwide. For example, in Barcelona,

Spain, the implementation of bike-sharing programs, pedestrian-friendly spaces, and protected cycling lanes resulted in a 30% increase in cycling trips between 2006 and 2016. In Bogota, Colombia, the implementation of a bus rapid transit system and pedestrian-friendly spaces resulted in reduced traffic congestion and improved air quality.

Policy changes and infrastructure improvements that support sustainable transportation can lead to significant improvements in the environment, public health, and transportation systems. By learning from successful case studies in other cities, policymakers and city planners can work to implement these changes in their communities, ultimately leading to a more sustainable and livable future. This is a lesson we'd like to see the civil engineers in the U.S. take to heart.

The challenge is to develop new technologies and systems that can meet our needs while also educating the public about all the benefits of this sustainable type of social planning. Especially here in the U.S. the term "Social Planning" comes with such a negative connotation, that typically equates to thinking our civic rights are being taken away or conjuring up visions of graffiti-laden subways. Trips to some of these countries would show that planned communities and public transit can be clean, safe, and affordable.

City/Social Planning

Industry 5.0 will revolutionize many aspects of business and society; however, none may be as singularly impactful as planning our cities of the future. Social planning plays a critical role and involves designing and managing urban spaces in a way that promotes environmental and economic sustainability.

Not only will there be a concerted effort to reduce transportation emissions, but new planning efforts will also reduce the need for unnecessary travel. Planning also includes new construction methods as well as energy-efficient homes and offices. Here are some ways that city planning can promote sustainability:

- **Green spaces:** Green spaces like parks, gardens, and green roofs can improve air quality, provide habitats for wildlife, reduce the urban heat island effect, and promote mental health and well-being.
- **Energy-efficient buildings:** Energy-efficient structures (buildings and homes) by establishing building codes and incentivizing developers to incorporate sustainable design features like solar panels, green roofs, and efficient insulation will reduce carbon emissions and energy costs, it's a win-win.
- **Waste management:** Sustainable waste management practices like recycling and composting can reduce the amount of waste sent to landfills, conserve resources, and reduce greenhouse gas emissions.
- **Water conservation:** Water conservation measures like low-flow fixtures, rainwater harvesting systems, and green infrastructure can reduce water usage, promote sustainable water management, and protect ecosystems.

Copenhagen is known for its green spaces, and efficient public transportation system. Vancouver has implemented policies to reduce carbon emissions, promote energy-efficient buildings, and protect its natural environment.

Mention sustainability and countries like Canada and Denmark are certainly in the conversation, however, there's also one that might seem less likely to champion environmentalism, but they may lead the way in city planning of the future.

An extreme example of this sustainable planning is The Line, in Saudi Arabia (https://www.neom.com/en-us/regions/theline).

In a country known for its oil production, The Line represents the absolute peak of sustainable living and a distancing from the fossil fuel industry that had provided much of the country's wealth.

The "Line" is a proposed futuristic city and economic zone that from the air, will look like a long, skinny structure (hence, the name) and it is part of Saudi Arabia's ambitious plans to diversify its economy and reduce its dependence on oil. The Line is envisioned as a 170-kilometer-long, zero-carbon city that would run on 100% renewable energy and be home to 9 million residents.

Figure 15 – Concept Rendering of "The Line" in Saudi Arabia

It's all part of a larger initiative called NEOM, which is a planned $500 billion megacity and economic zone that is being developed in the northwest of Saudi Arabia, near the border with Jordan and Egypt. NEOM is part of Saudi Arabia's Vision 2030 plan, which aims to modernize the country's economy and society and reduce its dependence on oil revenue.

The Line is being developed in close consultation with leading experts in sustainability, technology, and urban planning, and is designed to be a model for sustainable and livable cities of the future. The project is still in the planning and development phase, and it is not yet clear when construction will begin or when the city will be completed, but the fact that such an oil-rich country is making such a large statement on sustainability, tells us that the 5.0 revolution is certainly upon us.

Sustainable Food Systems

As we mention a few times in this book, regenerative farming practices are the cornerstone of a sustainable food system. By taking a holistic approach to farming, we can ensure that our crops are grown in a way that conserves resources and minimizes environmental impact. This means choosing seed varieties that are best suited to the local climate and soil conditions, using water conservation and soil fertility practices, and minimizing chemical inputs to protect human health and the environment.

Along with better agricultural methods are actions targeted at food waste. Approximately one-third of all food produced for human consumption is lost or wasted.

Every year, the world produces enough food to feed its entire population, yet an estimated 33% of all food produced for human consumption is lost or wasted. This is an alarming statistic that reveals the immense wastefulness of our current food system.

Every year, millions of tons of food are thrown away, leading to wasted resources and higher levels of methane emissions. Additionally, food insecurity is an often-overlooked consequence of food waste. To reduce the amount of food wasted in homes and in the food industry, individuals can practice mindful consumption and donate uneaten food to charities or compost it. Businesses can also invest in packaging solutions that minimize waste while maintaining quality control over their products.

A great example of this is a Florida-based company called Coffee Kreis. Founders and coffee lovers Ricardo & Daniela were unhappy with the amount of coffee grounds that are wasted every year, so they decided to do something about it. Being from Columbia, they knew a little bit about the coffee industry. They collect and repurpose used coffee grounds to manufacture, you guessed it, coffee cups!

They combine the grounds into natural polymers to make reusable cups for industry. I'm sure the cups can be used for a variety of drinks, but the coffee angle is just so cool. Less waste, better materials, and clever marketing. It's a fabulous and innovative solution. to learn more about them go to https://coffeekreis.com/

Supporting local farmers and producers can help to reduce the environmental impact of food transportation while supporting local economies. Buying locally sourced food is a great way to support the environment and local economies.

By purchasing produce, dairy, and other items from local farms and producers, we can reduce the environmental impact of food transportation while helping to support small businesses. Through buying locally sourced foods, we can also ensure that our meals are made with fresh ingredients that have been grown or raised in an environmentally conscious way.

The benefits of community-supported agriculture (CSA) programs, farmers' markets, and farm-to-table restaurants. Eating locally sourced food has become increasingly popular in recent years due to the numerous benefits it provides. Community-supported agriculture (CSA) programs, farmers' markets, and farm-to-table restaurants are all examples of ways to access fresh, seasonal produce.

One of the most promising businesses we've come across is Relish and Roots, located in Neenah, Wisconsin. Rhonda Mesko and her husband, Kevin saw the need (and the opportunity) to bring better food to their neighbors, all sourced from local farmers.

They provide meal "kits" all sourced with local produce, meats, and cheeses (it's Wisconsin ya know) and delivered to your door. Each week features a new menu with fully prepped meals as well as options for breakfast and snacks. If you're in the area, you can find them here at: https://relishandroots.com

As the global population continues to increase, the environmental impact of our food choices will become more of a concern. Fairly or unfairly, the meat and dairy industries have been targeted as significant contributors to greenhouse gas emissions. With all the debate surrounding this topic, it might be time to explore alternative protein sources that are both sustainable and nutritious.

Not to say we need to eliminate these traditional foods (we particularly like a good cheeseburger now and then), but plant-based meats, as well as high-protein plant foods like hemp seeds, offer us an opportunity to reduce our environmental footprint while still satisfying our dietary needs.

In the 18th century Hemp was a staple of American's lives. It was used for clothes, rope, paper, medicines, and food, and the Midwest was once known as the hemp belt of America.

Hemp's history in America dates back centuries, yet hemp in the 21st century is uncharted territory. Today it's making a resurgence, and there are few who know as much about the entire plant and its potential as Hemp Acres founder, Charles Levine.

For the past seven years, Charles has immersed himself in the plant; learning about hemp's history, nutritional properties, sustainable nature, how to grow hemp, how to process hemp, and hemp's innumerable applications. He was one of the first licensed hemp growers and the first licensed hemp processor in the state of Minnesota.

Charles built Hemp Acres from the ground up on a family farm in Waconia, Minnesota. The farm became his incubator to prove his hemp processing concept. Now, Hemp Acres is the largest wholesale producer of grain, botanical extract, and fiber ingredients in the nation. Charles is on a mission to widely introduce hemp back into the American market. Learn more about them at: https://www.hempacresusa.com/

Government policies and advocacy efforts can play a significant role in creating a more sustainable food system too. The importance of lobbying for sustainable food policies and initiatives and highlight examples of successful advocacy efforts.

A sustainable food system is essential for tackling climate change and feeding the world's growing population. Government policies and advocacy efforts have a critical role to play in creating such a system. Through lobbying, citizens can push for policies that promote sustainability, protect natural resources, reduce food waste, and create an equitable food system.

Additionally, by advocating for initiatives such as urban farming and community-supported agriculture projects, citizens can help build a more resilient food system that benefits all.

Industry 5.0 will certainly promote educating consumers about sustainable food systems and the positive impacts that choosing sustainable options can have on our environment. Thus, we can drive change and create a healthier, more equitable world for everyone.

Greater Equity and Social Justice

In a world where sustainability is an ever-growing priority, it is important to recognize how issues of equity and social justice are linked.

Living sustainably involves more than just taking care of the environment. It also means acknowledging and addressing issues of equity and social justice, which are closely intertwined with sustainability. In a world where resources are becoming increasingly limited, it is essential to recognize the connections between these two issues to create a more equitable future, especially for those populations that are considered "underserved".

To create sustainable solutions that will benefit all people, we must focus on creating greater economic and social equity for all. This means creating policies that will promote access to basic human needs, such as food, shelter, and healthcare. It also means creating a better education system, job opportunities for everyone, and equal wages for everyone regardless of gender or ethnicity.

As outlined in the UNSDGs, many issues need to be addressed to create a better future. Issues such as income inequality, access to education and healthcare, and social and environmental justice are all pressing matters that require immediate attention.

We talked about the importance of sustainable food systems, here we also need to address the fact that many people on this planet do not have reliable access to healthy food. In the U.S. it's known as a "Food Desert", typically urban areas that have no supermarkets or healthy food sales nearby. Adding to the problem are elderly and impoverished individuals that either cannot drive long distances to get to markets or cannot afford transportation to and from.

Sustainability is closely linked to issues of equity and social justice, in fact 9 of the 17 UNSDGs can be directly linked to social equality. In the 5.0 future, there will be a greater focus on creating more equitable and sustainable societies.

What Areas of Equality Will 5.0 Focus On?

Environmental Justice: The sustainability movement recognizes that marginalized communities often bear a disproportionate burden of environmental degradation and pollution.

Access to Resources: Sustainability initiatives can focus on ensuring equitable access to vital resources such as clean water, energy, food, and healthcare.

Green Jobs and Economic Opportunities: The transition to a sustainable economy offers the potential to create new job opportunities, particularly in renewable energy, energy efficiency, sustainable agriculture, and other environmentally friendly sectors.

Education and Awareness: Educating and raising awareness about sustainability and its interconnectedness with social justice issues can empower individuals and communities to actively participate in creating positive change.

Collaboration and Participation: The sustainability movement emphasizes the importance of collaboration and inclusivity. By involving diverse stakeholders, including marginalized communities, in decision-making processes, policies and initiatives can be more responsive to their needs and aspirations.

Reducing Inequalities: The sustainability movement recognizes the interconnections between environmental, social, and economic issues. This can involve advocating for fair distribution of resources, supporting social safety nets, and challenging discriminatory practices that perpetuate inequities.

It may be myopic, but a sustainable future for some and not for others is not our vision of sustainable development. Inequities have been a part of human history all along, but in the true spirit of Maslow's work, these situations are problems for all.

There have been security, health, and social impacts that affect all economic classes. Lack of education and other opportunities keep marginalized people in poverty and prevent talented people from rising to their full potential. Going back to Maslow, if someone is concerned about where their next meal is coming from, you can be assured that global sustainability is not high on their problem-solving matrix!

Ultimately, by integrating social equity as a core principle, the sustainability movement can work towards creating a more just and inclusive society that addresses the needs and aspirations of all individuals and communities, while simultaneously promoting environmental stewardship and long-term sustainability.

More Resilient and Adaptive Communities

In the face of our increasing environmental awareness, we know that communities must become more resilient and adaptive also. This means that they must be able to respond to the changing environment in a way that will ensure their continued survival and. By becoming more resilient, communities can better prepare for disasters and mitigate their risks.

To achieve this, our communities must be prepared to make changes in their infrastructure, policies, and practices to better prepare for future crises. Additionally, they must also have access to resources such as education, technology, and funding that can help them transition towards more sustainable practices.

To understand what the sustainability revolution will mean communities, we can look at organizations that focus on this area of study. One such association is the Post Carbon Institute.

From their website - Founded in 2003, Post Carbon Institute's mission is to lead the transition to a more resilient, equitable, and sustainable world by providing individuals and communities with the resources needed to understand and respond to the interrelated ecological, economic, energy, and equity crises of the 21st century.

Richard Heinberg is Senior Fellow of the Post Carbon Institute and is regarded as one of the world's foremost advocates for a shift away from our current reliance on fossil fuels. He has published five axioms of sustainability:

1. Any society that continues to use critical resources unsustainably will collapse.
2. Population growth and/or growth in the rates of consumption of resources cannot be sustained.
3. To be sustainable, the use of renewable resources must proceed at a rate that is less than or equal to the rate of natural replenishment (remember the 1.7 Earths calculation!).
4. To be sustainable, the use of nonrenewable resources must proceed at a rate that is declining, and the rate of decline must be greater than or equal to the rate of depletion.
5. Sustainability requires that substances introduced into the environment from human activities be minimized and rendered harmless to biosphere functions.

www.postcarbon.org

His observations are astute and beckon the need for "balance" in our quest to be more sustainable.

It seems to be a "no-brainer" that a society that uses more resources than can be replenished is ultimately going to run out. However, looking back at life in the 19th century, we can see that some early seeds of an unsustainable future were being planted.

As some of the largest cities were expanding (Paris and London especially), the natural resources near them were starting to be stressed. Forests and waterways were undergoing a rate of consumption far beyond what could naturally be replaced.

However, the British and French societies were primarily imperialistic, like many of the day. So, instead of looking inward to balance the use of resources, they simply exported the practices overseas to other colonies around the world. The need for sustainability didn't exist because new resources could be infinitely captured on the other side of the globe.

The push to lighten the load placed on our planet in 1800 would likely have been comparable to us worrying about stressing the natural resources on Mars in 2024. As a species, we simply don't have a history of looking that far into the future to identify unseen problems.

Expanding populations were dealt with the same way. Too many people? Overcrowded cities? Just ship them off to the New World. Since the accepted discovery of America in 1492 (this too can be heavily debated!), about 65 million people have left Europe to seek refuge elsewhere, mostly in North America.

The principals were economic; there were more opportunities in America, but the strategy remained the same. Problems at home? Simply export them somewhere else.

Today, we're running out of places to ship the problems to. In 1800 the world population was around 1 billion; today it's over 8 billion! While the rate of growth has slowed from 2% in 1970 to 1% today, the trajectory is still upward.

The Earth's population continues to expand, however, there's no New World to go to (until of course when we colonize Mars!). Meaning our finite resources will continue to dwindle.

Fossil resources are abundant on this planet, but they do have shelf-life and sooner or later we will run dry. Leaving our communities and society at risk. This is why interest in renewable energy has been a popular segment to study since the 1970s. In some forms (Hydro and Wind), we've had renewable energy sources for hundreds of years. However, to keep pace with our ever-expanding population, we turned to easier ways to power our lives like pumping hydrocarbons from underground and burning them to run our cities.

To truly be sustainable, we must move away from the established methods of consumption and adopt new axioms for renewable living. Can it be done? Yes. Will it be fast and easy? No way.

Did the Pandemic Change Our Thinking?

Indirectly, the COVID pandemic highlighted the need for sustainability, and we believe it is supported by several facts and observations. In every prolonged crisis, there are many predictable outcomes, but also some unintended consequences. As horrid as the pandemic was (essentially shutting down the world for nearly two years - early 2020 to mid-2021), it did prove some facts on the negative effects of the emergence, and even our dependence on technology.

Here are a few examples:

1. **Reduced carbon emissions:** During the COVID pandemic, many countries experienced a significant reduction in carbon emissions because of reduced economic activity and travel. This reduction highlighted the need to transition to more sustainable modes of transportation and energy production.
2. **Supply chain disruptions:** The COVID pandemic highlighted the fragility of global supply chains and the need for more resilient and sustainable supply chain management practices.
3. **Increased interest in outdoor recreation:** During the pandemic, many people turned to outdoor activities like walking, hiking, and cycling to stay active and maintain mental health. This increased interest in outdoor recreation highlighted the importance of preserving natural areas and promoting sustainable modes of transportation.

4. **Attention to public health:** It brought increased attention to public health and the linkages between human health and the environment. This has led to a greater recognition of the need for sustainable practices that promote both human and environmental health.

5. **Interest in sustainable living:** The pandemic has also led to an increased interest in sustainable living practices, including reduced consumption, waste reduction, and sustainable food production. This interest in sustainable living reflects a growing awareness of the need to live more sustainably and reduce our impact on the environment.

The pandemic also changed our way of thinking in a "punch to the gut" fashion. Would we have preferred a softer nudge? Yes, but as we discussed earlier, the radical change we need often comes with some discomfort.

OK, the big question we keep asking ourselves is: "When will, or when did the whole 5.0 thing get kickstarted?" Unlike Industry 3.0, where we put an exact date on the commencement, here in the fifth revolution, the date and time aren't so crystal clear. Some could argue that the line in the sand globally was the first Earth Day in 1970, or the signing of the Kyoto Protocol in 1997, others will argue for 2015/16 when the Paris Agreement was drafted and subsequently signed, and still others will point directly to the COVID pandemic.

We propose that whatever the driver was, or will be for 5.0 inception, that:

- Our thinking has changed.
- Our thinking is changing.
- Our thinking will continue to change.

Regardless of the timeline, the movement is still in its infancy, and the true thrust of this 5.0 revolution still lies ahead of us.

Can we Achieve a Net Zero Economy?

To answer this question, we might turn it around and ask, "What has doing very little to combat our assault on the environment done to get us to a net zero economy (local, regional, and global)?" Even with some sustainable practices in place, we're still trending in the wrong direction and really, how long can we keep this up? We learned lately how fragile and susceptible our economy can be and getting it to net zero is going to take an enormous, coordinated effort.

To start, we just endured a global pandemic that put into focus the negative effects we've had in the past 50 years or so of harming the environment. We got a crash course in conservation by way of the business slowdowns caused by COVID-19 and the actions to quell the spread of the virus.

By forced (and unforced) needs, we've lowered our carbon footprint over the two years of the pandemic in several ways; from less product consumption to shrinking global supply chain movement, and lower energy usage from more of us working remotely.

From 2020 to 2022, manufacturing was down, in turn, less energy was needed to run those factories. We saw local establishments hit hard, especially restaurants, gyms, and stores. This led to less transport of goods, foods, and people. While the result was a reduction in carbon emissions, the pandemic was in no way a viable, logical, or beneficial method to get us to Net Zero.

One of the unique aspects of Industry 5.0 is the fact that there is an endgame in mind, more specifically, this idea of a Net Zero Economy. We know what our goal(s) should be - Net Zero, but what is that exactly?

What do we mean by "Net Zero"? It sounds rather simple to define - an economy that produces (or offsets to equal) exactly zero carbon emissions. Most objectives give a timeline for achieving this by the year 2050.

For this book, we will use information from the Network for Greening the Financial System (NGFS) Net Zero 2050 Scenarios. These scenarios are templates of a variety of actions needed to get us to a net zero economy by 2050. As you can imagine, each scenario is interconnected and slight variations in one, can and will affect the others.

The scenarios outlined include a wide range of actions from cleaner power production, more efficient methods of travel and transport, less (and/or greener) packaging, cleaner manufacturing/production methods, carbon sequestering practices, and the use of bio-based materials to name a few.

So, if we take that timing as gospel, what needs to happen in the next 25 years or so to get us to Net Zero? Well, according to McKinsey's report "The Net Zero Transition: What it would cost, what it could bring", it will take over $9.2 trillion in annual spending to reconfigure our planet into a net zero state. The main sectors for infrastructure improvement are Power/Energy, Transportation, and Buildings.

Each of these sectors will take investment and innovation to transform them into net zero, or even net positive emissions. The Energy/Power sector has shown some movement in technology over the last 50 years.

Solar/PV power, wind, hydro, hydrogen fuel cells, and other technologies have shown promise, albeit on a smaller scale. To transform the world's energy supply into a net zero configuration will take enormous investment. Some estimates are about $60 trillion! Not only will it take a lot of money to transform, but there will also be a certain amount of waste along the way.

For example, what about new coal-fired power plants that are under construction or planned in the next few years? You may say, "There are no new plants planned in the U.S.!" True, but we are talking about a global power grid, and there are dozens of new coal plants on the books in China alone.

So, here's where the waste comes in. Say, we mandate clean energy in 2030 and beyond. What happens to the new power plants in countries like China? Do we shutter them years or decades before their lifespans are set to expire? What's the cost of building a new power plant, only to shut it down in just a few years? For each of China's largest plants, that's about $20B!

These factors are included in the NGFS' calculations for energy costs over the next decades. They propose that even with the high costs of transforming to clean energy, the initial cost increases would peak around 2040, then gradually begin to decrease over time. This results in costs lower than 2020 levels in 50 years.

On the transportation front, the cost savings would happen much sooner. The shift to EVs over ICE vehicles might happen in 5-10 years. Although today, the premium for EVs is higher, those costs could reach parity by 2025. Also, the lifecycle of a car is much lower than say a power plant. Not many cars from 20 years ago are on the road today, and many are less than 10 years old here in the U.S. where the average lifespan of a car today is 12 years. To say that all new vehicles by 2050 will have no tailpipe emissions is not much of a stretch.

As auto manufacturers switch to more carbon-neutral or even carbon-negative materials, combined with higher levels of renewable energy powering their factories, it's not hard to imagine the industry hitting net zero within the next 20 years, nearly a full decade before the estimates.

Building and construction round out the three sectors that will have the most impact on reaching a Net Zero economy by 2050. Somewhere in between the mobility sector (units replaced on a very regular basis) and power/energy (with a very long-life cycle for power plants), buildings can be energy efficient from the day of new construction or be rehabilitated into more energy efficient structures.

Sustainable construction got a lot of attention when the U.S. Green Building Council created the LEED program in 1994. It was started to encourage more sustainable practices of design and development utilizing tools and criteria for performance measurement. This sustainable construction is a combination of design to reduce energy consumption, as well as the use of more natural, bio-friendly materials.

Advances in technology are giving us better insulators, and more efficient lighting, heating, and cooling. So, getting to Net Zero will be a mixed bag of efforts and results, but technical advances and social awareness lead us to believe that Industry 5.0 will be going strong in the years to come. As a result, a Net Zero economy should be well within reach.

127

128

Chapter 10:

What Industry 5.0 Means to Manufacturing

Sustainability in Transportation

Transportation is foundational to human experience. Humanity has evolved from carriages, buggies, and bicycles into dozens of different types of scalable motorized activities. Cars, boats, and planes have amplified our ability to connect with people from all over the world. Of course, today, we have a much more complicated mobility infrastructure than just 100 years ago.

The mobility industry offers some of the best opportunities for sustainable manufacturing. Vehicles (this includes cars, trucks, trains, boats, and planes) are a bit unique as their carbon footprint goes far beyond the sourcing of raw materials and production processes to calculate carbon emissions.

The entire lifespan of a vehicle consists of consuming some type of energy (fossil fuels, electricity, etc.) and depending on the expected life of that vehicle, it can be many times the actual carbon footprint of the initial manufacturing.

Lightweighting

So, the transportation industry is looking at ways to reduce emissions at the factory, but also during their product's lifecycle. A big topic in the business is "lightweighting". Let's consider a few facts:

- There are approximately 100,000 flights around the globe every day.
- SpaceX is launching and lands rockets on a monthly basis.
- Tens of thousands of ships on the planet are moving goods and raw materials at any given time.
- In America alone, there are about 115 million cars on our roads.

These vehicles all have one thing in common. They are all heavy vehicles, with big engines (or large battery banks) that need lots of horsepower to propel them.

Lightweighting has become the cornerstone of mobility capabilities because:

- Lighter vehicles can accelerate faster.
- Lighter vehicles can go further.
- Lighter vehicles can carry more weight.
- Lighter vehicles get increased miles per gallon or miles per charge.

Studies have proven that a reduction in weight has significant implications on performance, and that in turn drives more efficiency as lighter vehicles travel further on the same amount of fuel (be it fossil or renewable). This shift will be seen across the mobility industries, first in automotive, then in sectors like marine and aerospace. Sustainable materials that reduce the weight and cost of vehicles will result in some big wins for us all.

Because so many new sustainable materials are bio-based, we're experiencing an amazing inflection point in the world today where material science is meeting with scalable agricultural supply chains. Similar to how renewable energy costs have fallen to parity with traditional energy production, natural materials are moving towards parity with, or becoming less expensive than, the traditional synthetic & mineral alternatives.

Every mode of transportation on the planet will benefit from the lightweighting movement, the bigger the vehicle, the more important lightweighting becomes.

Ultimately consumers are driving demand toward more sustainable transportation. This started with clean energy (like hybrids and electric vehicles) and has evolved into new, lighter, and greener materials. From the manufacturer's side, the materials revolution will result in a reduction in weight and costs, as well as a cleaner footprint to manufacture. For the consumer, the benefits will span from lower costs of use (less fuel) to safer, longer lasting vehicles.

Sustainability in Construction

Like in the transportation industry, consumers drive the shift toward more sustainable infrastructure and construction methods. This started with solar rooftops, but much like other industries, has shifted toward removing toxic materials from the walls, floors & ceilings of residential homes and commercial buildings. Right now, because there is no established, large-scale industrial biomaterial supply chain, there are not enough materials to meet the demand of the construction market. However, this may be the time that leads to change, as more land is being dedicated to crops used for raw materials than ever before.

Biomaterials have always been a part of the construction industry. In the beginning, we used them specifically, wood, stone, thatch, etc. As the industrial revolutions took hold, however, so did the use of non-bio and synthetic materials rise such as steel, carpeting, PVC and other plastics.

Today we are seeing construction advance by looking back to our roots, while still pushing the edge of technology. Hempcrete, composites made with hemp, bamboo or flax, cellulose insulation and even plant-based resins and paints are becoming more common in construction today. Not only do we see materials innovation in construction, but we're seeing them blended with process innovation as well.

A recent Bloomberg article touts a new neighborhood in Texas that is being constructed by robots using 3D printing technology! The homes are not only taking advantage of new materials, but they are also built with much less energy and waste than the traditional, manual processes.

https://www.bloomberg.com/features/2023-3d-printed-houses-austin-texas/

In the 1960s we thought about robots (that looked kind of human) serving us drinks and cleaning our homes. Today, those robots are building floors, walls, and roofs...and they bear very little resemblance to us!

Sustainability in Packaging

There are countless types of product packaging in use today and unsurprisingly, plastic makes up most packaging materials (up to 90% by some estimates). From consumer-scale boxes, plastic bottles, and containers in branded shapes and colors, to industrial crates and heavy-duty packaging meant to protect large, expensive machinery on its journey to the customer, plastic packaging is virtually everywhere.

Packaging is the most common way companies protect goods on their way to market, and it used to be a slightly overlooked aspect of the process when compared to product design and sales, but not today. Packaging began to move more into the forefront from a branding standpoint since the age of mass consumerism starting in the early 20th century, and protection of goods during transport was the core reason behind packaging to begin with. However, today packaging is getting a lot of attention from a sustainability perspective – as it should be!

Container design is an evolving multidisciplinary field that requires knowledge of branding, marketing, engineering, manufacturing, and more. When it comes to designing packaging one must consider the brand's image, the function of the product, regulations imposed by governing bodies & more. In 2024 and beyond, there will be even more focus on how damaging (or beneficial in some cases) to our environment that product packaging is.

Product packaging has evolved a great deal to accommodate the needs of consumers, but also the needs of manufacturers. Packagers have found lighter materials to protect goods – Styrofoam vs. cardboard for example. They have also found that heavier-duty pallets can carry more weight to accommodate larger loads on a truck. The problem is that the materials (like Styrofoam) of the late 20th century were not all that great for the environment, and most are still widely used today including wood, paper, and plastics.

As we've established, the use of petrochemical-based plastics and the clearing of old-growth timber is simply not sustainable. Recently, the need for health consciousness has served as the driving force behind some of the changes and banning some dangerous packaging materials, but now there is even more focus on materials that pose an overall danger to the health of our planet, be it consumer or industrial packaging.

Consumer vs. Industrial Packaging

The packaging used for consumer-packaged goods (CPG) is typically inexpensive and lightweight. The packaging for these consumer products is meant to give the customer relevant information on the product they're looking to buy. Traditionally, the information on this type of packaging illuminates the problem, solution, or how the product is different from the others. Consumer packaging is meant to position itself against competitors, so in some cases the packaging is clear to show the product inside, or its design is meant to stand out amongst all the other products on the display aisle at your local store, meaning that many times the packaging is unnaturally large for the amount of material it contains.

Industrial packaging is very different. The equipment that is purchased by large manufacturers is typically expensive, voluminous, heavy, and often even fragile. These large industrial machines may be as big as your garage, but that doesn't mean they can survive a drop off a loading dock or being bounced down the highway in the back of a semi-truck. This means there is very little room for failure when packing them up for transport.

Industrial packaging is typically engineered for longer journeys across varied mediums. For example, large electronic devices, say a rack of servers for a data center, need to be packaged to not only protect the device against drops but also long shipment voyages overseas (saltwater contamination), by air (extreme low temperatures) and eventually by truck (bumps and vibrations).

Industrial packaging must be robust, and sometimes the weight of this packaging can exceed the weight of the product that it's protecting! This is why new, lighter, more sustainable materials are being sought out by packaging engineers to replace the traditional materials like wood, foams and even asbestos.

Wood – The Most Traditional Material

For generations the crates and pallets that manufacturers relied on for their shipments were made from wood. When our GDP was 1/10 the size it is today, this was a viable solution. But today, there just aren't enough trees to cut down. Since demand is consistently increasing, and we know that there's a finite number of trees, manufacturers are forced to look for alternative solutions.

Recently, some manufacturers have realized that using wood as a shipping material comes with some major problems:

- A large percentage of the wooden pallets and crates break every year.

- Fixing these wooden parts is time-consuming and dangerous (sharp edges, rusty nails/screws, etc.).
- Wooden materials can rot when moisture is present.
- Continuously cutting down trees to make packaging products is not sustainable.
- New growth timber is not as robust as old growth, so the wood used today is gradually becoming weaker.

Since the world is beginning to transition toward a more sustainable future, leaders across manufacturing are actively looking for alternative materials to optimize their products and supply chains.

Fortunately, America is building reliable supply chains of bio-based materials, and these supply chains can support manufacturers by providing additives that increase the performance and reduce the carbon footprint of the raw materials already in use.

Bio-Based Solutions

There are many bio-based materials (sans traditional wood) that are being engineered and tested as better solutions to our industrial packaging crisis. One of the most promising is, not surprisingly, Industrial Hemp.

Industrial Hemp has a 10,000+ year history of being the strongest natural fiber in the world and it has proven to be useful in thousands of applications across almost every industry, albeit on smaller scales. Today we have biotech firms researching and developing it as a viable solution for industrial packaging; and engineering efforts are finding a multitude of new uses for this robust product.

Traditionally, this has been the most cost-prohibitive market for sustainable materials. I mean, who wants to increase their costs on packaging? The short answer is - no one. In the past, sustainable materials have traditionally carried a 30-150% premium over traditional materials. Many processors now can process bio-based fibers at scale and have helped the industry reach cost parity. This means that bio-based materials can be less expensive than existing petroleum-based products. This inflection point will open the door for organizations looking to package their products with sustainable materials.

Industrial packaging has many nuances that make it the perfect candidate for a material transition. As companies wake up to the fact that cutting down trees is not sustainable, they are actively testing wood replacements. Naturally, plastic is the material that is the most realistic alternative due to its cost, weight, availability, and durability.

One of the key metrics that are measured for industrial packaging is weight. A large portion of the weight of any shipment is the packaging. If we can reduce the weight of the packaging, we can increase the number of units that are shipped in each load. Reducing the weight of packaging instantly reduces logistics costs and carbon footprint.

For example, as car parts are shipped throughout the automotive supply chain, they rely on heavy and expensive packaging. In fact, 50%+ of the weight of the shipment from one automotive supplier to another can be packaging. As you can imagine, these car parts are large, so the packaging they rely on is clunky. Reducing the weight of the packaging is one of the easiest ways that a manufacturer can make its supply chain more sustainable.

Sustainable Packaging and Costs

Industry 5.0 will push manufacturers across the world to become "more sustainable." But traditionally, they will hesitate if there's an increase in cost.

Manufacturers work off thin margins, so cost increases can quickly flip their business model upside down. At times, competing at this level can be difficult. Many of the mined and synthetic goods used as additives in plastics are dirt cheap because they are abundant. How can an agriculture supply chain compete with minerals like talc and calcium carbonate? Exactly on what we just outlined – weight. More weight translates into more costs due to shipping, storage, and other logistics.

Bio-based materials can be up to 50% (or more) lighter than the synthetic materials that they replace. This means, a typical plastics application would need 1 pound of polymer and say a half-pound of additives, it would only need 0.2 to 0.3 pounds of bio additives to create the same volume (in cubic feet). This means that the sustainability metric we're measuring on is not "price per pound," it's "cost in use."

Beyond the usual specifications and characteristics, there is one more advantage to using natural materials that is paramount – reducing your carbon footprint! Every large company today has a "sustainability mandate." This mandate is a way to track a company's sustainability activities and results, and ultimately report on the actions they're taking to become more environmentally friendly.

Today, many of the top companies that are leading the sustainability movement are focused on measurably reducing their carbon footprints.

To do that, they only have a few options:

- Use less materials (which means selling fewer goods).
- Use recycled materials.
- Use clean energy.
- Use carbon-negative materials and additives to reduce the footprint of each product.

We are now realizing that the long-term path to carbon footprint reduction is to use carbon-negative materials. Since most companies plan on expanding production, they need to find a way to reduce the carbon footprint of the materials they rely on every day, and packaging is a great place to start. By using carbon-negative materials in packaging, we are essentially boosting the value of sustainability solutions with every increase in production, instead of amplifying the problems!

Manufacturers are quickly waking up to the material transition that's taking place. For some customers, industrial packaging has been an easy starting point that they've started to implement. For others, product development is being done right now on packaging products that will hit the market over the next few years. Either way, the time is now to explore the material transition that is going to deeply impact every part of the manufacturing sector.

Sustainability in the Manufacturing Process

A major shift we see coming from an operational perspective is from **Just in Time Manufacturing** towards the more sustainable edict of **Just in Case Resilience**. The recent pandemic put a huge strain on supply chains, and when you're reliant on that chain to work perfectly in harmony with your scheduling, you're betting that one of those many links won't break. Unfortunately, the pandemic broke a lot of links and decimated many businesses in its wake.

Just-in-time (JIT) is a production strategy that aims to minimize inventory and increase efficiency by producing and delivering products only as they are needed in the production process.

The goal of JIT is to reduce waste, improve quality, and increase responsiveness to customer demand. This is achieved by closely coordinating the flow of materials, information, and products between different stages of the supply chain so that raw materials arrive "just in time" to be processed and finished products are shipped just in time to meet customer demand.

The challenges of JIT are rooted in the amount of partner cooperation and general administration horsepower needed to run the organization efficiently. Many of these challenges lead to sustainability issues as well. Most notably they include:

1. Dependence on suppliers

2. Lack of flexibility
3. Vulnerability to disruptions
4. High costs of errors
5. Inventory management challenges

Dependence on suppliers: JIT manufacturing relies heavily on the timely delivery of raw materials and components from suppliers, and any disruptions in the supply chain can cause significant problems for the manufacturing process. We witnessed this first-hand during the pandemic. Supply chain failures were rampant and in turn, manufacturers took a huge hit. Some estimates put the global supply chain failures as high as $1T! This puts a spotlight on the need for more local, flexible, and resilient supply chains.

Lack of flexibility: JIT manufacturing is designed to operate as smoothly and efficiently as possible, which can make it difficult to adapt to changes in customer demand or production requirements. Let's compare this to ordering lunch at a fast-food restaurant. Most of these establishments make items ahead of time and prioritize those menu choices that sell more often (burgers, fries, etc.). If you had to wait for your order to be made after you placed it, that probably would eliminate the "fast" from fast food.

But what happens when sales are out of balance with the pre-prepped orders or the established run rates? Say, a news story came out the evening before highlighting a newly found disease in cattle. Obviously, the beef on hand would still be processed in a JIT organization, but the offtake would not be there. This results in a double hit, lost sales, and increased waste.

JIT manufacturers face this all the time. They build inventory that doesn't move, or they are faced with a sharp increase in orders but lack the raw materials to support them. Either way, the lack of flexibility hurts them in a few ways:

Vulnerability to disruptions

Since JIT relies on a delicate balance of materials, information, and products flowing through the supply chain, any disruptions can have a cascading effect that quickly disrupts the entire manufacturing process.

Case in point, the port of Long Beach in 2020/2021. The pandemic amplified the paint points here also. Massive shutdowns clogged ports and warehouses with inventory that wasn't moving. The delicate ballet of moving goods through the port was disrupted, and when the economy rebounded there was simply no way to ramp up or keep up with surging demand.

Lead times that typically ran days or weeks, turned into months! The pain that both consumers and manufacturers felt was daunting. We're still feeling the pain from this series of disruptions, especially with materials sourced overseas.

The High Cost of Errors

In JIT manufacturing, errors or defects in the production process can be very expensive to correct since they can cause a chain reaction of problems throughout the supply chain.

Let's look at electronics manufacturing. If you've ever cracked open an electronic device, what you see is a lot of components. Some electronics can contain hundreds or even thousands of parts. Let's also assume that just one of those components is defective. The entire device is rendered useless.

A faulty, or simply incorrect component, brings the production line to a halt. It might be from a defective batch, specified incorrectly, or as simple as a part number transposed. To make matters worse, if the component is sourced overseas, and lead times have stretched, the error might not be caught for months.

Multiply that by a factor of two or more when calculating the time to correct the error! There are engineering teams dedicated to solving problems on the production lines, however, when running at thin margins, those emergency projects can send you upside down in a hurry!

Inventory Management Challenges

JIT manufacturing requires a high degree of accuracy and control over inventory. Which can be difficult to maintain over time, especially as the scale of production increases. Inventory takes time, space, and money. Inventory turns are an important metric for any manufacturer.

Inventory turns (also known as inventory turnover) is a measure of a company's efficiency in managing its inventory. It is calculated by dividing the cost of goods sold (COGS) by the average inventory value for a given period, typically a year. The resulting figure represents the number of times that a company has sold and replaced its stock of goods during the period in question.

A high inventory turn rate indicates that a company is efficiently managing its inventory and selling its products quickly, while a low inventory turn rate may suggest that a company is having difficulty selling its products or is holding too much inventory.

Suppose a company has held inventory, because of a blip in production. Again, that one component that's holding up the line. Instead of moving the inventory, it's sitting in the warehouse, or even worse, clogging up the production line. Now those static materials are taking up space, time, and money. Equally important to the dollars they are wasting is that they are taking up space that new inventory should be capitalizing on.

Overall, JIT manufacturing requires a very high level of coordination, communication, and control to implement effectively. In a perfect world, JIT makes perfect sense. Businesses only invest in materials at the very time they are needed, and production operates without any missteps. However, we live in an imperfect world.

Just-in-Case Resilience

Just-in-case (JIC) resilience in manufacturing refers to a supply chain strategy in which a company keeps a manageable level of inventory on hand to respond quickly to changes in demand or unexpected events.

In this approach, the company relies on quick and frequent deliveries from local suppliers to meet customer demand, rather than relying on suppliers (overseas or regional) to deliver the materials just in time.

The advantage of JIC is that it minimizes the risk of inventory in motion. The disadvantage today is first costs can be higher, and usually are. However, we see local economies becoming the norm and not the exception in the 5.0 revolution, ultimately leveling costs out.

"Just in Case" (JIC) resilience is a process that prioritizes preparedness and risk mitigation, whereas "Just in Time" (JIT) is a process focused on minimizing waste and inventory by delivering goods or services exactly when they are needed.

While both JIC resilience and JIT have their merits in specific contexts, JIC resilience is often considered a better approach in certain situations. Here's why:

Risk Management

JIC resilience emphasizes proactive risk management. It recognizes that unexpected disruptions, such as natural disasters, supply chain disruptions, or economic crises, can occur. By preparing for such contingencies in advance, organizations can build resilience and better respond to disruptions, minimizing their impact. In contrast, JIT processes may leave organizations vulnerable to disruptions if they do not have backup plans or robust risk mitigation strategies in place.

Reducing Vulnerability

JIC resilience reduces vulnerability by incorporating redundancy and flexibility into systems. It allows organizations to maintain safety stocks, backup suppliers, and alternative production methods. This redundancy provides a buffer against unexpected disruptions and ensures continuity of operations. In contrast, JIT processes typically operate on thin margins and rely heavily on efficiency and optimization, leaving little room for contingencies.

Adaptability

JIC resilience promotes adaptability and agility. Organizations that prioritize resilience can quickly adapt to changing circumstances and pivot their operations when faced with disruptions. They are more capable of absorbing shocks, adjusting supply chains, and finding alternative solutions. JIT processes, on the other hand, may struggle to adapt swiftly as they are optimized for efficiency and may lack the necessary buffers and flexibility to handle sudden changes.

Long-Term Sustainability

JIC resilience considers long-term sustainability and the well-being of stakeholders. By mitigating risks and ensuring continuity, organizations can protect the interests of employees, customers, and the broader community. JIT processes, while efficient in minimizing waste and cost, may prioritize short-term gains at the expense of long-term sustainability and resilience.

Better Suited for Complex and Uncertain Environments

In complex and uncertain environments, where risks are difficult to predict and disruptions are more likely, JIC resilience is often more suitable. It acknowledges the inherent uncertainty of the operating environment and builds resilience measures to address this uncertainty. JIT processes, designed for stable and predictable conditions, may struggle to cope with the inherent variability and turbulence of such environments.

Sustainability in Supply Chains

The need for a global economy has increased the demand for products made in other countries and many of those are considered "Low-Cost Regions", or LCRs. These products are often made in factories with poor environmental protections, making the global environment suffer even more. But what if we rethink the problem and create a local supply chain?

We can produce goods locally, which will cut down on transportation costs, and does not require excess packaging to be shipped across oceans. Export packaging can add hundreds if not thousands of dollars to the transport costs and adds voluminous amounts of packaging and crating material.

Local production also helps reduce power usage. When sourcing from other parts of the world, the goods are typically warehoused while waiting for customs inspections. These warehouses consume power and combined with the current delays, goods can sit for weeks or even months in these warehouses, wasting power with every day in storage.

We call this shift towards local supply a "Circular Economy" and it has many benefits. A circular economy is designed to maximize resource efficiency by reducing waste and unnecessary depletion of our natural resources. It moves away from the traditional linear economic model of extract, produce, and dispose and moves toward local supply supporting regional sales, consumption, and recycling.

In the age of globalization, companies have been moving their production overseas to take advantage of cheaper labor costs. This trend isn't going anywhere, but there are some resources available that can help you reverse this trend for your business and save money.

In large corporations, reverse logistics has become a key strategy to reduce overhead costs. Companies need to make sure they coordinate their product returns with their suppliers, so they don't end up stuck with excess inventory and the associated depreciation expense. Imagine how hard it is to cancel or return goods to China vs. a supplier who is just across town.

In addition to the lack of local goods, the cost of importing goods from abroad is a major issue in developing countries. The trade imbalance between these countries and more developed ones has been a problem for decades.

One of the most promising solutions would be a system that increases the availability of credit to domestic entrepreneurs so they can start their own businesses and become involved in local production.

Your choice of materials can also add benefits. Choosing local, natural sources of materials will become increasingly important for manufacturers. By design, natural materials are a good choice for local sourcing, since many bio-products are inefficient to ship internationally anyway.

There's a new focus on sustainability, lowering carbon footprints, and generally being more aware of the environmental impact that our companies are responsible for. Sourcing natural materials is a great first step to meeting ESG mandates, and natural products are more inherently local.

We believe that many products made today can benefit from adding natural materials to the mix. Biomaterials can be grown virtually anywhere and can offer a substitute for so many materials from plastics additives to building materials to nanotech materials such as graphene! We have witnessed supply fulfillment in just hours by utilizing our local farms and processing facilities!

As more companies are focusing on predictability and sustainability, many are looking into sourcing their materials locally. Not only will these companies be able to better monitor the environmental impact of their supply chains, but they will also be able to provide better customer service by being able to quickly fulfill orders. By simplifying the supply chain, we can reduce sourcing costs and that will ultimately lead us to higher profits and happier customers!

A good read on the future of supply chain management can be found here.

https://www.heartland.io/sustainability-news/complete-guide-to-supply-chains-of-the-future-local-vs-global/

Today's Pain Points

Two Southern California ports account for nearly 40% of all goods entering the United States and as of the writing of this book, there are serious delays in and out of both (Los Angeles and Long Beach). NY/Newark, Savanna, Seattle, Houston, and Alameda make up a bulk of the remainder, with smaller ports dotted all along the U.S. coastlines.

Most of them have been impacted as well. We hear about the backups, both on the West Coast and East Coast and some reports show over 100 vessels waiting at sea outside these entry points. We see images of shelves empty or nearly empty in our favorite stores. However, the problem went much deeper than finding that perfect toy in stock this year; these delays are causing U.S. manufacturers huge headaches as well.

Figure 16 - Port of Long Beach, California

In the world of manufacturing today, timing is everything. Most manufacturers run on a "Just in Time" scheduling platform, meaning as they need materials for production, they show up on their docks. In the past this has allowed companies to reduce the amount of raw inventory on the shelves, lowering overhead costs and streamlining the production floor. However, when the materials don't show up on time, it's a disaster! If the ships containing those materials are stuck out at sea, then the goods they carry certainly are not going to show up on time! This is where the "chain" in the supply chain becomes important. Break one link and the chain fails.

Think about it as it pertains to building a house. The foundation must be in place before the framing. The framing takes place before plumbing and electrical, those must be complete before shoring up the walls, windows, doors, and so on. There's a predictable pattern of work to do in the proper order. If for some reason any one of those items is late, then the entire project gets delayed, and unused materials stack up. The worst-case scenario could be workers laid off or moved around inefficiently from job to job. It's the same for a manufacturer when the materials are late, everyone suffers.

With the rise of globalization, it seems that everyday Americans are becoming more reliant on goods imported from outside the U.S. From clothing to electronics, to cars, we consumers rely heavily on overseas products and many manufacturers have become dependent on foreign materials. However, this trend could have significant implications for the U.S. supply chains that count on these overseas materials showing up on time.

Supply chain efficiency has a big impact on the consumer. For example, a container ship carrying automobiles from Japan to the U.S., was diverted to Canada when the ship's captain went on strike. This is just one example of how disruptions in shipping can create major headaches for all parties involved in international trade, and this was just one boat! What happens when many container ships get delayed?

It doesn't take much to disrupt the effort as it is akin to a choreographed routine; each cargo ship moves in and out of port in a timely and efficient manner, allowing the flow to continue – think airplanes landing and departing at O'Hare. One major disruption and we have planes stuck on the tarmac and stacked at the gates!

The United States experienced a series of these shipping disruptions at the major ports of entry during COVID. This shortage led to a rise in freight and delivery costs. The problem is still affecting all of us in some manner, and it's not clear when (or if) the situation and prices will return to the pre-pandemic levels.

The Future of Local Supplies and Why It Matters

A local supply chain is a system of organizations, activities, and resources involved in the production and distribution of goods and services within a regional boundary – typically within a day's drive. The most common way it differs from an international supply chain is in the number of countries involved. Local chains contain operations within one country or region and rely mostly on rail and trucking to move goods from one point to another. International chains can encompass very large regions and are multinational by nature.

These multinational efforts are mainly handled via overseas shipping, utilizing large cargo vessels. These ships can take weeks, or months to get the materials to their desired location. Of course, once the goods hit an entry port, they essentially become regional and move the goods to the destination via rail or truck; this simply adds to the transportation time after the long ocean voyage.

To have a sustainable business, we need to consider our supply chains. In the modern world, the supply chain is no longer linear as it was in the past. Instead, it is now a complex network that has many interactions and different types of suppliers. This makes it harder for businesses to have an accurate picture of their total costs and environmental impact because they are not able to monitor every step in the chain.

What's more, most companies that grow into multinational corporations begin to rely on a global supply chain since they find it more cost-effective (on the surface) than relying on suppliers from one country or region only. However, those overseas routes are increasingly teaming with delays, and they are only getting worse.

While there are some benefits for global supply chains such as having access to a wide materials base, and some better "first-cost" points, those advantages can be quickly wiped out with a single disruption of the process. Local supply chains may offer a better solution, even if at first glance the costs may be higher.

One company in NY (Nanotronics) has redirected all supply chains inward and has been able to beat the competition to the punch. From an article in the New York Times – "There is nothing we have right now that is behind schedule," said Matthew Putman, the chief executive of the company, which makes items like robotic microscopes. "We don't rely on ships right now that are stuck at ports in Los Angeles." Nanotronics makes many of its components at its 45,000-square-foot office and factory space in Brooklyn. What it doesn't make, it acquires locally.

https://www.nytimes.com/2021/12/06/nyregion/nyc-companies-that-dont-rely-on-the-global-supply-chain-are-faring-quite-well.html

One of the beneficial aspects of choosing a local supplier is that they can be more responsive to customer needs. Also, when sourcing locally, you will often find that your suppliers are neighbors in your community and in many cases understand your business and its associated challenges better than someone on the other side of the globe.

This reduces the carbon footprint and environmental impact of your product(s). Even if they are not using bio-based or more natural materials, it is much easier to start that conversation with a local supplier. Plus, with today's higher focus on sustainability, they have the added incentive to search for more eco-friendly solutions from other local sources.

It is no secret that the effects of natural disasters are devastating. Hurricane Katrina, for example, caused widespread damage to homes and infrastructure including the port of New Orleans. That impact was felt for many years afterward. Local chains are more resilient in the face of these disasters.

The rising costs of transportation have been a concern for businesses. We are seeing a rapid increase in transportation costs due to our port delays simply because of the law of supply and demand. Less availability to ship products always means higher transport costs. However, with a more local supply chain, that impact is much lower. Also, with the development of innovative transportation/delivery technologies, such as self-driving trucks and drones, the shortage of drivers (which also adds costs), may be a thing of the past.

Local manufacturing has several advantages over overseas production, the most notable being the lack of import taxes as well as the costs of overseas middlemen. When you source within your own country, it is possible to save on those taxes. Some tariffs exceed 25% for imported products, and that's a huge burden when you consider most manufacturers run between a 20 to 35-point profit margin. We know of businesses that have been completely shuttered because of excessive tariffs.

Costly shipping also becomes irrelevant when goods are made close to where they will be sold. Sourcing locally also allows you to maintain better control over quality standards and safety regulations.

151

Chapter 11:

What 5.0 Means to Farming

Regenerative Agriculture

We spoke about the intersection of materials advancement and farming, as biomaterials are becoming more prevalent across many industries. To simply lean on agriculture in its current state would be selling our farmers short. Just as Industry 5.0 is pushing manufacturing into the future, it will have a major impact on farming as well. The term we see associated with sustainability is "Regenerative Agriculture".

Regenerative agriculture, also known as regenerative farming, is a sustainable agricultural practice that supports the natural life cycle of the land. It is an augmentation of traditional farming practices, which are based on the use of chemical fertilizers and tilling and has been shown to produce higher crop value.

In many ways, this regenerative method is better for the soil and ultimately better for the farmer's bottom line. Over time, yields per acre will increase and there will be a drastic reduction in human input (irrigation, pesticides, herbicides, labor, equipment, etc.). In some cases, the value per acre can be 2-3x just by going back to tried and true farming practices that were commonplace before the era of chemicals and genetic modification.

The regenerative approach to agriculture is clearly based on the principles of ecology. It recognizes that healthy soil is essential for healthy plants, animals, and human beings. The regenerative approach also recognizes that soil erosion and carbon sequestration are major problems facing our planet today.

This approach seeks to address these issues by promoting practices such as no-tillage (or low-tillage) farming, cover cropping, crop rotation, livestock integration (including poultry), composting, biological pest control, and water infiltration practices (such as rainwater harvesting).

It focuses on farming and grazing practices that, among other benefits, reverse climate change by rebuilding soil organic matter and restoring degraded soil biodiversity. This results in both carbon drawdown and an improved water cycle.

Regenerative agriculture practices are typically summarized into 5 main categories.

1. Don't disturb the soil through no-tillage, or minimal tillage practices.
2. Keep the soil surface covered via the application of crops that restore soil health.
3. Keep living roots in the soil, thereby building a thriving biological ecosystem.
4. Grow a diverse range of crops that compost to create a rich microbial community.
5. Bring grazing animals back to the land that stimulates plant growth and soil health.

NGO, The Carbon Underground, published this widely accepted definition of Regenerative Farming in 2017 –

"Regenerative Agriculture" describes farming and grazing practices that, among other benefits, reverse climate change by rebuilding soil organic matter and restoring degraded soil biodiversity – resulting in both carbon drawdown and improving the water cycle.

Specifically, Regenerative Agriculture is a holistic land management practice that leverages the power of photosynthesis in plants to close the carbon cycle, and build soil health, crop resilience and nutrient density. Regenerative agriculture improves soil health, primarily through the practices that increase soil organic matter.

This not only aids in increasing soil biodiversity and health but increases biodiversity both above and below the soil surface, while increasing both water holding capacity and sequestering carbon at greater depths, thus drawing down climate-damaging levels of atmospheric CO2 and improving soil structure to reverse civilization-threatening human-caused soil loss. Research continues to reveal the damaging effects to soil from tillage, applications of agricultural chemicals and salt-based fertilizers, and carbon mining. Regenerative Agriculture reverses this paradigm to build for the future.

https://thecarbonunderground.org/

Regenerative farming is a holistic, regenerative system of agriculture that embraces the principles of ecology. It can be seen as a new agricultural revolution or a revitalization of ancient practices that have been upgraded over time. Either way you look at it, Industry 5.0 will have a major impact on agriculture.

Sustainable agriculture has been practiced for centuries in local areas, but recent developments in equipment have made regenerative farming more accessible to larger operations too. The basics of this system include cover crop rotation, composting, carbon sequestration, and a focus on soil health.

At the highest level, regenerative agriculture focuses on the long-term health of the soil and the environment. It is a form of sustainable agriculture that can be traced back to ancient times.

We have seen an increase in awareness about the harmful effects of industrial agriculture on our environment, and regenerative farming offers an alternative to this harmful way of farming by focusing on sustainability, biodiversity, and healthy soil. For there to be meaningful change in farming practices, people must take a pragmatic approach to adopt these tried-and-true methodologies.

Let's imagine soil as the skin of the earth. Now ask yourself, do we humans have a history of a good skincare routine with our planet? The answer is clearly "No". We have seen topsoil erosion and compromise over the last century that outpaces the destruction of our farmlands across all human history. If we are going to reverse this trend, we need to integrate systemic changes in the farming methods we use today.

How Did We Get Here?

Modern large-scale agriculture (as we know it in America today) essentially started in 1862 when President Lincoln signed the Homestead Act. This allowed anyone to claim ownership of 160 acres of land in our heartland by proving they could sustain themselves for 3-5 years. It's worth noting that much of the land gifted by Lincoln to Americans was acquired during the Louisiana Purchase. Although the land was purchased by America from France, the original owners of the land were Indigenous people.

According to Lincoln's agreement, at the end of the term, the land was deeded to the new owners *if* they could prove their farming and/or ranching acumen was up to standard and could sustain them. This set in motion the widespread agricultural progress for America in the new territory west of the Mississippi.

In all, more than 160 million acres of public land, or nearly 10 percent of the total farmable land of the United States, was given away free to 1.6 million homesteaders.

For the first 50 years, the plan worked to perfection as small farmers and ranchers blazed their trails across the heartland. However, in the 1930s, America suffered through one of the worst tragedies, both agriculturally and culturally, in its history – the Dust Bowl.

Over the years, the farmers across North America had been over-tilling their soil while planting the same crops season after season. As farming became more commercial, and higher volumes of crops were needed to be harvested, we turned to the technology of the day (mechanized tilling, herbicides, and pesticides) to increase the output. However, the side effects of over-tilling (a term that didn't even exist then) were catastrophic!

Over-tilling by itself did not create the Dust Bowl, just like an airline crash is not caused by one component failure. Typically, many smaller failures add up and lead to larger, systemic ones.

Farmers of the day were tilling and planting the same crop over and over. By creating a monoculture (the growth of only one type of crop in each region), and without any cover crops to protect the land, wind erosion blew away the top layer of soil. Unknowingly, they were reducing the soil's ability to be resilient to pests, weeds, droughts, and other adversities. The reduction of organic matter content turned America's fertile soil lands into a desert.

Figure 17 - Dust Storm

Alongside over-tilling and planting the same crops over and over, America saw major droughts in 1934, 1936, 1939, and 1940. All of these variables, stacked on top of each other, evolved into a situation that created massive fallout for American farmers and food supply chains.

Nature was not solely responsible for the Dust Bowl either. Politics and culture played a huge role also. In the early 1900s, wheat was sold in marketplaces for a few cents per bushel. Most wheat farmers were of European descent where it was a more localized crop among other grains and grasses.

However, with the advent of war (World War I), Europe's grain routes (mostly from Russia) were blocked, and the U.S. stepped in to ramp up wheat production. Eventually, this guaranteed farmers $2 per bushel and created a mass market for wheat that previously did not exist.

How was that market supported? By leveraging the expansive original prairie grasslands of Kansas, Oklahoma, Texas, Nebraska, etc. Now, instead of varieties of crops produced by the small family plots, farmers inadvertently created vast monocultures by tilling and planting a single type of crop with no cover crops in sight.

To make matters worse, the economic collapse of 1929 sent farmers scurrying west for employment, leaving vast areas of land unplanted and ripe for a soil disaster. Bring on the droughts of the 1930s and it's easy to see how the perfect storm was unfolding.

> Note: *Cover crops are plants that are intended to cover the soil rather than to be harvested. They help farmers manage soil erosion, soil fertility, soil quality, water, weeds, pests, and diseases. By not planting cover crops, most (if not all) of the living organisms that keep soil healthy end up leaving because they have no food. Planting the same crop, harvesting, and tilling in constant cycles pulls the nutrients (and carbon) out of the soil and into the atmosphere. Carbon has gotten a bad reputation lately, but that's because there's too much in the atmosphere, and not enough in the ground!*

What Were the Outcomes of The Dust Bowl?

America's farmland went through a desertification process where the land degraded because biological productivity decreased. It's estimated that over 100,000,000 acres of once fertile land was essentially turned into dust. When fertile areas become arid climates, it's very difficult to reverse the effects.

Most of us think of the Dust Bowl as a singular event, however, the storms began in the 1930s and continued for nearly a decade. During that time, millions of people moved out of America's heartland because of widespread hunger and poverty. Those original homesteaders who had to prove themselves in the late 1800s to keep their land were ultimately evicted by mother nature herself.

Because of what was happening to farmers across America, Franklin D. Roosevelt decided to create the Soil Conservation Service (SCS) to revitalize the country's farmland. Today, we know this organization as the Natural Resources Conservation Service (NRCS).

Slowly but surely, this organization has helped support farmers, soil health, and the agriculture supply chains across America that the world relies upon.

So, from this natural disaster came a great organization that works with farmers every day. But the reality is, the dust bowl would have never happened if regenerative farming practices were used across America's agriculture industry. Even today, it can be difficult to convince farmers to use regenerative farming practices.

How This Led to Today's Farming Practices

The desertification of the heartland in the 1930s led to chemical and genetic technologies in the 1940s and beyond. Most of the chemical and genetic solutions were focused on introducing nutrients back into the soil. Much like the types of side effects humans get from taking drugs, adding lost nutrients to the plants created byproducts (or reactions) which then created more byproducts (and more reactions)! A vicious cycle was beginning.

The most notable undesired effect of introducing nutrients into a monoculture environment was the fact that weeds now had a new environment to thrive in. Crops can be seen as plants that humans have tamed to grow in certain areas, while weeds are plants that grow on their own, unassisted by humans.

The unassisted growth of weeds created an unintended nuisance – weeds competing against crops for nutrients and water. These weeds are supercharged with nutrients that are used as steroids for corn, wheat, or soy. This became a real problem for farmers across the heartland.

So, how did farmers learn to control the weeds? By again turning to technology in the form of weed killers or herbicides. These herbicides did exactly what they were designed to do, kill the weeds. Of course, the herbicides created another byproduct (or reaction). New variants of weeds become resistant to herbicides in one or two generations. So new, more powerful herbicides needed to be developed, and the cycle continued.

Another nuisance that farmers had to consider was pests (or insects). Again, our farming community turned to industry-leading technology, pesticides. These chemicals are designed to deter or kill harmful insects in farmland.

Crop-dusting (the act of spreading pesticides over a field before crops are planted), became common practice for farmers. These pesticides were designed to deter all different types of infestations.

As you may have guessed, much like herbicides, insects started to form a resistance to pesticides. Again, we have put ourselves into a never-ending cycle of genetic adaptations and chemical alterations.

Moreover, society began to see another byproduct that came by way of the increased use of chemicals in the fields. Now, not only do we know that crops are adversely affected by herbicides and pesticides (because they are poisons), but science has also shown the effect of these chemicals on humans. How did we attack this problem? Again, turning to technology in the form of genetic crop modification.

Genetics is a fascinating science that has always been shrouded in a bit of ambiguity. As the smallest unit of heredity, DNA has been studied for decades to try and understand how it works and what makes us who we are. Just like humans have genetic makeup, so do plants.

Like us, plant genetics form the characteristics of the organism. Are we tall, light-skinned, blue-eyed or are we shorter, husky, and tan? It's all in our genetics. Many times, plants have ideal, and less than ideal characteristics due to the conditions they are trying to survive in.

So, in the same way, humans evolved to survive, and so have our plant ancestors. By carefully studying and using genetic modification, researchers were able to develop crops with natural immunity to certain pesticides and herbicides. But again, byproducts reared their ugly heads.

Earlier we spoke about monocultures and the downsides of growing only one type of crop. Well, just like in humans, the crops' descendants take on the benefits of their parents. Unfortunately, they also take on the flaws.

What happens when the parents are too close together in the bloodline? Genetic mutations. Plants develop genetic weaknesses just like humans can. But, by insulating them from the weaknesses with additional herbicides and pesticides, we can temporarily strengthen the line. These chemicals are just band aids that never solve the root problem.

Think about it like this: A person that gets a kidney transplant is given a lot of drugs to help the body accept (or in most cases, simply not reject) the new organ. The body's natural defenses stack up against this threat to knock it down. However, the downside is that now other threats (viruses, disease, etc.) are more capable of attack because nearly all the body's defense mechanisms are being called upon to save the new organ. Transplant patients are often isolated for a time while the body heals and regenerates.

The plant's ability to adapt and survive through adverse conditions creates an environment for new threats to pop up all the time.

Of course, the next step, Maslow-like solutions are more technology, more pesticides, more herbicides, and further genetic modifications. As you can see, this is an endless cycle. Unfortunately, the biggest loser in this battle is our soil. The natural balance of our soil health got further off track throughout crop cycles and technologies. Our man-made solutions, while rapid and effective short term, have overwhelmed our soil's ecosystems and its ability to naturally recover and thrive.

We've leaned too heavily on genetic modification and chemical processing to put the necessary ingredients back into the soil by rotating in a whole new set of crops.

Countries with strong agricultural resources are investing in new technologies to increase their crop yields. But unfortunately, this has led to declining diversity in the types of crops being grown. The biodiversity of plants is directly impacted by human decisions, so we must keep track of the agricultural changes we make as we seek to grow biodiversity and soil health.

Of course, irrigation practices play a part too. Irrigation has smoothed over the rough patches of low rainfall periods. On the flip side, the overuse of water is leading us back to a potentially catastrophic event. We are taking more water from the aquifers than is being replenished by rainfall and snowmelt. One of our most critical natural resources is becoming scarcer from Kansas (underground aquifers) to California (diversion of rivers to supply irrigation needs).

In the end, plant diversity, natural pesticides, and weed control all took a back seat to innovations in chemical technology. The soil across the world is depleted and abused by years of mistreatment.

We are destroying the soil that houses 25% of all biodiversity on Earth. The soil that provides us with oxygen, produces food for us to eat, and stores water that can be used for drinking. The soil also absorbs incoming carbon dioxide which helps keep the earth's temperature cool. This is the type of carbon (sequestration) that we like!

One of the many reasons agriculture methods are problematic is because they require a lot of land. It has been estimated that one-third of the Earth's dryland surface is used for growing crops. That means that currently there are 5 billion hectares of land farmed globally.

Our governments and agriculture leaders need to invest in soil conservation and restoration practices; the future of the planet rides on it. The world's population is estimated to reach 9.7 billion by 2050.

This type of population growth will come with an increasing demand for food.

So, as the global population continues to grow, so does the need for healthy, sustainable agriculture practices. Today, virtually all the world's agricultural land exists in a degraded condition, which reduces the availability of nutrients in the soil. In Africa, it is estimated that forty million people are trying to survive on the formerly fertile land that has degraded to the point where it is essentially nonproductive.

The U.S. Department of Agriculture has found that farmers need to invest in soil conservation and restoration practices to meet the growing demand for food. Food security is a growing issue because of the world's rapidly changing population and changing climate.

The rapid growth in the global population combined with an increase in the demand for food has led to a decrease in farmland. This has increased the pressure to produce more food with less land. With this type of pressure on our farms and farmers, it is tough to visualize how we'll meet those demands while sustaining healthy ecosystems that minimize environmental impacts.

Topsoil is typically found in regions where rivers meet oceans and support plant life. Biodiversity is the variety of living organisms within an area, such as a species, family of species, or ecosystem. The biodiversity within the topsoil is the beginning of agricultural fields that provide the stability necessary to produce food for people.

Pesticides have been in use for a long time, but there has been a recent push to abandon them because they can cause a variety of health problems. According to the EPA, pesticides have directly impacted animal and human health. They add that the health effects of pesticides depend on the type of pesticide. Some, such as organophosphates and carbamates, affect the nervous system. Others may irritate the skin or eyes. Some pesticides may be carcinogens. Others may affect the hormone or endocrine system in the body. All in all, direct exposure to pesticides can be dangerous.

Industry 5.0 will lead us to this simple point – our soil is the basis of our existence. It's the medium in which plants grow. It contains our food, and it provides us with clean water. Soil is essential to life as we know it, so it's time we paid attention to its condition and treated our soil with a little more kindness. Regenerative agriculture processes are our first steps.

Is Regenerative Farming New?

No; there is nothing new about regenerative agriculture. The indigenous people across America were masters of regenerative agricultural processes! For centuries before the arrival of Europeans, the indigenous people of North America practiced a form of agriculture that sustained them for generations and defined their relationship with the land.

Contrary to popular belief, Europeans did not discover an "untouched land". This idea, known as the 'pristine myth' of the early settlers, is just that, a myth. Charles Mann, the author of "1491: New Revelations of the Americas Before Columbus," notes how this myth obscures the reality that Indigenous Americans were leading practices for hundreds of years that define sustainable agriculture and land stewardship today.

One of the agricultural systems the Iroquois practiced was called "The Three Sisters," and it involved growing corn, beans, and squash in close proximity to each other. This kept the soil's ecosystem diverse, as each plant had different characteristics, nutritional needs, and left behind varied biomass.

In this system, the corn stalks provided a natural trellis for the beans to grow on, which in turn helped the corn grow by adding nitrogen to the soil. The squash vines then acted as a 'living mulch' that could maintain soil moisture levels and keep weeds at bay. The three sisters could easily have been four, five, or a dozen – the more biodiversity, the better.

Because their land was their means to survival, indigenous peoples were true stewards of the environment. One of the most outstanding qualities of these communities is their deep connection to their surrounding land. For centuries, they had been protecting, preserving, and hunting in order to sustain themselves. Losing the resources and the land meant losing their homes, livelihoods, and, in extreme cases, it meant losing their lives. Today, they are also known for defending their land, forests, and rivers against the takeover for development and 'conservation' projects.

What Indigenous peoples are fighting for is their land, and all the plants and animals that live on it (as well as the plants and animals that live on neighboring lands). They understand this more than anyone else: without such landscapes, the Earth will eventually become dry and barren. Although they comprise less than 5% of the world population, Indigenous peoples protect 80% of the Earth's biodiversity. However, despite their critical role in ensuring a resilient and healthy planet for plants and animals, there is a lack of mass interest in their efforts.

If we are truly concerned about achieving global sustainability and protecting the world's biodiversity, we ought to be working more with indigenous peoples and communities to address these challenges. That starts with listening to them and recognizing their knowledge, experience, and culture.

166

Chapter 12:

What 5.0 Means to Business

Mandates, Reporting, and Regulation

Investors and analysts research almost everything about businesses prior to committing funds or providing guidance. Increasingly we see them focusing on sustainability goals and ESG. However, there are several avenues for collecting information and aligning business activities to mandates and regulations.

Sustainability mandates reporting and regulation refer to policies and requirements implemented by governments and organizations to monitor and regulate practices and performance. There are literally hundreds of these agencies across the globe, and reporting protocols vary widely. However, the basic aim of the mandates/regulations is similar - to ensure that businesses and entities are transparent about their environmental, social, and governance (ESG) impacts, and take measures to improve sustainability outcomes. Investors are increasingly looking at these reporting tools to better understand a company's commitment to sustainability.

Let's look at the five key aspects of sustainability mandates reporting and regulation:

1. **Reporting Requirements:** Sustainability mandates often include reporting requirements that oblige companies to disclose specific information related to their sustainability

performance. This can include reporting on greenhouse gas emissions, energy consumption, water usage, waste management, social impact, diversity and inclusion, labor practices, supply chain transparency, and other relevant metrics. Reporting frameworks such as the Global Reporting Initiative (GRI) and the Sustainability Accounting Standards Board (SASB) provide guidelines and standards for organizations to structure and report their sustainability data.

2. **Compliance and Disclosure:** Sustainability reporting mandates may require businesses to disclose their sustainability performance in their annual reports, financial statements, or dedicated sustainability reports. Compliance with these mandates ensures that relevant stakeholders, including investors, customers, employees, and the public, have access to accurate and comparable sustainability information. Additionally, regulatory bodies or stock exchanges may mandate certain companies to report on specific ESG factors or integrate sustainability into their corporate governance practices.

3. **Standards and Frameworks:** Various standards and frameworks have been developed to guide sustainability reporting and ensure consistency and comparability across organizations. These include the GRI Standards, SASB standards, Carbon Disclosure Project (CDP), Task Force on Climate-related Financial Disclosures (TCFD), and many others. These frameworks help define the metrics, indicators, and methodologies for reporting specific ESG factors, enabling organizations to align their reporting practices with widely accepted industry standards.

4. **Verification and Assurance:** Some sustainability mandates may require companies to obtain third-party verification or assurance for their sustainability reports (like carbon sequestration). Independent auditors or assessors review and verify the accuracy and reliability of the reported data,

ensuring that it complies with the relevant reporting standards and requirements. This verification adds credibility and trust to sustainability reporting and provides assurance to stakeholders that the reported information is accurate.

5. **Regulatory Compliance and Enforcement:** In certain cases, sustainability reporting mandates may be legally binding, backed by regulatory bodies or governmental agencies. Non-compliance with these mandates can result in penalties, fines, or legal consequences (think tax structure). Regulatory bodies play a crucial role in monitoring compliance and enforcing sustainability reporting requirements, ensuring that organizations adhere to the specified guidelines.

The aim of sustainability mandates reporting, and regulation should be to promote transparency, accountability, and continuous improvement in sustainability practices. By establishing clear reporting requirements and enforcing compliance, these mandates can drive organizations to assess, manage, and improve their environmental and social impacts, ultimately contributing to a more sustainable and responsible business environment.

To better understand how complex MR&R can be, we've created a glossary and definitions of some of the more popular agencies, groups, and business elements of sustainability. We'll break down and describe the sometimes-overwhelming acronyms (we do love our initials!). Fair warning, many groups are in Europe and definitions are cited from their publications, so European spelling might be in effect.

Sustainable Business Glossary

For those of you who would like to use the glossary primarily as a reference tool, it is copied into Appendix A. Feel free to skip ahead to Chapter 13.

BSR

Business for Social Responsibility

International business coalition and sustainability consultancy originally known as Business for Social Responsibility. Today, it's known as BSR. From their website, BSR is described as "...a sustainable business network and consultancy focused on creating a world in which all people can thrive on a healthy planet."

"Through our insights, advisory services, and collaborations, we enable business transformation to create long-term value for business and society."

BSR's focus areas include:

- Climate Change
- Equity, Inclusion, and Justice
- Human Rights
- Nature
- Supply Chain Sustainability
- Sustainability Management

https://www.bsr.org/

CDP

Formerly known as Climate Disclosure Project but now just CDP.

From their website, "CDP is a not-for-profit charity that runs the global disclosure system for investors, companies, cities, states and regions to manage their environmental impacts. Over the past 20 years we have created a system that has resulted in unparalleled engagement on environmental issues worldwide."

https://www.cdp.net/en

CDSB

The Climate Disclosure Standards Board

From their website, "CDSB is an international consortium of business and environmental NGOs. We are committed to advancing and aligning the global mainstream corporate reporting model to equate natural capital with financial capital."

"We do this by offering companies a framework for reporting environmental information with the same rigour as financial information. In turn this helps them to provide investors with decision-useful environmental information via the mainstream corporate report, enhancing the efficient allocation of capital. Regulators also benefit from compliance-ready materials."

"Recognising that information about natural capital and financial capital is equally essential for an understanding of corporate performance, our work builds the trust and transparency needed to foster resilient capital markets. Collectively, we aim to contribute to more sustainable economic, social and environmental systems."

https://www.cdsb.net/

CR&S - CSR

Corporate Responsibility and Sustainability - Corporate Social Responsibility

The two terms here are very similar, and typically cross-reference definitions when searching. According to Learning to Give.org, CR&S/CSR is, "... any action a corporation does to benefit the relationship between a corporation and the community, and to make a positive difference in the community with employee engagement, financial support, and volunteerism. Corporate social responsibility is a business trying to do well in the community through responsible actions."

https://www.learningtogive.org/resources/corporate-social-responsibility-and-sustainability

CSO

Chief Sustainability Officer – the most senior executive in the business responsible directly for sustainability

Most of us are very familiar with the C-suite positions. CEO, COO, CFO and such. However, newer to the scene is the CSO, or Chief Sustainability Officer. There are other CSOs - Chief Security Officer, Chief Sales Officer, etc., but for this discussion we're focusing on sustainability (obviously!).

The CSO will create, author and develop company strategies to address issues such as energy use, resource conservation, recycling, pollution reduction, waste elimination, transportation, education, and building efficiency. They also serve as the sustainability champion, often overseeing training efforts for all functions within the organization.

CSRD

Corporate Sustainability Reporting Directive – proposed EU replacement for NFRD

From the European Commission on Finance, "EU law requires all large companies and all listed companies (except listed micro-enterprises) to disclose information on their risks and opportunities arising from social and environmental issues, and on the impacts of their activities on people and the environment.

This helps investors, civil society organizations, consumers, and other stakeholders to evaluate the sustainability performance of companies, as part of the European green deal entered into force. This new directive modernizes and strengthens the rules about the social and environmental information that companies must report. A broader set of large companies, as well as listed SMEs, will now be required to report on sustainability – approximately 50 000 companies in total.

The new rules will ensure that investors and other stakeholders have access to the information they need to assess investment risks arising from climate change and other sustainability issues. They will also create a culture of transparency about the impact of companies on people and the environment. Finally, reporting costs will be reduced for companies over the medium to long term by harmonizing the information to be provided."

https://finance.ec.europa.eu/capital-markets-union-and-financial-markets/company-reporting-and-auditing/company-reporting/corporate-sustainability-reporting_en

DE&I

Diversity, Equity and Inclusion

DE&I is a conceptual framework that claims to promote the fair treatment and full participation of all people, especially in the workplace, including populations who have historically been under-represented or subject to discrimination because of their background, identity, disability, etc.

From Wikipedia "Diversity" describes a wide variety of differences that may exist amongst people in any community, including race, ethnicity, nationality, gender and sexual identity, disability, neurodiversity, and others.

"Equity" is the practice of providing fair opportunities via personalized approaches based on individual needs, thus aiming to "level the playing field" by taking into account the different starting points of different individuals. Therefore, "equity" aims to achieve fairness by considering each individual's trajectory and context, and should not be confused with the notion of "equality" which aims to treat everyone the same.

"Inclusion" specifies the desired outcome, namely, ensuring that individuals find opportunities and spaces to participate, regardless of their differences.

https://www.dictionary.com/browse/dei

https://en.wikipedia.org/wiki/Diversity,_equity,_and_inclusion#cite_note-1

EPR

Extended Producer Responsibility

Extended Producer Responsibility is a concept where manufacturers and importers of products should bear a significant degree of responsibility for the environmental impacts of their products throughout the product life-cycle, including upstream impacts inherent in the selection of materials for the products, impacts from manufacturers' production process itself, and downstream impacts from the use and disposal of the products.

A great example of this is a car with an internal combustion engine. The manufacturer is not responsible for the carbon emissions to build the vehicle, but the fossil fuel emissions of its anticipated lifetime on the road.

Producers accept their responsibility when designing their products to minimize life-cycle environmental impacts, and when accepting legal, physical, or socio-economic responsibility for environmental impacts that cannot be eliminated by design.

https://www.oecd.org/env/waste/factsheetextendedproducerresponsibility.htm

ESG

Environmental, Social and Corporate Governance

We see ESG mentioned a great deal in the finance and investment world. This is because it is becoming increasingly important to portfolio analysts and advisors as to stability and growth of firms, especially with the 5.0 revolution upon us. ESG as described earlier is essentially:

1. Environmental: The environmental aspect of ESG focuses on a company's impact on the natural environment. This includes factors such as carbon emissions, energy efficiency, waste management, pollution, resource consumption, and climate change adaptation. Assessing a company's environmental performance helps identify its efforts to mitigate environmental risks, promote sustainability, and contribute to the transition to a low-carbon economy.

2. Social: The social aspect of ESG refers to a company's impact on society, including its relationships with employees, customers, communities, and other stakeholders. It encompasses factors such as labor practices, human rights, diversity and inclusion, employee health and safety, product quality and safety, community engagement, and philanthropy. Evaluating a company's social performance helps determine its commitment to social responsibility, ethical practices, and positive social impact.

3. Governance: The governance aspect of ESG focuses on the systems and structures that govern a company's operations and decision-making processes. It includes factors such as board composition and independence, executive compensation, shareholder rights, transparency, risk management, and corporate ethics. Evaluating a company's governance practices helps assess its accountability, integrity, and alignment of interests with shareholders and stakeholders.

As mentioned above, ESG factors are increasingly considered by investors, regulators, and other stakeholders as important indicators of a company's long-term value and sustainability. They provide a deeper look into a company's impact on the environment, society, and its overall governance framework. ESG analysis is increasingly important to investors to help make more informed decisions, and it enables companies to manage risks and thereby seize new opportunities in the pursuit of responsible business practices.

FASB

Financial Accounting Standards Board

Established in 1973, the Financial Accounting Standards Board (FASB) is the independent, private- sector, not-for-profit organization based in Norwalk, Connecticut, that establishes financial accounting and reporting standards for public and private companies and not-for-profit organizations that follow Generally Accepted Accounting Principles (GAAP).

The FASB is recognized by the U.S. Securities and Exchange Commission as the designated accounting standard setter for public companies. FASB standards are recognized as authoritative by many other organizations, including state Boards of Accountancy and the American Institute of CPAs (AICPA). The FASB develops and issues financial accounting standards through a transparent and inclusive process intended to promote financial reporting that provides useful information to investors and others who use financial reports.

The Financial Accounting Foundation (FAF) supports and oversees the FASB. Established in 1972, the FAF is the independent, private-sector, not-for- profit organization based in Norwalk, Connecticut, responsible for the oversight, administration, financing, and appointment of the FASB and the Governmental Accounting Standards Board (GASB).

https://www.fasb.org/facts

GRI & GSSB

Global Reporting Initiative

GRI was founded in Boston (USA) in 1997 following on from the public outcry over the environmental damage of the Exxon Valdez oil spill, eight years previously. Our roots lie in the non-profit organizations CERES and the Tellus Institute, with involvement of the UN Environment Programme. The aim was to create the first accountability mechanism to ensure companies adhere to responsible environmental conduct principles, which was then broadened to include social, economic and governance issues.

The first version of what was then the GRI Guidelines (G1) published in 2000 – providing the first global framework for sustainability reporting. The following year, GRI was established as an independent, non-profit institution. In 2002, the GRI's Secretariat relocated to Amsterdam (The Netherlands), and the first update to the Guidelines (G2) launched. As demand for GRI reporting and uptake from organizations steadily grew, the Guidelines were expanded and improved, leading to G3 (2006) and G4 (2013).

In 2016, GRI transitioned from providing guidelines to setting the first global standards for sustainability reporting – the GRI Standards. The Standards continue to be updated and added to, including new Standards on Tax (2019) and Waste (2020), a major update to the Universal Standards (2021) and the continued roll-out of Sector Standards (2021 onwards).

https://www.globalreporting.org/

Global Sustainability Standards Board

The GSSB has sole responsibility for setting the world's first globally accepted standards for sustainability reporting – the GRI Standards. Established as an independent operating entity under the auspices of GRI, GSSB members represent a range of expertise and multi-stakeholder perspectives on sustainability reporting.

The GSSB works exclusively in the public interest and according to the vision and mission of GRI.

https://www.globalreporting.org/standards/global-sustainability-standards-board/

IASB, IFRS, IIRC, ISSB, & SASB

International Accounting Standards Board

The International Accounting Standards Board (IASB) is an independent, private-sector body that develops and approves International Financial Reporting Standards (IFRSs). The IASB operates under the oversight of the IFRS Foundation. The IASB was formed in 2001 to replace the International Accounting Standards Committee (IASC). A full history of the IASB and the IASC going back to 1973 is available on the IASB website.

Under the IFRS Foundation Constitution, the IASB has complete responsibility for all financial reporting-related technical matters of the IFRS Foundation including:

- Full discretion in developing and pursuing its technical agenda, subject to certain consultation requirements with the Trustees and the public
- The preparation and issuing of IFRSs (other than Interpretations) and exposure drafts, following the due process stipulated in the Constitution
- The approval and issuing of Interpretations developed by the IFRS Interpretations Committee

https://www.iasplus.com/en/resources/ifrsf/iasb-ifrs-ic/iasb

International Financial Reporting Standards

The IFRS Foundation is a not-for-profit, public interest organisation established to develop high-quality, understandable, enforceable and globally accepted accounting and sustainability disclosure standards.

Our Standards are developed by our two standard-setting boards, the International Accounting Standards Board (IASB) and International Sustainability Standards Board (ISSB).

https://www.ifrs.org/

IIRC International Integrated Reporting Council

The International Integrated Reporting Framework and Integrated Thinking Principles have been developed and are used around the world, in 75 countries, to advance communication about value creation, preservation and erosion.

The cycle of integrated reporting and thinking result in efficient and productive capital allocation, acting as a force for financial stability and sustainable development.

Integrated reporting aims to:

- Improve the quality of information available to providers of financial capital to enable a more efficient and productive allocation of capital
- Promote a more cohesive and efficient approach to corporate reporting that draws on different reporting strands and communicates the full range of factors that materially affect the ability of an organization to create value over time
- Enhance accountability and stewardship for the broad base of capitals (financial, manufactured, intellectual, human, social and relationship, and natural) and promote understanding of their independencies
- Support integrated thinking, decision-making and actions that focus on the creation of value over the short, medium and long term

The Integrated Reporting Framework and Integrated Thinking Principles are maintained under the auspices of the IFRS Foundation, a global not-for-profit, public interest organisation established to develop high-quality, understandable, enforceable and globally accepted accounting and sustainability disclosure standards.

https://www.integratedreporting.org/the-iirc-2/

International Sustainability Standards Board

A proposed new body under IFRS. The International Sustainability Standards Board (ISSB), established at COP26 to develop a comprehensive global baseline of sustainability disclosures for the capital markets, today launched a consultation on its first two proposed standards. One sets out general sustainability-related disclosure requirements and the other specifies climate-related disclosure requirements.

https://www.ifrs.org/news-and-events/news/2022/03/issb-delivers-proposals-that-create-comprehensive-global-baseline-of-sustainability-disclosures/

Sustainability Accounting Standards Board

SASB Standards guide the disclosure of financially material sustainability information by companies to their investors. Available for 77 industries, the Standards identify the subset of environmental, social, and governance issues most relevant to financial performance in each industry.

Effective August 1, 2022, the Value Reporting Foundation–home to the SASB Standards–consolidated into the IFRS Foundation, which established the first International Sustainability Standards Board (ISSB). SASB Standards are now under the oversight of the ISSB. The ISSB will build upon the SASB Standards and embed SASB's industry-based standards development approach into the ISSB's standards development process. The ISSB actively encourages preparers and investors to continue to provide full support for and to use the SASB Standards until the SASB Standards become the IFRS Sustainability Disclosure Standards.

https://www.sasb.org/

IBE

Institute of Business Ethics

The IBE is an important partner to any business wanting to preserve its long-term reputation by doing business in the right way.

All organisations need to demonstrate they are trustworthy in order to operate effectively and sustainably. Reputations are not based solely on the delivery of products and services, but on how an organisation values its stakeholders. Having a reputation for acting with honesty and integrity not only differentiates an organisation, it makes it more successful.

Since 1986, the IBE has advised organisations on how to strengthen their ethical culture by sharing knowledge and good practice, resulting in relationships with employees and stakeholders that are based on trust.

We achieve this by:

- Acting as a critical friend to organisations we work with
- Advising senior business leaders and those with responsibility for developing and embedding corporate ethics policies
- Supporting the development of these policies through networking events, regular publications, research and benchmarking as well as training
- Providing guidance to staff through bespoke training and decision-making tools
- Educating the next generation of business leaders in schools and universities.

The IBE is a registered charity funded by corporate and individual donations.

https://www.ibe.org.uk/

IPCC

Inter-Governmental Panel on Climate Change

Created in 1988 by the World Meteorological Organization (WMO) and the United Nations Environment Programme (UNEP), the objective of the IPCC is to provide governments at all levels with scientific information that they can use to develop climate policies. IPCC reports are also a key input into international climate change negotiations. The IPCC is an organization of governments that are members of the United Nations or WMO. The IPCC currently has 195 members. Thousands of people from all over the world contribute to the work of the IPCC. For the assessment reports, experts volunteer their time as IPCC authors to assess the thousands of scientific papers published each year to provide a comprehensive summary of what is known about the drivers of climate change, its impacts and future risks, and how adaptation and mitigation can reduce those risks. An open and transparent review by experts and governments around the world is an essential part of the IPCC process, to ensure an objective and complete assessment and to reflect a diverse range of views and expertise. Through its assessments, the IPCC identifies the strength of scientific agreement in different areas and indicates where further research is needed.

https://www.ipcc.ch/about/

NGOs

Non-governmental organizations.

An NGO, or Non-Governmental Organization, refers to a non-profit, voluntary organization that operates independently from

182

government entities and is typically driven by a specific mission or cause. NGOs are often created by individuals or groups to address societal, environmental, or humanitarian issues and work towards the betterment of communities and the world at large.

The world is full of non-governmental organizations (NGOs) that are dedicated to improving the lives of people, animals, and the environment. From Amnesty International to Greenpeace, from Médecins Sans Frontières to World Wildlife Fund and Oxfam, these renowned NGOs have made it their mission to make a positive difference in the world. But there are many other lesser-known NGOs that strive every day to do their part in making this planet a better place.

Non-governmental organizations (NGOs) play a critical role in tackling some of the most pressing social and environmental issues of our time. They strive to stand up for those who have been neglected or overlooked, advocate for human rights, and work to create a more sustainable future. From providing food aid to developing countries to advocating for the rights of women and children, NGOs are essential players in creating positive change in our world.

SDGs

Sustainable Development Goals of the United Nations

The 2030 Agenda for Sustainable Development, adopted by all United Nations Member States in 2015, provides a shared blueprint for peace and prosperity for people and the planet, now and into the future. At its heart are the 17 Sustainable Development Goals (SDGs), which are an urgent call for action by all countries - developed and developing - in a global partnership. They recognize that ending poverty and other deprivations must go hand-in-hand with strategies that improve health and education, reduce inequality, and spur economic growth – all while tackling climate change and working to preserve our oceans and forests.

The SDGs build on decades of work by countries and the UN, including the UN Department of Economic and Social Affairs

https://sdgs.un.org/goals

TCFD & TNFD

Taskforce Climate Financial Disclosures - How companies should report on their climate impacts

One of the essential functions of financial markets is to price risk to support informed, efficient capital-allocation decisions. To carry out this function, financial markets need accurate and timely disclosure from companies. Without the right information, investors and others may incorrectly price or value assets, leading to a misallocation of capital.

The Financial Stability Board (FSB) created the TCFD to develop recommendations on the types of information that companies should disclose to support investors, lenders, and insurance underwriters in appropriately assessing and pricing a specific set of risks—risks related to climate change.

https://www.fsb-tcfd.org/about/

Taskforce on Nature-related Financial Disclosures – how companies should report on their nature impacts

The mission of the Taskforce on Nature-related Financial Disclosures is to develop and deliver a risk management and disclosure framework for organisations to report and act on evolving nature-related risks, with the ultimate aim of supporting a shift in global financial flows away from nature-negative outcomes and toward nature-positive outcomes.

https://tnfd.global/

UNGC

United Nations Global Compact

The United Nations Global Compact is a voluntary initiative launched by the United Nations in 2000. It encourages businesses and organizations to adopt sustainable and socially responsible policies and practices. Participants commit to ten principles in areas such as human rights, labor, environment, and anti-corruption. The UNGC serves as a platform for companies to engage in dialogue, share best practices, and collaborate on sustainability issues.

https://unglobalcompact.org/about

VRF

Value Reporting Foundation – (merger of SASB and IIRC)

The Value Reporting Foundation (formerly the International Integrated Reporting Council - IIRC) is an organization that promotes integrated reporting as a means for companies to communicate their broader value creation story, including financial and non-financial information, to stakeholders. Integrated reporting provides a holistic view of an organization's strategy, governance, performance, and prospects, integrating financial, environmental, social, and governance (ESG) information in a single report.

https://www.valuereportingfoundation.org/

This list is by no means exhaustive, but can be exhausting to figure out what business should be reporting, and to what agencies. Many of you reading this book may have intentions of garnering more investor dollars, increasing the capitalization of your firm, or looking to increase your brand's value by committing to sustainability goals, and reporting those to the proper channels. Jumping into sustainability reporting can be a difficult initiation, especially when considering so many external agencies, frameworks, and standards.

However, with the right guidance and support it doesn't have to be as daunting.

To determine the best way to embark on sustainability reporting for your company, consider the following steps:

1. Assess your company's context and priorities: Understand your company's specific sustainability goals, industry, stakeholders, and regulatory requirements. Identify the key environmental, social, and governance (ESG) issues relevant to your operations and value chain. This will help you focus on the most significant areas for reporting.

2. Research reporting frameworks and standards: Investigate different sustainability reporting frameworks and standards to find the ones that align with your company's goals and priorities. Commonly used frameworks include the Global Reporting Initiative (GRI) Standards, the Sustainability Accounting Standards Board (SASB) standards, the Task Force on Climate-related Financial Disclosures (TCFD), and the International Integrated Reporting Framework (IIRC), among others. Each framework has its own focus and requirements, so assess which one(s) are best suited to your needs.

3. Consider sector-specific guidelines: Some industries have specific reporting guidelines tailored to their unique sustainability challenges. For example, the Sustainability Reporting Guidelines for the Extractive Industries (GRI G4 Guidelines), the Equator Principles for the finance sector, or the Carbon Disclosure Project (CDP) for carbon-intensive sectors. Look for any sector-specific guidelines that may be applicable to your industry.

4. Engage stakeholders: Consult with internal and external stakeholders, such as employees, customers, investors, and industry associations, to understand their expectations and reporting needs. Engaging stakeholders early on will help

shape your reporting approach and ensure that it addresses their concerns and interests.

5. Develop a reporting strategy: Based on your assessment and research, develop a sustainability reporting strategy tailored to your company's goals and priorities. This strategy should include the chosen reporting framework, key performance indicators (KPIs), data collection and management processes, reporting frequency, and communication channels.

6. Set goals and targets: Define measurable and time-bound sustainability goals and targets aligned with your company's strategy and stakeholder expectations. These goals should be specific, achievable, and relevant to your business. Establishing clear targets will guide your reporting efforts and help track progress over time.

7. Collect and analyze data: Implement systems and processes to collect relevant sustainability data across your organization. This may involve gathering data on energy consumption, emissions, waste management, social impact, diversity, and other performance indicators. Ensure data accuracy, consistency, and transparency to build credibility in your reporting.

8. Report and communicate: Prepare your sustainability report using the chosen framework and guidelines. Clearly communicate your sustainability goals, performance, progress, and initiatives to your stakeholders through various channels, such as annual reports, dedicated sustainability reports, websites, and stakeholder engagements.

9. Continuously improve: Sustainability reporting is an ongoing process. Continuously monitor and evaluate your sustainability performance, engage with stakeholders for feedback, and use the reporting process as a tool for identifying areas for improvement and driving positive change.

Remember, sustainability reporting should reflect a company's unique context and priorities. It's essential to customize the approach and evolve it over time as understanding of sustainability deepens and investors' expectations evolve. Seek guidance from sustainability professionals or consultants if needed, who can provide specific expertise and support throughout the reporting journey.

190

Chapter 13:

How 5.0 Will Build Brand Value

As a society, we are becoming increasingly aware and concerned about the effects of our choices on the environment, as well as the problems that arise from emitting GHGs into our atmosphere. As more consumers realize the power they have in shaping what types of businesses thrive, they're demanding that companies take responsibility for their impact on the planet. But before we tie the two together, let's look at the importance of brand equity and its relation to brand value.

What is Brand Equity?

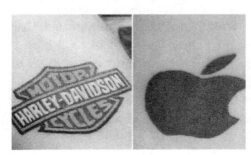

Figure 18 - Harley Davidson and Apple Tattoos

Brand equity is a term that was first introduced by marketing professionals in the 1980s and sometimes confused with brand value. It refers to the importance of a brand name, and how much more consumers are willing to pay for a particular product or service. Brand equity can also be thought of as the intangible value that the brand's perception holds in the consumers' minds.

It refers to a value premium that a company generates from a product with a recognizable name when compared to a more generic equivalent. Companies can create brand equity for their products by making them memorable, easily recognizable, and superior in quality and reliability. Mass marketing campaigns also help to create brand equity, but it's more of a relationship with the consumer that creates the higher equity. Good examples are Apple, Harley-Davidson, and Red Bull. Think about each and their customer bases. A good rule of thumb is that if customers tattoo the logo on themselves, brand equity is most likely very high!

Higher brand equity commands a higher price, more consumer loyalty (to the point of evangelism) and leads us on the path to building higher brand value. Think of off-brands and how they compete – it's almost always on price.

Companies with high brand equity don't compete on price, they operate on a much higher level than that. Ultimately, competing on price is a race to the bottom.

When a company has positive brand equity, customers willingly pay that higher price for its products, even though they could get the same thing from a competitor for less. Customers, in effect, pay a price premium to do business with a firm they know and admire. Because the company with brand equity does not incur a higher expense than its competitors to produce the product and bring it to market, the difference in price goes to their margin. The firm's brand equity (what the consumer thinks) enables it to command higher brand value (the price that consumers are willing to pay), hence why it is so important.

Think of a few examples of widely known brands such as Apple, Google and Nike. Each of these is a well-known brand, but it goes beyond just recognition and equity in the consumer's minds. These brands stand for something, and that alignment with the customer is valuable – very valuable! For example, Apple's brand value is estimated at $355 B. That's not hard assets, or quantified purchase orders, or even real estate. That is solely the value of Apple's brand name!

Since "Brand" is a significant asset to the company, it has the power to maintain their customer base, attract new customers, and increase sales. Successful brands cannot sit on their hands once they reach a significant point in the customers' minds; they need to be protected for them to retain that value. This is why we see the most successful brands continue to promote, advertise, and maintain awareness in the business arena.

Brand is value, brand is trust, and in the business world, brand is everything.

Where Sustainability Fits into Today's Business Brands

Sustainability is the future of building brand value. The word "sustainable" has been tossed around a lot lately, but it can mean different things to different people. Some consider it energy transformation (renewables vs. fossil), or community involvement (sponsoring a youth league), and others feel it's elimination of discrimination in the workplace. We believe it's all the above and more. A great saying is simply – Do things right and do the right things!

Today, a company can be said to be sustainable if it meets these criteria:

- It is profitable (Doing Well).
- It creates a healthy environment for its workers, customers, communities, and it uses resources responsibly (Doing Good).

This all means conducting their business without harming the planet, society, or individuals.

How do forward-looking companies achieve this? Well, first by creating a sustainability strategy. A good first action for many businesses is hiring a sustainability champion. Many times, this position is at the director level or higher. Most Fortune 500 companies now boast a Chief Sustainability Officer in their boardroom.

This position is focused on strategies such as:

- Responsible Energy Use
- Reduction of Waste and Waste Materials
- Efficient Shipping and Transportation
- Community Outreach
- Diversity and Inclusion
- Recycling and Resource Use
- Materials Innovation

The idea of sustainability is often associated with environmentalism or corporate responsibility. However, sustainability goes beyond that and includes social responsibility. Many companies are now building sustainability into their mission statements and publicly reporting on things like ESG mandates/efforts.

To see where sustainability fits in business, we need to dissect the term from a corporate perspective. In his book, "Making Sustainability Work", Marc Epstein notes nine principles of sustainability that businesses will need to pay attention to, and in turn grow their brand equity. Below are excerpts of the nine principles from Mr. Epstein's book.

1. Ethics

Ethical companies establish, promote, monitor, and maintain fair and honest standards and practices in dealings with all of the company stakeholders and encourage the same from all other stakeholders, including business partners, distributors, and suppliers. Ethical companies set high standards of behavior for all employees and agents, and have in place effective systems for monitoring, evaluating, and reporting on how the company does business . The reporting of ethical violations to appropriate authorities is also actively promoted. Ethical companies create codes of conduct, develop ethics education programs, and honor internationally recognized human rights programs.

2. Governance

The governance principle is a commitment to manage all resources conscientiously and effectively, recognizing the fiduciary duty of corporate boards and managers to focus on the interests of all company stakeholders. This duty is of primary importance and is superior to the interests of management. The company follows practices of fair process and seeks to enhance both financial and human capital while balancing the interests of all of its stakeholders. The company encourages the achievement of its mission while being sensitive to the needs of its various stakeholders. Its mission must be clearly stated and widely understood and must recognize the interests of multiple stakeholders. The company must have a strategy and performance metrics that are consistent with its mission. The mission, strategy, policies, practices, and procedures are communicated openly and clearly to employees. Decision - making processes are engrained within this principle as performance is directly related to a particular course of action taken by the company. Companies that value governance evaluate the CEO and senior management on financial and nonfinancial performance and have a board structure that represents a wide range of stakeholder views.

3. Transparency

While the governance principle relates to internal management issues, the transparency principle is about disclosure of information to company stakeholders. Transparent companies provide full disclosure to existing and potential investors and lenders of fair and open communication related to the past, present, and likely future financial performance of the company. Transparent companies broadly identify their stakeholders. Indeed, companies embracing this principle recognize that they are accountable to internal and external stakeholders, understanding both their informational needs and their concerns about the company's effects on their lives.

4. Business relationships

Companies must encourage reciprocity in their relationships with suppliers, by treating them as valued long-term partners in enterprise, enlisting their talents, loyalty, and ideas. Companies endorse long-term stable relationships with suppliers in return for quality, performance, and competitiveness. Companies select their suppliers, distributors, joint-venture partners, licensees, and other business partners not only on the basis of price and quality but also on social, ethical, and environmental performance.

5. Financial returns to investors and lenders

The company compensates providers of capital with a competitive return on investment and the protection of company assets. Company strategies promote growth and enhance long-term shareholder value. The interests of investors and lenders must be explicitly recognized, and companies must develop formal mechanisms to foster an ongoing dialogue with their investors.

6. Community involvement and economic development

Increasingly, companies recognize that it is in the best long-term interest of both the company and the community to improve the community, community resources, and the lives of its members. Thus, the company fosters a mutually beneficial relationship between the corporation and the community in which it is sensitive to the culture, context, and needs of the community. The company plays a proactive and cooperative role in making the community a better place to live and conduct business.

7. Value of products and services

This principle requires companies to specify their relation and obligations to their customers. A proactive stance on this principle requires the company to respect the needs, desires, and rights of its customers and ultimate consumers, and to provide the highest levels of product and service values, including a strong commitment to integrity, customer satisfaction, and safety. Companies create explicit programs to assess the impacts on their stakeholders of the products and services they provide.

8. Employment practices

Adopting this principle means that companies engage in management practices that promote personal and professional employee development, diversity, and empowerment. Companies regard employees as valued partners in the business, respecting their right to fair labor practices, competitive wages and benefits, and a safe, family - friendly work environment. Thus, companies strive to increase and maintain high levels of employee satisfaction and respect international and industry standards for human rights. To do this they offer programs such as tuition reimbursement, family leave time, day care, and career development opportunities.

9. Protection of the environment

To follow this principle, companies must define their commitment to the natural environment. For proactive companies, it means striving to protect and restore the environment and promoting sustainable development with products, processes, services, and other activities. Companies must be committed to minimizing the use of energy and natural resources, and decreasing waste and emissions. At a minimum, the company fully complies with all existing international, national, and local regulations and industry standards regarding emissions and waste. It also entails a commitment to maximize the use and production of recycled and recyclable materials, the durability of products, and to minimize packaging. Increasingly, companies have recognized that sustainability values and principles are important for long-term corporate profitability and are using them to define their sustainability strategies.

Epstein, Marc J.; Rejc Buhovac, Adriana. Making Sustainability Work. Berrett-Koehler Publishers.

When think about sustainability, it's easy to focus primarily on principle #9. After all, that's where a lot of effort (and PR) has been centered. However, to truly be a sustainable business, we need to look at all these aspects that Epstein points out. Looking deeper into ESG scoring, you will see many metrics beyond carbon emissions, most of which are outlined in principals 1-8.

Weighing Long-term Outcomes vs. Short-term Costs

Can sustainability lead to higher brand equity, brand value and a more profitable business? The short answer is, "Yes". However, when diving into all nine of Epstein's principles, it's easy to see there may be conflicts between long term outcomes and short-term costs.

Environmental Stewardship

Implementing sustainable practices helps preserve natural resources, reduce pollution, and minimize ecological damage. While there may be initial costs associated with adopting eco-friendly technologies or processes, the long-term outcome is a healthier environment, mitigated climate change impacts, and improved ecosystem resilience. This benefits not only business but also society as a whole, ensuring a more sustainable future for generations to come.

Cost Savings

Although there might be short-term costs involved in adopting sustainable practices, businesses can realize significant long-term cost savings. Energy-efficient technologies, waste reduction measures, and resource conservation initiatives can lead to reduced operational expenses, lower energy bills, minimized waste disposal costs, and optimized resource utilization. Over time, these savings can outweigh the initial investments and enhance the company's profitability.

Brand Reputation and Customer Loyalty

Sustainable practices resonate with an increasing number of consumers who prioritize ethical and environmentally conscious businesses. By demonstrating a commitment to sustainability, companies can build a positive brand reputation, attract socially responsible customers, and cultivate long-term customer loyalty. This can result in increased market share, brand differentiation, and a competitive edge in the marketplace.

Regulatory Compliance and Risk Management

Governments and regulatory bodies are increasingly imposing environmental regulations and standards. Embracing sustainability proactively can help businesses stay ahead of regulatory changes and avoid costly penalties or legal issues. Furthermore, sustainable practices often involve risk management strategies that enhance resilience to environmental disruptions, such as climate-related events, supply chain disruptions, and reputational risks.

Innovation and Adaptability

Embracing sustainability encourages businesses to seek innovative solutions and adapt to evolving market demands. Companies that integrate sustainability into their core strategies often drive innovation, develop new products and services, and uncover untapped market opportunities. This forward-thinking approach positions businesses for long-term success and resilience in an ever-changing business landscape.

In short, while there may be start-up costs associated with sustainability initiatives, the long-term benefits will ultimately outweigh the first costs. Environmental protection, cost savings, improved brand reputation, customer loyalty, regulatory compliance, risk management, and enhanced innovation are all on the table for the forward-thinking business. Presenting these benefits in clear and concise (meaning leave behind the deep reporting KPIs and focus on what it means to the bottom line) can help stakeholders understand the value and importance of prioritizing sustainability in business decisions.

Sustainability and Your Brand

Many businesses will face challenges with reaching their sustainability goals, however, the upside will be substantial. From their book, "The Sustainable Business Handbook", David Grayson, Chris Coulter, and Mark Lee suggest that sustainability needs to be baked into your business strategy and your daily tactics. It's not simply an annual report from a lone-wolf department, sustainability needs to be integrated into all aspects of your company, and when it's ingrained into all you do, it becomes your "Brand"!

The authors surmise that "Sustainability must be short term as well as long term, tactical as well as strategic. The business case for sustainability matters because more sustainable companies better anticipate, prioritize, and address emerging risks and opportunities including new standards and regulations, while deep trust reservoirs make them more attractive to suppliers, customers, and partners, improving competitiveness.".

These total business relationships lead to "deeper engagement, better access to information and enhanced understanding of societal expectations, supporting better strategy and accelerating research and development, innovation and growth."

The Sustainable Business Handbook: A Guide to Becoming More Innovative, Resilient and Successful By: David Grayson, Chris Coulter, and Mark Lee

What are the steps necessary to move your brand forward toward sustainability? Honestly, they're the same as most strategic initiatives. We need to set goals, assess the current situation, identify the gaps, then map out the path to close the gaps. Let's look at this in a little more detail.

1. **Goal setting:** Establish clear, specific, and measurable goals that align with the business's mission and strategy. This step

involves defining what the business wants to achieve, why it wants to achieve it, and by when.

2. **Strategy development:** Develop a comprehensive plan for achieving the goals that include the resources, activities, and timeline needed to achieve them. This step involves determining how the goals will be achieved and the specific steps that need to be taken.

3. **Resource allocation:** Allocate the necessary resources, including budget, personnel, and technology, to implement the strategy and achieve the goals. This step involves making the investment required to achieve the goals and ensuring that the resources are effectively used.

4. **Implementation:** Put the plan into action and start executing the strategy. This step involves starting the activities and projects needed to achieve the goals and making any necessary adjustments to the plan along the way.

5. **Monitoring and evaluation:** Regularly monitor progress towards the goals and evaluate the results. This step involves tracking the progress of the business toward its goals, identifying any issues or challenges, and making any necessary adjustments to the plan.

6. **Continuous improvement:** Continuously improve the process of goal achievement by learning from successes and failures. This step involves using the lessons learned to refine the approach to goal setting, strategy development, and implementation, and to improve the chances of achieving future goals.

Goal Setting

Most strategic leaders will tell you, "If you don't know where you're going, you have little chance of getting there!" The goal setting is simply painting a picture of where you want to arrive, and what it's like once you get there. The more detailed and specific you can be with that picture, the better.

There are many publications on goal setting and strategic planning. One of the most popular would have to be Stephen Covey's, "The 7 Habits of Highly Effective People". The book sold over 40 million copies, so there's a good chance it's on your bookshelf, or someone's that you know!

The first two of those habits are mantras for goal setting:

1. Be proactive.
2. Begin with the end in mind.

Some say that being proactive isn't a step, it's a mindset. We argue that it's both! We all know people who tend to be more proactive, and many times those same people are known to have "leadership" qualities. It's no coincidence that "leaders" tend to be more "proactive". Is it that some folks are born with the proactive gene, or is it a matter of experience that leaders must take the bull by the horns? Leaders don't approach problems in a passive manner. They take control, make decisions, and take action.

Beginning with the end in mind. From a sustainability perspective, you might get stuck here because your company may have little or no history with sustainable issues. When you're writing a marketing plan, the first thing most marketers look at is last year's plan. Financial, Sales, and Operations tend to work the same way. For us working in sustainability, this year's plan might be the first.

If so, there are some ways to help map out your path. A great place to start is looking at direct/indirect competitors to see if they publish any sustainability objectives, ESG reporting, or other internal mandates.

If you don't find anyone in your space that sparks ideas, there are some general sustainability pioneers that you can lean on. Some of our favorites are:

1. Patagonia - https://www.patagonia.com/our-footprint/
2. Unilever - https://www.unilever.com/planet-and-society/sustainability-reporting-centre/

3. Google - https://sustainability.google/commitments/
4. Microsoft - https://www.microsoft.com/en-us/sustainability
5. Ford - https://corporate.ford.com/social-impact/sustainability.html
6. Toyota - https://global.toyota/en/sustainability/
7. Ikea - https://about.ikea.com/en/sustainability
8. Proctor and Gamble - https://us.pg.com/environmental-sustainability/
9. Intel - https://www.intel.com/content/www/us/en/corporate-responsibility/corporate-responsibility.html
10. Nestle - https://www.intel.com/content/www/us/en/corporate-responsibility/corporate-responsibility.html

If those aren't enough, Corporate Knights publishes the Global 100 Most Sustainable Companies!

https://www.corporateknights.com/rankings/global-100-rankings/2022-global-100-rankings/100-most-sustainable-corporations-of-2022/

And if you need some personal motivation for you and/or your team, here are some great reads to get the creative juices flowing:

1. "The 7 Habits of Highly Effective People", Stephen R. Covey.
2. "Think and Grow Rich" by Napoleon Hill
3. "Getting Things Done: The Art of Stress-Free Productivity" by David Allen
4. "The Power of Habit: Why We Do What We Do in Life and Business" by Charles Duhigg
5. "The Lean Startup: How Today's Entrepreneurs Use Continuous Innovation to Create Radically Successful Businesses" by Eric Ries
6. "Drive: The Surprising Truth About What Motivates Us" by Daniel H. Pink

7. "The One Thing: The Surprisingly Simple Truth Behind Extraordinary Results" by Gary Keller and Jay Papasan
8. "Atomic Habits: An Easy & Proven Way to Build Good Habits & Break Bad Ones" by James Clear
9. "The Success Principles: How to Get from Where You Are to Where You Want to Be" by Jack Canfield
10. "Mindset: The New Psychology of Success" by Carol S. Dweck
11. "Transformational Change" by Tom Wentz

Industry 5.0 and the drive toward sustainability will affect businesses in several ways. Reputation and brand value will be paramount and companies that prioritize sustainability and have a strong sustainability track record are more likely to attract and retain customers, employees, and investors. Sustainability can enhance a company's reputation and brand value, leading to a competitive advantage.

Your firm's financial performance will improve. Companies that invest in sustainability can reduce costs, improve efficiency, and increase revenue. Sustainability can also help companies manage risk and increase resilience, leading to long-term financial stability and success.

You won't need to worry as much about regulatory compliance if you're committed to sustainability. Companies must increasingly meet sustainability regulations, such as emissions standards and waste management requirements. Companies that comply will find themselves on the right side of history. Those who do not comply with these regulations may face fines, legal action, and reputational damage.

Consumers will demand your products and services. Consumers are increasingly demanding sustainable products and services, and they are willing to pay a premium for them. Companies that respond to this demand by offering sustainable products and services can tap into this growing market and increase their competitiveness.

Supply chain management will be less of a headache. Companies are increasingly expected to manage their supply chains sustainably and to work with suppliers to reduce their environmental and social impacts. Companies that do not manage their supply chains sustainably may face reputational damage due to public perception, or loss of product positioning because of the resistance to acquire lower carbon materials.

To foster a positive impact on society, companies need to think about whether their products and services are sustainable and whether they have an ethical supply chain. but how do you know if your supply chain is sustainable and/or if it is on the path to reduce CO2 emissions? It's a tough question and it will require more cooperation between businesses to sort it out. Here lies the opportunity to not only be more sustainable, but to share that progress with your customer base and even other companies. We are aware of sustainable forums, where industry leaders (and yes, competitors) share their findings on sustainability freely with others in the same industry space. This is the type of cooperation that will fuel our vision of 5.0!

What if you not only became a carbon neutral company, but along the way shared those values with your customers and in turn, helped them become more sustainable too?

It is important for businesses to be cognizant of the impact they have on society. If you are seeking to create a positive impact, consider these strategies.

- Create a business plan with a clear vision of the company's long-term sustainability goals.
- Organize operations to not only meet customer demands but reduce your impact on the environment.
- Continuously improve operational efficiencies all along your value chains.
- Take care of your employees.

Reports show that consumers are willing to pay more for products from companies they consider are doing social or societal good. That means the more sustainable your business is, the more customers are willing to buy from you, and that they are willing to pay more too. This is the essence of brand equity and brand value!

The "Gap" in Brand

In marketing we look for "gaps" to exploit. If there were only two automobiles on the market, one super luxury sedan and one sub-compact, there would be a huge gap in the market to fill - coupes, SUVs, sports cars, etc. would round out the market offering plus many more.

In the era of sustainability, it is important for every company to take responsibility for its own actions. What we see in sustainability is that the standards the customer (and even our business leaders) want environmentally conscious companies to meet, compared to how those companies perform, is very different. Leaving a "gap" in the market.

According to Forbes, 90% of CEOs agree that sustainability will be vital to their company's success. In the same article they pose that 88% of business students believe environmental issues are paramount. However, it's reported that less than 60% of companies have a sustainability strategy! Far less than that can report carbon neutrality.

With figures like these, it's easy to see why sustainability is such a hot topic, and why there is such an opportunity to help others on their sustainability journey

Think about the brands you place the highest value in. Do you trust them? Yes! Do you tell others about them? I would guess again, yes! Are their values aligned with yours? Certainly!

Sustainability is rapidly becoming a fundamental aspect of business today, and if you can not only create a business that is more sustainable, but along the way, help your customers achieve it, you'll both reap the rewards!

The quest for sustainability lies in leading the charge. You could find more efficient ways to use electricity, look to local supply chains, or seek out more natural materials. These are certainly steps in the right direction, however what if you didn't just accomplish these things internally, but rather shared accomplishments with your customers. Wouldn't that add value? Wouldn't your customers find this helpful? Wouldn't this position you as a sustainability thought leader?

As a default, if you become more sustainable as a company, your customers become more sustainable by purchasing your products and services. Why not market that advantage and why not position yourself against the competition accordingly? By being a thought leader, you will reinforce the power of your brand and add value to your company. You will build credibility, trust, and most likely establish a following of evangelists for you and your business.

Customer Loyalty = Brand Actualization

Customer loyalty is the key to the success of any business. For a brand to survive in the competitive market, it needs to establish strong customer loyalty. It is not only about providing excellent products and services but also about giving customers an experience that far exceeds their (rising) expectations.

The key to developing customer loyalty is obviously by providing quality products and services. However, the buying decision is influenced by the customer's perception of the product or service as well as their perception of you and your company as solution providers. The solutions may not always be in the form of a tangible product. Customers often are looking for information, training, insights and a "leg-up" on their competition. This all adds up to the customer's experience with your brand.

You may not be competing directly with Apple, but chances are there are many other competitors in your space. So, you don't necessarily need to out-market Apple, but you should be evaluating your competition and looking for any area to elevate your business in your customer's (and prospect's) eyes. By aligning your products with expectations, offering exceptional customer service, and giving your customers all the information, they need to solve their problems (after all, solving customers' problems is the reason you're in business), you can build brand value to outpace the competition.

Brand equity can be built through various channels of advertising and marketing, word-of-mouth, etc. These are all good ways to create a strong brand, but we feel the differentiator is thought leadership. If you are the referent expert in a certain business area then you become the thought leader, and when customers bump up against challenges, they will look to you first to help them overcome them.

Industry 5.0 will be the proving ground for those willing to take leadership roles in sustainability. Today, many businesses know they need to be more sustainable, but not all know how to achieve that. If you can offer a clear path to sustainability, meaning you can educate, and communicate to, your customer base on your dedication to sustainable business practices, it's more likely your clientele will ultimately come to rely on your products/services and in turn become loyal customers - or even evangelists. Get those tattoo guns ready!

210

Chapter 14:

What 5.0 Means to Investors

Let's start at the beginning. Investors, no matter what type they are, angel, debt, equity, investment banker, fund manager, or venture capitalist, are all looking for the same thing – return on their investment or ROI. A former boss of mine had a great saying, "Make sure you put all of your children to work for you!". In other words, make sure every dollar you earn is working to increase its value.

ROI is not just maximizing revenue gains on the investment dollars, but also minimizing risk; because no matter what the investment, there is always some underlying risk.

Estimates are that over $5 trillion will be invested annually in sustainability-related businesses and activities. This could provide a huge shift in investor sentiment when it comes to companies and their commitments to a better environment.

This trend will not be limited to investors, but consumers and employees as well. The bottom line is that if companies want to thrive in the next few decades, they will have to have a keen focus on their sustainability strategies and implementations.

So, how do investors, large and small, maximize returns and minimize risk? Basically, it's in the research. They need to know a few things about the companies they are investing in like:

- What is the market reach and opportunity for this company and/or products?

- Is the company innovative and does it develop breakthrough products?
- Is the company or product considered "disruptive"? Meaning, does this product make current products obsolete (think word processor/typewriter or automobile/horse and buggy)?
- Is there, or will there be, significant demand for their products?
- Is there a path to gain market acceptance? Can they move past the early adopter stage to a broader, more mainstream market?
- Are there competitors that operate in the same space, and how will they fight them off?
- What are the capabilities of the management team?
- Does the team have a diverse set of experienced advisors to guide them through rough times?

Note: we categorize "services" as products throughout this book

Investor Options

All of this is important as investors weigh their options. The companies that can check off all the boxes have the advantage of lower risk and line of sight to profitable returns.

However, we do recognize that having a great idea is not enough, the company and its leaders must be marketing-led in their approach to business. This means that the potential market must drive activity such as:

- Product development
- Brand awareness
- Shaping attitudes
- A consumer-centric focus on all the above.

We can think back to the video player wars between Sony's Betamax and the JVC's VHS format. Most experts agreed that Betamax was technically superior in every way to VHS, however, JVC understood that broad market appeal would be vital to success. The VHS tapes, while with lower picture quality, could record 2 hours as opposed to 1-1.5 for the Betamax; meaning that full movies could be housed on a single VHS tape. Video and audio quality gave way to the customer's experience.

Therefore, the VHS format found its way onto far more video store shelves than Betamax because they could put twice as many movies in the same shelf space. The leaders understood the power of marketing and product alignment with consumer needs – eventually equaling a much broader market reach. JVC licensed its technology to many partners and took on Sony. Due to advantages beyond the actual video quality (run time, content availability, pricing, and eventually rental market dominance) the marketplace spoke, and investors took notice.

History of Investment Wins

History shows us that many investments that might have seemed risky at the outset, were well thought out and researched. This is especially true during times of economic downturn. It seems counterintuitive, but the worse the market is, the more chance there is of profit. Nathan Rothschild, a 19th-century British financier and member of the Rothschild banking family, is credited with saying that "The time to buy is when there's blood in the streets."

Stock markets follow some predictable patterns and have always recovered from downturns...always! However, when we are in a depression, recession, or even a mild correction, it's human nature to be cautious and a bit pessimistic. This is when savvy investors can make huge gains, by backing those companies that will create new products, new industries, and even new movements. Those downturns always led to periods of prosperity, and those companies who were prepared (and had investors) at the starting line reaped huge benefits.

The late 70s were a time of runaway inflation and investor caution in the U.S. but those who invested in Steve Jobs' and Steve Wozniak's idea of small computers for the individual profited greatly. In 1977, Mike Markkula, an angel investor saw the future of this "home computing" and invested $250k in Apple. By 1980, the economy turned, computers took off, and today, that share was worth billions.

Investor boldness doesn't need to be tied to socio-economic conditions, sometimes it is just the ability to see the future. In 1998 Andy Bechtolsheim, co-founder of Sun Microsystems, put $100k into a company that didn't even exist yet. Why? Because he could see the future of the Internet's power over commerce. That company? Google.

History is rife with examples of investors seemingly taking huge risks with not only unknown companies but with completely unknown industries! What are those unknowns today? We believe it's in the sustainability space and there will be a lot of winners.

Investing in Innovation

Innovation is the lifeblood of most industries. It's the competitive edge that propels companies like Apple, Google, and Amazon. Innovation and disruption help bring about positive changes in society (case in point, ESG). ESG mandates are directing our society toward a greener and more sustainable future. We have also seen innovation in areas like medical devices that have led to advances that extend our lifespans and improve our quality of life.

Innovation is most associated with new technologies, new manufacturing methods, and new adaptations of materials. It can also be an outcome of "gaps" in the marketplace. These gaps, for example, could have been transportation related. In the early 1900s, most people moved about by horsepower (the original horse power that is) and there was a "gap" between how people got around, and how they wished to travel; the automobile filled that gap.

50 years later there was a gap in the outright power and speed of those automobiles, and the safety they provided. The innovative

products that filled that gap included seat belts, airbags, crumple zones, and even RADAR speed detectors. Gaps in the market always represent opportunity, and savvy investors look for, and identify those gaps.

As with most innovative ideas, it's not just one technique or technology advance that spurs growth, it's usually a combination of technologies, materials, and ideas that foster the advancement. This is why we believe that sustainable materials innovation will be at the forefront of investment speculation for years to come.

In the same way that the industrial revolution relied on multiple technologies and ideas (steel, oil, electricity), we believe material advancements will take place on a few fronts. We see general improvements in product quality and lifespan, products that take less energy and resources to produce, to raw material supply chains that are more localized and include more bio-based materials.

These innovations will intersect and bring about new materials, better products, and more efficient methods to manufacture them. Whatever the innovations, expect them to be disruptive.

Product Development and Disruptive Technology

Product development is paramount in gaining a competitive edge in manufacturing. Think back 10 years and ask yourself, "Is any leading manufacturer still producing the same portfolio of products"? The answer is – probably not!

Makers of cars, computers, washers and dryers all tend to introduce new products at a regular cadence. However, how often is that introduction something truly innovative and disruptive? Compare the first iPhone to the release of the iPhone 13. Both were necessary for Apple to keep a competitive edge, both required a ton of resources to launch and included innovative ideas, but only one was disruptive.

The term "Disruptive Technology" first popped on the scene in the mid-1990s, but disruptive technologies have been around for hundreds of years. Think of the cotton gin, the steamboat, or even the wheel (although we don't know who to credit for that one)!

Today, we may overuse the word "disruptive" when talking about product development, because the word has so much power. However, consistent development is not always innovative disruption. Companies, even those with steady levels of development, must be on the lookout for disrupters. Investors must be on the lookout for them as well.

Let's go back to the videotape era to see a perfect example of disruption. When Blockbuster was approached by a novel technology company that sent digital copies of movies to subscribers (first CDs then via the Internet), they (Blockbuster) were still in a comfortable phase. No one at Blockbuster seemed too interested in the digital path this new company was taking, and in turn, declined to invest in them. That company? Netflix.

Was the Netflix model disruptive? You bet (and Blockbuster bet wrong). However, Blockbuster at the time was still developing a relatively new business model, even though it was widely accepted in the marketplace.

From a conservative investor standpoint, it might have looked like Blockbuster was a safer, more consistent investment (and at that exact moment, it probably was!). But those investors who saw the disruptive opportunity that Netflix offered, profited handsomely.

Another note on disruptors; they are usually small and/or startup companies. Why? Because by nature, they look for niche opportunities where they can outperform the status quo. The most successful then turn that niche into widespread market acceptance of their innovations.

Why Investors Should Look at Sustainable Businesses

It's widely accepted that businesses are focusing more on sustainability and the associated carbon footprint reductions that will be needed to get to a net zero economy in a few decades. Just like the Netflix example, there will be large organizations that make moves in the area, but there will also be disrupters, and we believe that there will be many of them. Why? Simply because there are so many aspects to the movement. Add that to the fact that we see the movement as a business revolution, and you can rest assured that tens, if not hundreds of thousands of new businesses will sprout up, and a percentage of them will be widely successful. One area we see as having a lot of potential is materials, and more specifically, the previously mentioned, sustainable materials.

Investors will look into materials innovation because it is an industry that has the most potential to grow exponentially in the coming years, and has many opportunities to be "disruptive". There are many thousands of materials in use today, and some date back hundreds of years. This opens the door for disrupters.

Innovations in the materials industry are also one of the most important future factors for many sectors, including automotive, aerospace, building products, packaging, and consumer goods.

In the past, investors have been investing in innovative technology like AI and AR/VR, and they are most likely the future of consumer-focused markets like entertainment and electronics. But these technologies alone are not going to be able to solve the world's biggest problems.

To tackle climate change, pollution, population growth, food distribution, and worldwide healthcare issues, we will need a steady stream of new eco-friendly materials. Let's face it, we live in a consumption-based economy and that's not changing anytime soon.

ESG, Sustainability, and Market Opportunity

Sustainability, ESG, and renewable energy are all terms that have been receiving a lot of attention lately (both positive and negative).

From the Environmental angle, most companies are looking to measure emissions from standards called Scope 1, 2, and 3. Scopes 1 and 2 are internally controlled and revolve around power usage and conservation to limit greenhouse gases. Scope 3 emissions are the external properties (like the raw materials used) that are much harder to control and measure. Because of this, companies that are focused on the Scope 3 efforts will be filling a huge void, and there lies the investment opportunity!

Furthermore, an ESG mandate can either be retrospective or prospective. Retrospective ESG mandates require companies to examine the behaviors that have already taken place whereas prospective ones focus on activities that are yet to occur. Prospective, or proactive mandates look ahead to the future, to set a strategy for increasing a firm's sustainability. Again, here is where materials innovation will be front and center.

Managing scope 3 emissions is about finding ways to reduce their impact on the environment through steps like buying responsibly sourced materials. This means that companies that can measure, track, and demonstrate the positive effects of their bio-friendly materials (e.g., lowering the carbon footprint), could see the largest opportunity for growth over the coming decades.

Everyone agrees that to maintain life on this planet as we know it, we need to be more mindful of how we take care of it. Sustainability is simply learning to live in harmony with the Earth. However, there is resistance to mandating ESG activities, not because of the measures themselves, but because we typically push back on anything that is labeled as a "mandate". But the data tells us that change is needed, and a portion of that change will certainly be mandated.

Human activity over the last 150 years or so (since the first Industrial Revolution) has been improving technology, improving our lifestyles, and on the downside, damaging our environment. It's understandable, as early on during the revolution, we didn't have the data on how the planet was suffering, nor the means to collect and interpret that data. In turn, we did not fully understand the negative impact we were having on our environment. Thankfully today that has all changed.

Sustainability is now on the front burner, and getting the attention it deserves. Along with the data and attention comes action. On the corporate front, that action is in the form of those ESG measurements and mandates. An ESG mandate is a requirement to comply with specific environmental, social, and governance standards. These requirements can be implemented at either the company level or by regulators themselves.

Estimates are that over $5 trillion will be invested annually in sustainability-related businesses and activities. This could prove a huge shift in investor sentiment when it comes to companies and their commitment to a better environment. This trend will not be limited to investors, but consumers and employees as well. The bottom line is that if companies want to thrive in the next few decades, they, and their investors, will have to have a keen focus on their sustainability strategies and implementations.

The Shift from Negative Screening to Positive Screening, and Ultimately to Proactive Engagement with ESG

Investors in sustainable companies have seen a shift in how they gauge opportunities. Early on, the investors would exclude companies from their portfolios that did not meet standards for sustainability or had some negative press tied to environmentally unfriendly activities. They would screen out or take a "negative screening" approach to those companies that had a bad reputation and simply look to invest in other directions.

Then, sediment shifted to a "positive screening" viewpoint, meaning companies that had better reputations for environmental awareness and activities, now got another look when it came to investment dollars. Companies that had a reputation for positive environmental actions were actively considered a better choice for investment.

Today, it's all about corporate strategy and the proactive measures that companies take and report on, to be sustainable. Now, it's not sufficient to simply have a good reputation for sustainability, you must prove it. Investment managers include ESG factors in their fundamental analysis and identify ESG strategies as paramount to a company's success.

Investors are now looking at the management team's commitment to sustainability with the same intensity as they examine their operations, finance, sales, and marketing plans. They are looking for compliance, especially as it relates to new SEC reporting requirements.

Investing in Manufacturing Innovations

Manufacturers make products, products are made from a collection of raw materials, and raw materials have been slow to adapt to the changing landscape that focuses on climate change.

Today, we still make products from many of the same materials we used 50 years ago, wood, steel, and petrochemicals (oil). Many textiles are made of natural materials like cotton, or man-made polymers like nylon. Homes are constructed with wood, concrete, and stone. Skyscrapers and bridges contain large amounts of steel. However, there's a shift in thought towards raw materials, as our current path is unsustainable.

There are only so many trees to cut down, raw ore to be mined and oil to be pumped out of the Earth. I know landowners who contract with loggers to harvest hardwood. These trees are sometimes 200 years old or more. Do we simply say, "Come back in a few centuries, and we will have more trees for you"? Of course not, even though wood is considered renewable, it simply cannot grow at the pace we need to sustain our planet's raw materials needs.

Nor can we mine or drill for the resources we will need to satisfy the demands of the future. We will need materials innovations that can keep pace with our society, and that bring more meaning and weight to the word, "Sustainability ".

We will need to find new, bio-friendly, and bio-sourced materials that don't add to the weight of our material shortages, and supply chain interruptions we see today. In other words, we need more in the way of materials innovation to keep pace with our consumption patterns and at the same time, reduce the negative impact we have on our environment.

Companies that invest in new materials innovation for the future, will certainly see growth and may even "leapfrog" the current competition. History shows that the most profitable companies in the world are constantly investing in research, development, and innovation. These investments are key to staying ahead of the competition, keeping up with technological advancements, and creating new markets.

Materials innovation is not just about creating new materials, it's about rethinking how we use them and how we can do more with them. It's about finding ways of using less material and making what we already have go further.

This is why investing in manufacturing innovation is investing in our future – because it will help us meet some of society's biggest challenges, from avoiding climate change to leveling social inequality, and eventually ending poverty and food insecurity.

Increased levels of manufacturing and our human consumption of those products have led us to this critical inflection point. We know consumption will only continue to rise, the answer is in creating new materials that are more eco-friendly to make, more eco-friendly to use, and more eco-friendly to dispose of (if we dispose of them at all)!

In the past, sustainability practices were only adopted for the sake of environmental stewardship. But more and more companies are adopting these practices to get a competitive edge in their industry.

This is why savvy investors are setting their sights on companies that will challenge the status quo.

Carbon Markets

What are Carbon Markets? They are a powerful tool for reducing greenhouse gas emissions. They work similarly to any stock and/or futures market, by setting the cost of emitting carbon and creating an incentive for businesses to reduce their emissions. These markets can create a financial incentive for companies to make more sustainable choices, and it not only helps the environment but also boosts economic growth as businesses invest in low-carbon technology and infrastructure.

They work by allowing countries and companies to trade emission allowances so that those who can reduce their emissions more cheaply can do so and sell the resulting surplus allowances to those who cannot.

As the world grapples with the daunting challenges posed by the effects of our first four industrial revolutions, finding effective solutions to mitigate greenhouse gas emissions and achieve global sustainability goals has become paramount for governments, businesses, communities, and individuals alike.

Amidst all of this, carbon markets have emerged as one of the most effective and vital tools in the international effort to combat the emissions of greenhouse gases (GHGs). They are in place, but mostly voluntary and primarily used in Europe and Canada. There are efforts underway in New Zealand, South Korea and China. However, there are some notable absentees from this list including the United States, Russia, and India.

By harnessing the power of market mechanisms to incentivize emissions reductions and promote sustainable practices, carbon markets offer a promising avenue towards a low-carbon future. Let's explore the concept of carbon markets, their evolution over time, and their potential effectiveness in driving transformative change on a global scale.

There are two general approaches to placing a value on carbon - Tax or Trade. When researching them, you'll find they seem to be mutually exclusive. Today, that means either "forcing" or "incentivizing" the reduction of GHGs. We would also like to explore a hybrid approach - maybe a system that can get the markets up and running quickly with a proper amount of regulation and standardization (tax), as well as creating incentives for everyone to participate in a free-market carbon structure (trade).

Taxation

Taxing carbon emissions? OK, it sounds heavy-handed and anytime you use the word "Tax", the conversations will be emotionally and politically charged. We get it, but let's take a dive into what a carbon tax system would look like.

From his book, Cap-and-Trade versus Carbon Tax - Ugur Akinci, describes that "Carbon tax is a tax on the carbon content of fossil fuels (coal, oil, gas, etc.). It's about levying a monetary penalty on those industries that produce carbon dioxide (CO_2) because of burning carbon-based fuels."

While Akinci notes that while the cap-and-trade scheme provides an incentive for some companies to produce greenhouse gases by purchasing carbon credits, the carbon tax intends to prevent CO_2 release in the first place.

The idea of a "carbon tax" has gained so much traction that in 2007 a Carbon Tax Center was founded in Washington D.C. According to the Carbon Tax Center (CTC), a carbon tax is the most economically efficient means to convey crucial price signals and spur carbon-reducing investment. It is necessary, the CTC claims since the cap-and-trade scheme with offsets cannot deliver the needed emissions reductions - www.carbontax.org

Akinci, Ugur. Cap-and-Trade versus Carbon Tax: Carbon Pricing Issues and Selected Country Implementations.

A comprehensive "preview" of what carbon taxing policy might include, comes from a statement signed in 2019 by a host of influential economists.

The Following is From, The Wall Street Journal 1/17/2019

Economists' Statement on Carbon Dividends Global climate change is a serious problem calling for immediate national action. Guided by sound economic principles, we are united in the following policy recommendations.

1. A carbon tax offers the most cost-effective lever to reduce carbon emissions at the scale and speed that is necessary. By correcting a well-known market failure, a carbon tax will send a powerful price signal that harnesses the invisible hand of the marketplace to steer economic actors towards a low-carbon future.
2. A carbon tax should increase every year until emissions reductions goals are met and revenue neutral to avoid debates over the size of government. A consistently rising carbon price will encourage technological innovation and large-scale infrastructure development. It will also accelerate the diffusion of carbon-efficient goods and services.
3. A sufficiently robust and gradually rising carbon tax will replace the need for various carbon regulations that are less efficient. Substituting a price signal for cumbersome regulations will promote economic growth and provide the regulatory certainty companies need for long- term investment in clean-energy alternatives.
4. To prevent carbon leakage and to protect U.S. competitiveness, a border carbon adjustment system should be established. This system would enhance the competitiveness of American firms that are more energy-efficient than their global competitors. It would also create an incentive for other nations to adopt similar carbon pricing.

5. To maximize the fairness and political viability of a rising carbon tax, all the revenue should be returned directly to U.S. citizens through equal lump-sum rebates. Most American families, including the most vulnerable, will benefit financially by receiving more in "carbon dividends" than they pay in increased energy prices.

Note: The full signatories list can be found at:
https://clcouncil.org/economists-statement/

Economic Efficiency

Carbon taxes are a way of encouraging lower carbon emissions by setting a cost for each ton of greenhouse gas released into the atmosphere. This encourages companies to invest in renewable energy sources and reduce their emissions. Market-based incentives encourage businesses and individuals to decrease their emissions, thus creating a proper balance between the environment and business operations.

Carbon taxes are a cost-effective way to reduce emissions when compared to direct regulations or subsidies. This makes them an attractive option because they rely on market forces, rather than costly regulations, to ensure that emissions are reduced in the most efficient manner. It gives great flexibility to market participants as they can decide the best way to reduce their emissions and still save costs.

Market Signals

Placing a taxable cost on carbon emission helps set the market's expectations of what it will cost to emit these greenhouse gases. This pricing system motivates businesses and consumers alike to invest in cleaner technology, energy efficiency, and green alternatives. By incentivizing sustainability, innovation can be rewarded, and this has a trickle-down effect that encourages producers and consumers alike to establish more eco-friendly habits. This, in turn, leads to a big transformation in the economy at large.

Scalability and Speed

Carbon taxation has the capacity to be modified and adapted to different sectors of the economy, making it a viable option for curbing carbon emissions. AI-driven solutions are useful across many industries, energy sources, and geographic regions. This wide application helps to reduce emissions effectively and on a large scale, which is necessary to address climate change efficiently.

A Carbon tax is a fast-acting solution to address the pressing environmental issues we are currently facing. It's much easier to implement compared to other policy measures, making it an ideal choice for those who feel that urgent action is needed (and most of us agree that action needs to be taken sooner rather than later).

Revenue Generation and Flexibility

A carbon tax can be a great source of revenue for governments as it gives them the flexibility to invest in clean energy technologies, fund research, development for sustainable solutions, and finance social environmental programs. The downside is that taxes are great political fodder, and this system can easily be attacked by one side or the other, citing many government programs that intended to tax our way to prosperity that have failed miserably.

However, this strategic use of revenue generated from a carbon tax *can* help create a sustainable environment for the future. Deployed properly, tax revenues in this manner can help lessen the economic consequences, provide aid to struggling industries, and foster a transition towards a low-carbon economy that is fair and equitable.

Long-Term Certainty

Carbon taxes can help businesses make informed decisions in the long term by creating a clear pricing structure. This encourages sustainable investments and allows organizations to plot a course with greater certainty. Carbon pricing is a reliable way to reduce emissions and help businesses plan; it creates stability and encourages long-term decision-making. Especially in industries with extended investment cycles, such as energy, manufacturing, or transportation, having a predictable trajectory of carbon prices can make a huge difference (both in the tax and trade systems) in planning business protocols and/or investment portfolios.

Carbon taxes are often promoted as a cost-effective way to reduce emissions; however, their efficacy may be subject to change depending on the design, how well it is implemented, and if there are any supplementary policies in place. To reach their emission reduction goals effectively, countries with diverse contexts may need to apply bespoke solutions that integrate various policy tools.

Will 5.0 be jump-started by a pure carbon tax system? We don't know, but the likelihood is high, as governments could quickly see new revenues streams from this type of program. However, don't count out the pure market forces of a carbon trading future.

Cap and Trade

A cap and trade carbon market is a market-based approach to address and regulate carbon emissions. It is designed to reduce greenhouse gas emissions by placing a limit, or cap, on the total amount of emissions that can be released within a specified period.

Under this system, emissions allowances are allocated or sold to participating entities, such as companies or organizations. These entities can then trade their allowances, allowing those with lower emissions to sell their excess allowances to those needing additional permits. By creating a financial incentive to reduce emissions, cap and trade carbon markets encourage businesses to adopt cleaner technologies, improve energy efficiency, and invest in sustainable practices.

This market mechanism provides flexibility, encourages innovation, and aims to achieve emissions reductions in a cost-effective manner while promoting the transition to a low-carbon economy. Here are some real-world examples of carbon cap and trade:

- European Union: The EU Emissions Trading System (EU ETS) is the largest and longest-running carbon market in the world. It covers multiple sectors across the EU member states and has been instrumental in reducing emissions since its establishment in 2005.
- California, United States: California operates a cap-and-trade system, known as the California Cap-and-Trade Program. It covers various sectors, including electricity generation, transportation, and industrial activities. California's market is linked with the Canadian province of Quebec, creating the Western Climate Initiative.
- Quebec, Canada: Quebec implemented its cap-and-trade system in 2013, known as the Quebec Cap-and-Trade System. It covers sectors such as electricity, industrial processes, and transportation. Quebec's market is linked with California's as part of the Western Climate Initiative.
- New Zealand: New Zealand operates an emissions trading scheme (NZ ETS) that was established in 2008. It covers several sectors, including energy, industry, and forestry. The scheme has undergone revisions to strengthen its effectiveness over time.
- South Korea: South Korea launched its nationwide emissions trading system, the Korean Emissions Trading Scheme (KETS), in 2015. The market covers various sectors, including power generation, petrochemicals, and steel production.
- China: China has established multiple regional pilot emissions trading schemes in cities such as Beijing, Shanghai, and Shenzhen. These pilots are precursors to the national emissions trading system, which was launched in 2021.

Cap and trade have some serious potential. We see the voluntary markets above gaining traction every day. While it is challenging to predict with certainty, the likelihood of such an evolution based on current trends and discussions in the field is promising.

The likelihood of a global, standardized carbon market largely depends on the level of international cooperation and consensus among countries. If countries can align their climate goals and policies and work together to address climate change collectively, it increases the chances of developing a standardized carbon market. The Paris Agreement is a step in this direction. If countries involved actively pursue their commitments it will surely create momentum for a global carbon market.

Some existing linked cap and trade systems, such as the California/Quebec agreements and the European Union Emissions Trading System (EU ETS) have implemented linkages between their markets. Linking carbon markets allows for the exchange of emissions allowances, fostering a more integrated and interconnected system. If more countries and regions establish linkages, it can lay the groundwork for a global carbon market.

Efforts are underway to harmonize and standardize carbon markets across regions. Organizations like the International Carbon Action Partnership (ICAP) and the World Bank's Partnership for Market Readiness (PMR) are working towards establishing common methodologies, accounting systems, and best practices. These initiatives facilitate the exchange of knowledge and can contribute to the eventual development of a global carbon market.

The advancement of technologies related to carbon measurement, reporting, and verification (MRV) will play a role in the development of a global carbon market. We will cover some promising technologies in chapter 18, Engineering Earth. Improved transparency and accuracy in tracking emissions will not only build trust among countries but make it much easier to facilitate the exchange of emissions allowances between partners and traders.

While these factors indicate some potential for the evolution of cap and trade carbon markets into a global, standardized carbon market, challenges and barriers still exist. These include political differences (those driving for taxes alone), divergent national priorities, and the need for more robust, transparent governance structures. However, as the urgency to address sustainability grows, and we start recognizing the benefits of cooperation, the chances of Industry 5.0 ushering in a global carbon market are undeniable.

Is There a Compromise Between Tax and Trade?

Compromise is nothing new, especially here in America. The United States government was built on famous traditions of compromise.

The "Great Compromise" or "Connecticut Compromise" reached during the Constitutional Convention of 1787 was necessary to address the competing interests of small and large states in terms of representation. It sought to strike a balance between the principle of proportional representation based on population and the desire of smaller states to ensure their interests were adequately represented.

The result was two chambers of congress: the House of Representatives is apportioned among the states based on population. The compromise also established the Senate, where each state is represented by an equal number of senators, regardless of population. Each of our states, regardless of size, has two senators. This protects the interests of smaller states like Vermont, Rhode Island and Wyoming, and also prevents larger states like California or New York from dominating the legislative process by sheer numbers alone.

At the time, it was most likely one of the most complicated compromises to maneuver, however a compromise between carbon tax and trade might be even more elusive. Why? Here are a few reasons:

1. **Policy Philosophies:** Cap and trade and carbon taxing represent different policy approaches and philosophies. Cap and trade set a specific emissions limit (cap) and allows the trading of emission permits, creating a market for emissions reductions. On the other hand, carbon taxing imposes a price

on each unit of carbon emitted. These differing approaches can lead to ideological differences and preferences among policymakers, making it more difficult to find common ground.

2. **Political Dynamics:** The political landscape often involves a range of stakeholders evangelizing for opposite interests and priorities. Industries and businesses may have different views on the most appropriate policy instrument, but speaking to our experts, most seem to favor an open trade system as opposed to a pure tax.

   Most we spoke with prefer the market-based approach of cap and trade, which offers flexibility and allows for cost-effective emission reductions, while others may advocate for the simplicity and transparency of a carbon tax. Balancing these competing interests and reaching a compromise can be challenging, especially when there are powerful lobbying forces involved.

3. **Economic Implications:** Both cap and trade and carbon taxing have economic implications, and different stakeholders may perceive these implications differently. Industries and businesses may be concerned about the potential impact on their competitiveness, profitability, and costs of compliance.

   The distributional effects of policy instruments can also be a point of contention, as certain sectors or regions may be disproportionately affected. Reaching a compromise that addresses these economic concerns and ensures a fair and equitable outcome for all parties involved can be complex.

4. **Complexity of Implementation:** Both cap and trade and carbon taxing require robust infrastructure, monitoring, and enforcement mechanisms to be effective. Implementing either system involves establishing accurate emissions inventories, developing compliance frameworks, and

creating administrative bodies to oversee the functioning of the policy. The complexity of implementation can make it difficult to find a middle ground that satisfies the requirements of both systems.

While a compromise between these two policy instruments may seem unlikely, it's worth noting that hybrid approaches have been proposed and implemented in some jurisdictions. For example, elements of cap and trade systems, such as market mechanisms, can be incorporated into a carbon tax system to enhance cost-effectiveness and flexibility. However, reaching a comprehensive compromise that satisfies all stakeholders and combines the best aspects of both approaches remains a very complex task.

In the context of cap and trade, "market mechanisms" refer to the economic mechanisms and principles that govern the trading of emissions allowances within the carbon market. These mechanisms facilitate the buying and selling of emissions permits, allowing participants to trade their allocated or purchased allowances.

The key market mechanism used in cap and trade systems is the trading of emissions allowances, also known as carbon credits. These allowances represent the right to emit a specified amount of greenhouse gases. Participants, typically companies or organizations, can buy or sell these allowances in a secondary market, creating a market price for carbon.

The market mechanisms in these systems function based on the principle of supply and demand. As the total number of allowances is capped, creating scarcity, the price of allowances can fluctuate based on market forces. If a company has surplus allowances because they have successfully reduced their emissions, they can sell those allowances to other entities in need of additional permits to comply with their emission limits. This trading allows for a more efficient allocation of emission reduction efforts.

Market mechanisms also foster innovation and cost-effectiveness. Companies that can reduce emissions at a lower cost than the market price of allowances have a financial incentive to do so. Conversely, companies facing higher costs can opt to purchase allowances instead of making costly emission reductions. This flexibility encourages emission reductions to occur where they are most economically feasible, driving overall cost savings and emission mitigation.

Overall, market mechanisms within cap and trade systems promote the efficient allocation of emission reductions, encourage innovation, and provide economic incentives for transitioning to a low-carbon economy. Tax systems force compliance with strict regulations.

A hybrid approach might be a mandated system in which a governing body determines values and levels of carbon emissions, while individuals and corporations can participate in a structure to build the market through private investment (like the Green Bond market today).

A Green Bond is a financial instrument designed specifically to raise capital for sustainable and environmentally friendly projects. It is a type of bond where the proceeds are earmarked for financing projects that have positive environmental and climate impacts.

Although Green Bonds are a good start, they only include projects that have been approved, so there are severe limitations on the scope of businesses that can participate. A true hybrid approach to carbon markets would be inclusive of all that can contribute to a greener economy.

Whichever way we go, tax, trade or hybrid, the values will depend on reporting standardization, transparency, and regulation of the market value of carbon.

234

Chapter 15:

How 5.0 Will Correct the Ills of the First Four Revolutions

Why is 5.0 a Natural Evolution of 1-4?

Industry 5.0 stands on the shoulders of the first four industrial revolutions, and because we studied 1-4, we now understand that the negative outcomes of mass industrialization can't continue unchecked. Science shows us all the alarming facts of the damage we've done to the planet from the soil to our water and the air:

- Carbon in the atmosphere - up 47% since the 1800s.
- Plastics in the ocean - 8 million tons each year.
- Wildlife populations - down 60% in just 50 years.
- Food - ⅓ of all produced each day is wasted or lost.
- Earth's resources - being consumed at almost twice the rate the planet can provide.

All of these and thousands more data points tell us we not only need to stop, but we also need to reverse our course! The only logical way to accomplish the reversal of the first four industrial revolutions unintended consequences, is to ignite the fifth! the famous philosopher, Lao Tzu famously said, "The journey of a thousand miles begins with a single step". We've taken some steps...we need to take a lot more!

The reason being that there is still a feeling of resistance to the term "sustainability", especially in the business community. Not to mention the recent negative connotations associated with acronyms like ESG, DEI and CSR. This low-lying reluctance to jump aboard tells us that the movement is not fully embraced. Compare that to how completely the digital revolution took hold. Were there some that resided? Yes! Are they still in business? Most likely not! If fact, show me one successful global or regional company that hasn't wholly adopted computers. We doubt there are any!

The good news is that the 5.0 movement gains momentum every day, even if we're not calling it that…yet! We know this because we live it, and the velocity of leads and interest in our sustainability programs and products have been growing at a breakneck pace.

We Really Don't Have a Choice

The industrial revolutions of the 1800s and 1900s brought about unprecedented economic growth and technological advancements but also had such detrimental impacts on the environment and society. Left unchecked, the decay will continue. Industry 5.0 will play a crucial role in reversing the damage caused during those periods. Specifically, that damage is felt in many ways:

Air and Water Pollution: The rapid industrialization during these periods led to increased emissions of pollutants into the air and water. Factories and power plants released large quantities of pollutants, including sulfur dioxide, nitrogen oxides, and particulate matter, contributing to air pollution and smog. Industries also discharged untreated waste into water bodies, leading to water pollution and ecosystem degradation.

Automobiles and other fossil fuel-based transportation have greatly increased levels of toxins in our air. Agriculture practices have contributed to both air and water pollution.

Deforestation and Habitat Loss: Deforestation started before Industry 1.0, but the rapid industrialization of 1.0 and 2.0 ramped the process up, with the increased demand for raw materials, leading to widespread deforestation to make way for agriculture, mining, and urban expansion.

Because such large areas of forests were cleared, this resulted in the loss of habitat for numerous plant and animal species. Deforestation also disrupted ecosystems, reduced biodiversity, and contributed to climate change by reducing the capacity of forests to absorb carbon dioxide.

Natural Resource Depletion: With pollution and deforestation, come reductions in other natural resources, especially the finite one oil, coal, gas and other valuable minerals. The increased demand for these resources led to overexploitation and depletion of resources. This depletion has long-term consequences, including reduced availability of resources, land degradation, and ecosystem disruption.

Climate Change: This is the term we're probably most familiar with. All the problems are synergistic, however rapid climate change has the potential to fracture our delicate balance on the planet.

The burning of fossil fuels, such as coal and oil, for energy during the industrial revolution released significant amounts of carbon dioxide and other greenhouse gases into the atmosphere. This has contributed to the accumulation of greenhouse gases, leading to global warming and climate change. The consequences of climate change include rising temperatures, sea-level rise, extreme weather events, and disruptions to ecosystems and biodiversity.

Loss of Biodiversity: The expansion of industrial activities, the conversion of natural habitats into agricultural land or urban areas, and the negative effects of pollution have resulted in the loss of biodiversity.

Once thriving species have faced habitat destruction, fragmentation, and loss, leading to declines in populations and, in some cases, complete species extinction. The loss of biodiversity has far-reaching ecological consequences, affecting ecosystem stability, pollination, nutrient cycling, and overall ecosystem health.

Social Impacts: The industrial revolution brought about significant social impacts, including poor working conditions, exploitation of workers, child labor, and income inequality. The rapid urbanization and migration of people to industrial centers often led to overcrowded and unsanitary living conditions, contributing to social and health challenges.

To be fair, it wasn't all detrimental, it's important to acknowledge that the industrial revolutions also brought about positive advancements and improvements in living standards. We don't want to sound as if the entire era of 1-4 was one big slam-fest on the Earth, and as business leaders, we certainly believe in the free-market society that helped fuel them.

However, the damage caused to the planet and society during these periods highlight the need for sustainable practices and a transition towards more responsible and environmentally conscious industrial and economic systems. We now have the opportunity, and obligation, to change our course.

All these issues, if looked upon as independent challenges, are quite enough to drag humanity down by themselves. We know however, that each in turn "pile on" to each other and the negative effects start to grow exponentially. This viscous cycle is one we don't easily stop, so acting is vital. Looking at them collectively, it's easy to come to the conclusion of the title here and understand that "We really don't have a choice"!

239

240

Chapter 16:

Why Innovation is Crucial to a 5.0 World

When Thomas Edison famously invented the lightbulb in 1879, it was truly a miracle of science. Up until then, to get light we needed to burn something and create a flame (kerosene, wood, etc.).

The invention was a fully self-contained light machine that you could hold in your hand. It was, dare we say - revolutionary! Not only was it a significant invention on its own, but the lightbulb also spurred the entire electrification and power generation industries. lightbulbs are literally in use everywhere, and we could have stopped there, but our friend Maslow says, "not so fast"! As life changing as incandescent electrified light was, there is also the downside of its terrible inefficiency.

The incandescent lightbulb is suffering its demise partly because of the broad adoption across the globe. Every year there are over 7 billion bulbs sold and that's a fraction of what is in use, and they consume a lot of power. Much of that consumption is lost as heat, up to 98%. Here we see an innovation, the LED bulb.

Consider this, an LED light bulb is about 95% efficient, meaning that only 5% of the energy used is wasted (as heat). Compared to the incandescent bulb's 2% efficiency (remember that 98% lost as heat!), we can see that LEDs are exponentially better when it comes to energy efficiency.

Here's where innovation has interacted with a traditional innovative product to create an even larger marketplace - all driven by sustainability.

Industry 5.0 will move fast and far. We see it entirely possible that some, even some innovations born at the beginning of the revolution will be obsolete and replaced later down the line.

Innovation and Commercialization

Innovation sometimes comes from unfamiliar sources. Innovation will be a critical element of the next business revolution, that's not up for debate as almost everyone agrees. What we may not all agree on is where that innovation will come from.

When you think of giant leaps forward, a few recognizable companies might come to mind - Apple, Amazon, Google, and 3M. So, it's easy to connect innovative products with large, established companies. However, that might not always be the case (and might not always be the case with the companies above). Sometimes we rewrite history in our minds!

How so? Well, think about each of these titans of industry in their early days. At the beginning of Apple, Steve Jobs and Steve Wozniak had the idea that home computers would become more than just a specialty technology item that limited itself to engineers, technicians, and general computer hobbyists. They saw a world where everyone could partake in the digital revolution. Looking back today it seems obvious to us, but in 1976 nothing could be further from the truth.

Most computer companies were focusing on the established markets of mainframes. And really, who wouldn't? Big companies were the only markets for giants like IBM and DEC. DEC not sound familiar? Digital Equipment Corporation or DEC, went bankrupt in 1998. DEC was a major American computer company that played a significant role in the early days of the computer industry and had revenues in the 80s of $14B! Just ten years before some disruptive innovation tanked them.

All computer manufacturers (like IBM and DEC) were looking to take part in this enormous B2B market share, while the average American was striving just to purchase a new car or television set. A computer was something the military used - they were intimidating, looked like a piece of military equipment, and came with a military-like price tag.

Apple made computers friendly, useful, and beautiful...they still do! The Apple II made its debut in 1977 and sold over 6 million units, and in 1984 they introduced the Macintosh and dominated home computing for nearly a decade. However, the story doesn't end there. By 1997, Apple was floundering and on the brink of collapse. A small team of Apple design engineers (15-20 of them) developed the breakthrough iMac, and the company hasn't looked back since. So, in essence, Apple was a start-up twice! It's tough to not rewrite history in our minds and think that Apple's innovations have all been spawned from the behemoth we know today.

Google dominates the web, but that was not so in 1998, the year it launched. There were established search players like Yahoo, Dogpile, AltaVista, and Excite. But ask most today who invented web search and the answer is most likely, "Google". Why? Because we rewrite history in our minds to suit the present-day reality.

Think we don't rewrite history in our minds? How about this. In 1984, the best basketball player the world has ever seen, and quite possibly the best competitive athlete in history, Michael Jordan, was not drafted #1 or even #2. He was third.

Meaning all the NBA analysts, scouts, coaches, and executives could not see what the future held. Michael saw it, his coach Dean Smith saw it, and so did Michael's parents, but virtually no one else did.

However, ask anyone today, and they'll tell you that coming out of UNC, we ALL knew Michael Jordan was special and would dominate the NBA like no one before, or since. And most will tell you they are certain he was drafted #1.

So, back to the point of innovation - much of it comes from small, unheard-of companies, or even one lone entrepreneur who is way ahead of his or her time. Large companies do innovate, but many of those innovations are product extensions or enhancements (iPod, iPhone 2-x, iPad, etc.).

When starting out, these innovators have it rough - they don't have the name or resources to get their ideas into the public realm. And virtually all of them go through tough times accompanied by a very bumpy path to success. We heard a story from an investor group the other day about an entrepreneur they passed on in the 1990s. One thing they remembered was thinking what an odd-sounding name he had. That name was "Elon", yep Elon Musk. As brilliant as Mr. Musk was, many investors couldn't recognize the true innovator that lay just beneath the surface of the guy with the funny name.

Back to a favorite book of ours by Peter Thiel (who created PayPal and brought Elon onboard through acquisition of his similar online banking company "X") - Zero to One, where he talks about the central element of real innovation. Going from Zero to One.

Thiel, Peter, and Blake Masters. Zero to One: Notes on Startups, or How to Build the Future. Crown Business, 2014.

What is the Zero to One concept? The central thesis is the idea that progress doesn't happen on its own - someone must make it happen. Someone must think of a solution in a totally new way. This is where the "zero to one" phrase from the title comes in. It refers to the fact that most things are simply copying or iterating on something that's already been done, One to n.

Our earlier example: The myriad of new, improved typewriter designs over 100 years was all horizontal progress as they improved an existing technology. Going from the typewriter to the Word Processor was vertical progress (Zero to One). This "computerized" version of personal publishing virtually put all the traditional typewriter companies out of business.

Vertical progress is doing something no one has envisioned before. The famous saying from Henry Ford is that if you asked customers what they wanted before the automobile was invented, they'd tell you "I want a faster horse".

This "vertical" progress is where the next industrial revolution will take hold, and many of those individuals, small companies, and large corporations that will be responsible for it may not even be on our radar yet in 2024!

What are some examples of the next wave of innovation? It's a difficult task, as by nature innovation is many times unexpected, but here are some of the breakthroughs we will see, and need.

Electric Vehicles

EVs are nothing new, they've been around since the 1970s, right? Ah no, here we rewrote history in our minds again! The world's first electric car dates all the way back to the 19th century. In the late 1880s, Thomas Parker, a British inventor, and engineer, is credited with building the first practical production electric car. He converted a horse-drawn carriage to electric power in 1884. This early electric car featured a high-capacity rechargeable battery and a small electric motor.

Today's EVs are mostly powered by Lithium-Ion batteries, and you'll hear a few specifications that sound similar but refer to different characteristics.

The first is **Energy Density**. This is the amount of energy the battery can hold. Like most electric energy, it's measured in Kilowatt hours. Essentially, how much power can be contained in the cell(s)?

The other key stat is **Power Density**. They sound almost the same, but as Energy Density is the total power, Power Density is the rate at which the battery cells can deliver (or absorb) power. Sound confusing? Let's clear it up.

In electricity courses, the rates and flows of electric current are usually taught comparing it to water traveling through a hose...not a perfect correlation, but the physics are kind of the same.

For Energy Density, think of a large water tank sitting next to a smaller one. The larger one can hold more water than the smaller one. Seems obvious right? So higher Energy Density is simply the ability or capacity to hold more power (a larger tank).

Power Density refers to the flow of power. Say the large tank had a 1-inch diameter hose connected to it, and the smaller tank had a 3-inch diameter hose. The hose size controls the amount of "flow", or in electric terms, the amount of current. Even though the big tank has more Energy, the smaller tank in this case can push (or pull) more power because of the larger hose size. Pushing refers to the energy going to power the car while pulling is the rate at which the battery can be recharged (or pulling power back into the battery cell).

So, with batteries, as with most electric devices, there are tradeoffs between the chemistries. Some have great **energy density**; others have better **power density** and many times those are mutually exclusive.

Both are important to EV technology, you want both high energy and high power, and the research is pushing both to get better, along with stability, safety, etc.

So, where's the innovation heading? Well, let's face it, EVs need to get better - a lot better! We might even be as bold as to not call them EVs, but alternative power vehicles that include hydrogen, fission, or fusion.

Electric motors used in EVs have tremendous power conversion capacity. We recently toured Ohio State's Center for Automotive Research (yep, CAR) and were shown a mobile electric motor, not much bigger than your average lawnmower engine. This small motor could convert as much power as the average V6 internal combustion engine!

The problem is an imbalance in our technology. You see, the internal combustion engine is fueled by gallons of gasoline. That gas has enormous energy potential. However, the engine is only about 40% at best. So, we waste about 60% of our energy in the form of heat.

On the other hand, that super-efficient electric motor can convert almost 90% of the incoming power. The problem is the batteries we use are bulky, heavy, and take a long time to recharge.

So, the next wave might be powered by batteries that are bio-based, or we might fire up our Mr. Fusion (yes, a nod to the movie, Back to the Future Part II!). Either way, we need to get to a point where the EV (alternative) is substantially better than today's internal combustion technology.

We need to go from across town on a single charge, to across the country. We'll need battery charging from hours (or minutes) to seconds, or no need for recharge at all! We will also need a transformation to renewable energy sources for vehicle power.

Someday, we'll see vehicles charge up almost instantly (from sources that are not fossil-based) and it will travel thousands of miles on that single charge. No tailpipe emissions (the push), and none from the generation and transfer of power (the pull)! Once we solve this imbalance (and charge times), EVs will dominate the market.

Recycling Overview

We're going to spend a bit of time here on the recycling topic for two reasons:

1. Recycling has been around for a while and most (if not all) of us have participated in some type of recycling effort.
2. Even though these programs are established (for decades in some cases), as a society, we are nowhere near the level of

recycling (quantity or quality) that we need to be. Nor are we as efficient with the actual recycling processes, but the good news is we're trending in the right direction!

Many of us have separate recycling bins at home, at work, and at school. It seems simple enough that we put materials into those often blue-colored containers, and they magically get recycled on the other end. However, the recycling process is extremely complicated and very labor-intensive.

A recent tour of the Outagamie County Recycling Center in Appleton, Wisconsin opened our eyes to the vast complexities and rules of recycling. Yes, there are rules, and they are there for good reasons.

In order the rules are:

1. No plastic bags.
2. Empty and rinse your bottles, then replace the bottle caps.
3. Cut cardboard into 2' by 2' squares.
4. No electronics.
5. No shredded paper.

#1 was kind of a shock, however the plastic bags (or any type of plastic film), gum up the mechanical processes. They have to shut down the lines a few times a day to clear the bags from the internal gears and shredders! So, how do we attack bags and films? Chemical recycling, with a great example a little later.

There are good reasons for the other four and without getting into the details, the best way to learn is to visit your local recycling center. Most are more than happy to give you a tour and teach you some lessons!

There are several areas of innovation that will greatly benefit the recycling processes, and the materials we think of when recycling are paper, glass, and even wood. However, most of the innovation will be centered around plastics recycling simply because of the sheer amount that we use. Not to mention the overwhelming variety of polymers out there which adds to the complexity of recycling this material.

This may or may not be news, but plastics don't play well together in the recycling process. Because they are molecularly different, they need to be sorted, separated, and cleaned prior to recycling. Another problem is that it's very difficult for consumers to know what types of plastics are in the products we buy and the packaging that they come in, so 100% accurate sorting on the consumer end is nearly impossible.

The fact is that there are many methods of recycling plastics (mostly due to the chemistry involved in the chemical makeup of the polymers themselves) be it mechanical, chemical, or a combination of both. There's a need to simplify the process, and innovation is the key here.

Some high-level items that will improve plastics recycling include:

1. **Improved Sorting Technologies:** Since by recycling, we're usually breaking the polymer materials down to their original base (monomers), they need to be sorted by like-types. By utilizing cutting-edge artificial intelligence, machine learning, and robotics technology, advanced sorting technologies are being developed to maximize the efficiency and accuracy of separating materials for recycling purposes. This will boost the sustainability efforts of many industries and communities.

2. **Chemical Recycling:** Pioneering developments in chemical recycling enable the depolymerization or deconstruction of intricate materials into simpler elements – the original molecular building blocks - thus widening the scope for recyclability. This will be particularly beneficial for plastics that are traditionally difficult to recycle using known mechanical processes (like packaging films and shopping bags).

3. **Sustainable Packaging:** Designing packaging materials that are more easily recyclable and utilizing renewable or biodegradable materials will reduce the environmental impact of today's enormous amount of packaging waste. Innovations in this area will involve developing alternative materials or redesigning existing packaging to optimize recyclability.
4. **Closed-Loop Systems:** Promoting the development of closed-loop recycling systems, where materials are recycled back into the same product, will reduce the demand for virgin, carbon-rich resources. This approach will be particularly impactful for plastics (but metals too) ensuring a more circular economic model.
5. **Consumer Education and Engagement:** New, innovative approaches to educate and engage consumers about proper recycling practices will help improve our anemic recycling rates. Smart recycling bins, mobile apps, and gamification will all be part of the innovative technologies used to incentivize and reward recycling behaviors. This is a great way to make people more conscious of their environmental impact.
6. **Advanced Recycling Infrastructure:** Upgrading processing equipment and implementing better collection systems in recycling facilities will enhance their capacity, efficiency, and effectiveness to process a wider range of materials, like films and flexible packaging so that those can also be added to the curbside recycling systems.

Industry 5.0 will push people to become more sustainable recycling will be at the forefront of the conversation. Recycling plastic waste will be an opportunity for anyone wanting to become more sustainable in their day-to-day activities. This is why we believe there will be relatively wide adoption of recycling practices across the world.

So, what are some of the details? By and large, there are two main types of material feedstock used in plastics recycling:

Post-Industrial Resin (PIR)

This plastic is the extra waste that is trimmed off and reclaimed during the manufacturing process. Post-industrial is closer to virgin plastic than post-consumer because it tends to be clean material, does not yet contain residual from its 1st life, is processed far less, and can be separated much easier.

Post-industrial resin is plastic waste from the manufacturing process that is collected at the moment of discarding and sent to recycling. Almost all recycled plastic is Industrial plastic waste from a manufacturing process that creates the bottle used for your shampoo and milk or the film used to make bubble wrap and plastic bags. Due to the fees associated with sending plastic waste to a landfill there is an incentive to recycle and reuse as much as possible.

What most people don't realize is that most of the plastics recycling supply chain (80%+) consists of post-industrial resin. Only a small fraction (10-20%) is post-consumer resin.

Post-Consumer Resin (PCR)

This plastic is used by the consumer for its intended purpose, has reached its end of life, and is then tossed into a recycling bin, along with other recyclable materials such as paper, metal, and glass. It is often mixed in use, and then mixed again as it's discarded into a central collection bin.

This means that post-consumer resin requires a lot more touching and processing. Recycling post-consumer resin has become a complicated process of collecting, separating plastics from other recyclables, sorting the plastic types (water bottles are different than shampoo bottles than plastic bags than prescription bottles, cleaning and then possibly milling, melting, and compounding).

Post-consumer resin is plastic waste from everyday products like packaging and consumer goods. Almost all this plastic is thrown away in a trash bin, with minimal opportunities for recycling.

Some recyclers focus specifically on post-consumer resins, and others focus only on post-industrial resins. There are even recycling companies that focus specifically on ocean plastics or on creating circular economies of plastic within large organizations. Plastic recycling has now become a booming industry; it's no longer about just collecting empty water bottles. But the development of the plastic recycling ecosystem and infrastructure must continue to evolve to manage more of today's packaging formats.

Innovations in Recycling

Most of us think of plastics recycling as simply grinding down and melting plastics to simply reuse the material and mold it into new products. While that is a piece of the cycle, there's much more to recycling. There's no single solution to recycling as each polymer requires different methods and sorting plastics is a tough task – think about recycling a multilayer laminate!

For our discussion, we are looking at two basic types of plastic recycling - mechanical and chemical.

Mechanical Recycling

Mechanical recycling (heat melt, grind, etc.) is the most common type of plastic recycling in use today. It uses established technologies and can be very labor intensive, especially when using post-consumer materials for the feedstock, as this is our waste collected in various forms and conditions.

The collection of post-industrial resins is much easier, as this is typically done within a plastic manufacturing facility. This "clean" scrap material is then used to make plastic products, replacing a portion of new virgin resins.

Mechanical recycling has other limitations, such as collection, sorting, and the fact that the material cannot be completely restored to its virgin state easily and that the polymers suffer degradation during the process. This limits the use cases for mechanically recycled feedstock, and points to the uptick in innovations regarding chemical and biological recycling.

Mechanical recycling, the most common and with established supporting infrastructure, still has inefficiencies built in. During the process of sorting, washing, grinding, and melting, not all contaminants get removed. Also, there is great stress on the polymer under heat. This means that the output of plastic products is almost always downgraded to goods of lesser quality than virgin materials.

To reap the full rewards of plastics recycling, additional technologies and processes are needed to complement mechanical recycling to increase the amount, type, and form of plastics that can be recycled.

Chemical and Advanced Recycling

Unlike traditional mechanical recycling, which involves melting and reshaping plastic materials, chemical recycling employs a range of thermal and chemical processes to deconstruct and convert the plastic polymers into their original molecular building blocks that can be used as the materials to produce plastics or other materials, keeping the plastic in productive use. Advanced recycling relies on heat alone, using no actual chemicals, which we will highlight in a case study later.

This transformation allows for a broader range of plastics, including mixed or contaminated plastics, to be recycled, reducing the burden on landfills and incineration. Chemical recycling holds the potential to significantly improve the circularity of plastic waste.

Researchers from the University of Delaware's Center for Plastics Innovation (CPI) have developed a direct method to convert single-use plastic waste — plastic bags, yogurt containers, plastic bottles, bottle caps, packaging, and more — to ready-to-use molecules for jet fuel, diesel, and lubricants.

The work is led by Dionisios Vlachos, Unidel Dan Rich Chair in Energy and Professor of Chemical and Biomolecular Engineering. Vlachos' research focuses on circular economy and waste derivatization, multiscale modeling, simulation, and distributed (bio)chemical manufacturing,

He focuses on using a novel catalyst and unique process to quickly break down these hardest-to-recycle plastics, known as polyolefins. Polyolefins account for 60 to 70% of all plastics made today. The catalyst itself is a hybrid material, a combination of zeolites and mixed metal oxides.

Zeolites are known to have properties that make them good at creating branched molecules. Zeolites are found in things like water purification or softener systems and home detergents, where they counteract minerals like calcium and magnesium, making hard water softer and improving the laundry process.

Mixed metal oxides, meanwhile, are known for their ability to break down large molecules at just the right amount without overdoing it. The antacid in your medicine cabinet, for example, is a metal oxide used to break down, or neutralize, the acid causing your upset stomach.

"Alone these two catalysts do poorly. Together, the combination does magic, melting the plastics down and leaving no plastic behind," Vlachos said. "This makes them ready-to-use molecules for high-value lubricant or fuel applications."

Another real-world example of the advancements in chemical recycling, or more precisely "Advanced" recycling, is being pioneered by a company called Nexus Circular. They are focusing on plastics that are notoriously difficult to handle like films and flexible packaging.

They employ an established technique called Pyrolysis, a proven technology that has been used for over 50 years in the chemicals and plastics industries. Using only heat without oxygen at atmospheric pressure to convert the long chains of the used plastic molecule into shorter chains in the form of gas.

This gas is then cooled into its components and the result is pyrolysis oil, which is then used by plastic producers to make virgin-quality resin from 100% recycled content, displacing and reducing the dependence on fossil-based resources. Nexus' pyrolysis-based chemical recycling process enables plastics to be repeatedly recycled into their base monomers, again and again creating a circular loop. Those base monomers are then converted into various polymer chains.

Nexus is continually looking for new avenues to divert hard-to-recycle plastics from landfill, such as healthcare plastics. By nature, those "sterile" materials used in our doctors' offices, and hospitals are typically single-use, and most times go directly to landfills. In a partnership with Berry Global, Nexus is recycling items like flexible fluid containers, tubes, gowns, surgical cloth, and packaging. The recycled materials can be used to make new healthcare items, making the process truly circular...like their name says!

There are a broad range of complementary Reduce, Reuse, and Recycle strategies that are currently being implemented to develop a circular economy for plastics. These strategies value plastic as a resource that can be used again and again and are helping to build the recycling ecosystem to keep plastic out of landfills and prevent leakage into our environment.

Nexus' version of advanced recycling is an innovative technology that can address a broad range of hard-to-recycle plastics that are not able to be recycled through traditional mechanical recycling processes and are (too) often landfilled.

However, even with some recycling challenges, many manufacturers today are trying to reduce the amount of virgin plastic they use in the products they make, and recycled plastic could be a perfect solution to reduce the amount of virgin plastic they're using.

How Much Gets Recycled?

Since a large percentage of all plastics are not recycled, this means they stay around for centuries in landfills or our oceans. What is even more alarming is that most post-consumer plastics that we collect for recycling actually find their way to our already overflowing landfills!

How much plastic gets recycled? This is shocking, but according to National Geographic, an astonishing 91 percent of plastic isn't recycled. Of course, this means that only around 9 percent is being recycled. That equates to about 3 million tons annually, which on the surface may sound impressive – until you realize that over 30 million tons (yes, that's 60 billion pounds) of plastic simply goes to waste!

While recycling has a foothold in the plastics community, there are some challenges arising, such as not enough raw plastics to meet recycling demands. The world is facing a shortage of recycled plastics. This feels a little bizarre as we just mentioned the fact that not much of the overall plastic waste produced gets recycled!

There are many reasons for this occurrence – other countries refusing to buy our recyclables, less plastic making it to the recycle bins, and the ever-complex (and expensive) process of recycling plastics.

As more companies begin adopting recycled plastic, there will be a growing need for larger supplies of plastic from recyclers. Today, most waste plastic from corporations' manufacturing lines is already recycled. This means that new recycled plastic sources will need to come from consumer recycling efforts, or post-consumer resin.

This is where the problem lies, because humans are notoriously bad at changing habits in general, and they are especially bad at changing habits when the benefit is not instant gratification. If consumer behavior is unable to change at the rapid pace of corporate consumption, there will be a major shortage of recycled plastic in the coming years.

This shortage will certainly have a negative effect on our society, like an increase in pollution and an increase in costs. However, we need a renewed focus on recycling plastics, as it will always be important to reduce our environmental footprint and ensure that there is less plastic waste that goes into landfills or oceans.

The Impact of Recycled Plastic Challenges

In a world where there is more plastic than there are trees, our current recycling efforts just don't cut it. Environmental sustainability has been the buzzword for decades, but it's time to switch gears and get smart about how we're going to get out of this mess.

In theory, recycling plastic is a great idea. You take a plastic water bottle and turn it into two new bottles, right? But the reality is the world has reached a point where the demand for plastic is far outstripping our ability to produce it, as well as the ability of our planet to maintain it.

While recycling initiatives are making a difference, there is not enough effort to keep up with the demands. The recycling process can also be time-consuming and expensive, meaning that sometimes it's cheaper to just make new plastic, which should send a chill down our collective spines!

We are running out of recycled plastics because of two reasons, first is supply and second is consumer behavior. Supply-wise, there is a problem with plastic recycling plants (mechanical) worldwide. They are running out of raw materials because people are throwing away more plastics than ever before.

Another factor that contributes to this shortage is the lack of clean recyclable plastics in circulation. Clean recyclables are just that, plastic containers that have been rinsed thoroughly before they get thrown into the bins. Cleaning individual dirty containers is a nightmare for mechanical recyclers because it adds more labor, equipment, and overall costs.

Consumer behavior-wise, people just don't know how important recycling is anymore – they just throw it away without thinking twice about it. If only consumers knew that by tossing their recyclables in trash cans, they're potentially depriving future generations of plastic products, then this planet would be a much better place. The problem is that we don't see used plastic as a resource, we see it as trash!

It is estimated that by 2050, the demand for plastic will have increased by 4x the baseline 2020 demand and there will be more plastic than fish in the oceans. The effects of this are already being seen on the health of humans and animals alike. Many companies have created products with recycling plastics in mind, however, it seems these efforts are not achieving the desired impact. This is a huge problem, and we need to either find ways to recycle more plastics to reduce this shortage and/or find better, more bio-friendly ways to make plastics in the first place!

The shortage is a major issue and it has been predicted that by 2030, the world will be producing more plastic than it can recycle. This increase in production will inevitably lead to a plastics shortage as demand for new plastics far outstrips the recycling capacity. As such, we need to start preparing for this upcoming crisis now.

There are three key areas we should focus on:

1. Building up our recycling infrastructure and capacity
2. Reducing our dependence on single-use plastics
3. Rethinking the way we design and market products to minimize their environmental impact.

Numbers one and two are essentially expanding the current solutions that are in place today, number three may be the best long-term choice as there is still a finite amount of raw petrochemical polymer material available to us (oil). New, renewable sources are certainly the future of plastics.

Continued research, development, and collaboration across industries and sectors will be crucial to drive sustainable advancements for the immediate future and beyond. Innovations need to span the collection, sorting, and actual process of returning the materials to their "virgin" states.

New Materials

Maybe the single-most-important category of innovation as it relates to our lower-carbon future is new materials. Material science will see many innovations that promote sustainability, particularly in the realm of bio-based, low (or no) carbon materials.

Materials innovation is constantly on the move. From the beginning of recorded history, humans have been working with tools and their associated materials. We fashioned stone axes, knives, and spears to level the playing field with stronger, bigger and faster animals (try taking down a mastodon with your bare hands!). We wove textiles to make clothing and we treated wood with pine tar and other sealants to make boats and shelters. Our entire existence has been advanced by understanding how to manipulate materials and make them work better for us.

By definition – "Materials Innovation" is the process of developing new materials with specific properties that solve previously unsolvable problems. It's important because this type of innovation has changed the world and not only made things easier for us, but it's also made life as we know it possible in ways that were not even conceivable before. The U.S. government has even recently appropriated grant funds for scientific discoveries in the field of materials innovation with a concentration on sustainable and biomaterials.

We might think of the scientific side of materials innovation as a recent occurrence, but we have been working with and improving materials since the beginning of the industrial revolution (and really, even long before that). Today, we are always looking for a better material to improve our lives; whether that means clothing that lasts longer, houses that are easier to heat a cool, and vehicles that travel farther on fuel, or use no fossil fuel at all!

The Early History of Materials Innovation

The great Irish playwright, George Bernard Shaw had this wonderful quote – "The reasonable man adapts himself to the world; the unreasonable man persists in trying to adapt the world to himself. Therefore, all progress depends on the unreasonable man. "

Unreasonable humans have been "progressing" by innovating materials for millennia. The ancient Egyptians invented linen while the Incas created cloth from llama wool. There are many other examples of innovations from early history including paint, glass, and cement.

Pottery and ceramics go back over 16,000 years and the first bronze weapons were manufactured about 2,000 B.C.! As early as the year 900, the beginnings of what we know as the periodic table began to appear in the very first classifications of chemical elements.

More recently were the discoveries of rubber, cement, and chemical substances – all leading to advancements in things like transportation, housing, and agriculture. No matter what the material(s), it seems that humans have always had a compulsion, or a need to improve the world around them (Abraham Maslow strikes again!).

Materials innovation has always been a prevalent factor in the progress of civilization. The past few decades have seen some of the most groundbreaking developments in materials engineering, from light-weight carbon fiber to more efficient solar cells. Because we now better understand some of the negative aspects of our recent progress, these new materials are helping to reduce our dependence on fossil fuels and make our world a little greener.

But if we back up about 100 years or more, what was the result of materials innovations, especially in the late 19th and 20th centuries? Sure, they allowed for the mass production of goods, transportation, and housing expansion in areas beyond the urban centers, but most of them came with a high-carbon footprint or wreaked havoc on the environment to extract and process them.

The first two revolutions were a time of drastic changes to the political, economic, and social spheres. These revolutions were fueled by advances in technology. Steam power and mass production led to the creation of factories, which in turn led to a more mobile workforce and the mass production of goods. This led to even greater advances during Industry 2.0 that allowed people to move out of densely populated areas to more rural settings, eventually spawning great migrations westward across the United States. The new materials that they spawned, and their uses were almost endless, but we know now that the unprecedented progress came with unintended consequences.

What Price Have We Paid for our Progress?

The news is full of bad stories about the environment and climate change. Many of these are connected to industries that have a negative impact on the planet such as mining, farming, logging, and oil drilling. These activities have certainly led to human advancements, and life as we know it would be impossible without the innovations in materials that span all these industries. We have made huge progress, but it has come with a high price tag.

We've decimated some of our natural resources. Trees, farmland, rainforests, etc. The overaggressive purge of the land has taken a toll. Estimates are that about 10,000 acres of rainforest is destroyed every day, and between 2015 and 2020 we lost over 10 million hectares of old growth timber!

Today, the push for sustainability is causing us to reexamine the way we use our natural resources and how we develop products and materials. Industry 5.0 will push us to pay greater attention to our effects on the planet. Today we are ushering in the movement to truly leave the Earth a better place for future generations.

But there is one area where caution is advised and we need to reexamine our reliance on this particular resource, or we may face some dire consequences. Don't worry, new thinking (and materials technology) can prevail. With this in mind, we can also see how biomaterials will impact the manufacturing of the homes and buildings of the future. The resource we're talking about is wood, and Industry 5.0 will affect our concept of forestry and wood production - let us explain.

A Word About Wood

Is wood renewable? Yes. Is wood sustainable? No, not in the current ways we exploit the resources. Our current path of forestry, actually "de-forestry" is a better description, will bring us close to exhausting wood resources. We've already destroyed a lot of old-growth timber, and replanting new trees takes decades to return the forest to its natural state.

The problem is we don't wait decades and we don't plant the variety of plant life back into our tree farms. It's much like monocropping in agriculture. Replanting trees is a great idea, as long as we give them the time and ecological diversity needed to maintain the planet. The problem is most times, we don't. Call us tree-huggers, but we need to seriously consider the rate and volume of trees/forests we harvest. The movement here isn't new, but we see a ramping up of the cause.

A Brief History of Tree Hugging

Tree hugging is closely associated with the hippie movement of the 1970s. The definition of a tree hugger is an environmental campaigner. This movement was based around the symbol of a person embracing a tree in an attempt to prevent it from being cut down. But hippies were not the original tree huggers. So, where did they come from?

The first known tree huggers were called Bishnois who represent a sect of Hinduism that resides in Northern India. In 1730, Foresters came through town to cut down trees that would be used to build a palace. The Bishnois were not willing to part ways with their sacred trees and, in response, led a physical protest.

During this protest, their leader, Amrita Devi, wrapped herself around a tree to stop the foresters from cutting it down. In response, the Foresters attacked her and the trees with their axes. In support of their leader, 363 other Bishnoi's sacrificed their lives for the trees. Eventually, the foresters admitted defeat.

These were the seeds that sprouted (yep, more puns) the tree-hugging movement hundreds of years ago.

Social Benefits of Trees

Figure 19 Tree-lined Neighborhood

We all know that trees are beautiful to look at. They make our neighborhoods look aesthetically pleasing and create a reminder that nature is both green and living. Communities are not just a bunch of concrete buildings put in the same general area. Communities have parks, lawns, and scenic views that create an experience that people want to come back to.

Trees are foundational to that experience. Removing them is removing the living things that civilization has relied upon for millions of years.

Here are a few of the social benefits that trees provide:

- Trees filter pollutants from the air.
- Trees cool the atmosphere.
- Trees filter rainfall and the sun's ultraviolet rays.
- Trees provide shade and comfort to all living things.
- Trees increase recreation opportunities.
- Trees absorb sounds.

Economic Benefits of Trees

Saving trees is a lot more economically beneficial than cutting them down. If we can reduce our expenses as a society by saving trees, then why would we look to remove them?

There are many reasons why having trees in our local communities is valuable to all the living things that surround it.

Here are a few of the economic benefits that trees provide:

- Trees prevent flooding and damage to neighborhoods.
- Trees reduce energy costs in winter by creating a wind barrier.
- Trees improve air quality which reduces cardiac disease, strokes, and asthma.
- Trees reduce energy costs in summer by providing shade to buildings.
- Trees improve human health and reduce medical costs.
- Trees improve a neighborhood's property values.

Today, cutting down a large tree takes only a few seconds. The problem is that the tree took many years to grow. Here's another example of the unintended consequences of the First Industrial Revolution. We created machinery that can plow down a forest in record time, however, we haven't created a process to grow trees back at the same rate. We are moving closer toward an imbalance every day.

During the early 1900s, there were billions of acres of forest land to feast upon. Today, we are tracking deforestation at the rate of over 37 million acres per year!

Figure 20 Logging Operation

Losing forests and the increasing human population have a direct correlation to disaster. To put it into perspective, in the time it took to read this paragraph, we lost another 20 acres of forest.

The Amazon rainforest alone provides about 9% of the world's oxygen. Today, it's being both cut down and burned down. The forests in California and other regions are consistently burning to the ground from hotter temperatures, poor forest management, and a lack of rain.

A mature tree produces as much oxygen in a season as 10 people inhale in a year. Their ability to convert carbon dioxide into oxygen has been well-documented throughout history. This begs the question, why are we actively cutting down trees at such an alarming rate? Here are a few of the environmental benefits that trees provide:

- Trees conserve water and prevent water pollution.
- Trees replenish underground water reserves.
- Trees provide habitats for birds and insects.
- Trees create food for bees, birds, and other animals.
- Trees reduce wind speed.
- Trees stabilize soil to prevent erosion.
- Trees absorb up to one-third of particle pollutants within a 300-yard radius.
- Trees reduce urban flooding and keep pollutants out of waterways.
- Trees reduce evaporation rates.

Protecting trees is something that will certainly be an aspect of Industry 5.0. We anticipate a shift in thinking about our forests, and what will be lost if we destroy them. By shifting to industrial uses of crops like hemp, bamboo, and flax, we can offset some of the use of traditional woods - especially where wood flour and particles are used.

New Plastic Materials

The plastics industry gets a lot of attention in the carbon reduction conversation, and most of that talk is negative. However, we understand that as a society, we simply cannot "flip the switch off" on plastics. They are vital to our survival as a species, and eliminating plastics is unrealistic. I know that might sound a bit dramatic but take a walk around any hospital, now in your mind remove all the plastics. The results would be devastating. No flexible IV tubes, no handheld heart monitors, no lightweight pharmaceutical packaging and no easily fabricated sterile containers! Hospitals are just one example, but it's hard, if not impossible, to imagine a world today without these polymers.

Our view is that we need plastics, and in turn we need to make the plastics we use less harmful to the environment. The way to do that is by incremental innovation, augmenting those plastics with bio-based materials allowing us to shift to greener, decarbonized materials that do not harm the environment. The innovation comes in not only devising ways to incorporate these bio-based additives in everyday plastics, but ever increasing the amount of bio-content over time. At some point we will be able to neutralize the carbon emissions of plastics, and eventually even reverse it.

The materials sector is one of the most important industries in the world and it continues to grow at a rapid pace, but it is also the most capital-intensive sector, with investments required in assets such as equipment, buildings, and property. Materials are the building blocks of everything around us and it's estimated that the materials industry is worth $2 trillion.

Products are the centerpiece of the world economy, they fuel markets, industries, and countries. To make a product, there are a myriad of materials involved. These materials can range from metals to plastics to mined materials. The development of new environmentally friendly materials is something that will have a significant impact on the products made in the future, because the consumer today is much more "judgmental" than at any other time in history.

Do we Need more Solutions such as Bio-friendly Plastics?

The short answer is, an emphatic YES! Bio-friendly plastics are the organic equivalent of traditional plastics. They are made with renewable, sustainable materials such as hemp, corn, or soybean. These materials can be easily grown and harvested, meaning they do not require any form of mining or drilling to procure them. Simply grow and harvest!

Pure polymers completely made from biomaterials are available, but the technology is not quite there to replace our established plastics materials. One potential downside to this type of plastic is that it doesn't last as long as the traditional materials and doesn't have the mechanical properties needed for commercial use.

However, we can use these natural materials as plastics additives, and essentially gain (or even improve) the same properties as plastics that use petrochemical or mined additives. This is shaping up to be the best overall solution by coming up with sustainable alternatives for plastics that can also serve as building blocks for the materials we currently produce from petroleum. We are strong proponents of biomaterials like hemp as it can be grown very quickly with limited resources to supply the additives we need for plastics, and in turn reduce our carbon footprint at the same time!

The Bio-based Additives Opportunity

Bio-based additives offer a sustainable and green solution to the growing chemical and plastic industry. They're made from renewable resources that are abundantly available. The market is expected to grow significantly in the coming years as consumers become increasingly aware of the environmental effects of chemicals and plastics.

Biotechnologies are key to the future development of sustainable products in all sectors. One of the sectors in which biotechnology can be heavily used is plastics manufacturing. Biotechnological innovation is needed to replace fossil-fuel based polymeric materials with bio-based ones which are more environmentally friendly, biodegradable, and recyclable. Current research work is aimed at finding out more ways to use these biomaterials as an additive material for plastics production.

The bio-based materials that are most widely studied for usage as additives in plastics manufacturing are plant oils and lignin-derived polymers. In general, these plastic additives can be classified into two categories – those that improve quality of the final product and those that reduce cost of the process itself or improve production rates.

As of the writing of this book, all raw material supply chains are pinched. Plastic, metal, wood, petroleum, minerals, and synthetic materials are all experiencing lower supply and higher pricing.

This is opening a massive opportunity for recycling supply chains across the world to step up to the plate to innovate and outcompete the virgin raw material supply chains.

Bio-based Composites

Bio-based composites will combine natural fibers, such as flax, hemp, or bamboo, with an all-bio-based resin matrix. These composites will be used in various applications, including construction, automotive parts, and consumer products. They will offer much-improved sustainability, reduced weight, and far lower (or no) carbon emissions compared to today's traditional composites. Today, we see a multitude of composites on the market, solving many sustainability challenges for traditional materials. Like bioplastics, look for science to push the development of these materials at a rapid pace.

Sustainable Textiles

Innovations in material science led to the development of totally sustainable textiles made from bio-based fibers. Fibers like bamboo, hemp, and organic cotton are being used as alternatives to synthetic fibers, reducing the environmental impact of the textile industry.

Cellulosic Materials

Cellulose is the most abundant organic compound on Earth, and it has limitless uses for new products. Cellulosic materials are derived from plant-based sources, such as wood, hemp, agricultural waste, or recycled paper. They will have far-reaching applications in packaging, automotive, consumer, and construction materials. Cellulosic materials will offer far greater sustainability benefits due to their renewable and recyclable nature.

Bio-based Coatings

Bio-based coatings will use natural ingredients based from plant/vegetable oils (hemp, flax, soybeans, etc.) as alternatives to conventional petroleum-based coatings. These coatings will offer similar, or superior performance properties while reducing reliance on fossil fuels and minimizing environmental impact.

Biodegradable and Renewable Packaging

Advances in material science will lead to the development of biodegradable and renewable packaging materials such as Polylactic Acid (PLAs are derived from natural resources like sugarcane or cornstarch). These include bio-based films, molded pulp packaging, and compostable materials, which provide biodegradable alternatives to single-use plastics and reduce waste.

Additive Production Methods

Getting the Most Out of New Materials

A lot of attention has been directed towards 3D printing over the past decade or so, for good reason! 3D printing began as a great alternative to prototyping as samples could be quickly produced in small quantities. However, advancements in this technology have moved 3D printing from purely prototyping to full production.

Its commercial production is rapidly becoming a viable solution to materials in construction and other manufacturing processes. One reason is because of its efficiency and accuracy. However, the decision to move to more 3D printing has a deeper impact on sustainability, as it is considered an "additive manufacturing". Let's look at that.

For most of the industrial revolutionary periods, we maintained a "subtractive" manufacturing philosophy. Meaning, we carved away raw materials to create the shapes and structures that we needed. Think of carving a canoe, or milling steel parts, or chiseling away at stone. Michelangelo's famous quote was "Every block of stone has a statue inside it, and it is the task of the sculptor to discover it. I saw the angel in the marble and carved until I set him free." In other words, he "chopped away" the material that wasn't the angel.

This was our approach to manufacturing, by seeing the parts we needed, locked up inside a slab of marble or a sheet of steel we set forth to "set them free." However, that process in itself is inefficient and wasteful, even if we recycle the scraps (which is not always done), the energy and labor to do so is excessive beyond the original need. This setting something free is otherwise known as "subtractive" manufacturing. We "take away" or remove the unneeded parts of the whole.

Additive manufacturing means we only create what we need with minimal raw materials. 3D printing is the perfect example. We can supply a filament of materials (typically plastics, but use of other materials is underway) that are fed into a nozzle that builds up, layer by layer, the part we need. No waste, no carving, no chiseling, and much lower energy use!

Entire homes are being 3D printed along with car parts, tools, clothing, even food! All with little, or no waste, and quality that is on par with traditional manufacturing methods. Additive manufacturing will be a staple process in our 5.0 world.

A Case Study on Materials and Cooperation

A conversation on new materials would not be complete without mentioning some of the synergistic opportunities leading us into Industry 5.0. A perfect example is one we are very close to, in fact, we're contributing members!

Three companies who were working independently on new materials are now standing together to lead the material innovation space. Mito Material Solutions, Endeavor Composites, and Heartland Industries on the surface do have a few things in common (sustainable materials innovation) but would have not pooled our efforts together except for a shining business accelerator program that began in 2022. The program was GoMove and the accelerator was Greentown Labs.

Greentown Labs is the largest Greentech accelerator in North America, with locations in Somerville, MA and Houston, TX. They have more than 200 startups between the two locations, offering the expertise, resources, and support they need to change the world. GoMove was a sponsor program funded, and led by two industrial giants, BASF and Magna International.

The thrust of the program was to decarbonize automotive plastics and there are no better partners to work with! BASF provides the science and raw materials. They are simply the largest chemical company on Earth. Magna is one of the largest automotive suppliers in the world, and even manufactures complete vehicles for OEMs like Mercedes-Benz, Toyota and Fisker.

Being chosen for GoMove meant these startups were in elite company, with over 150 applications submitted and only five chosen! Each offered market-ready solutions for lower carbon plastics on their own, but as GoMove progressed, they began to see opportunities to work together and multiply their sustainability efforts.

Mito's main business is functionalizing graphene. We hear a lot about graphene but moving it from expensive concepts in a lab to production-ready applications in a factory is a chore. Without getting too deep in the weeds, Mito has perfected a process to make their graphene soluble, meaning it can be easily functionalized in raw materials. Raw materials like industrial hemp.

This is where Heartland comes in. Heartland is a material science company that engineers natural fibers into additives for plastics. These fibers make the plastic lighter, stronger and with a much lower carbon footprint, in some cases, negating the polymer's carbon footprint altogether!

To bring the process together we look to Endeavor Composites. With Heartland providing the natural fibers, and Mito improving the characteristics using graphene, we needed a way to manufacture a useful material in large quantities, and more specifically, a material that can be manufactured on an industrial scale.

This is where Endeavor's process of matting comes into play. Endeavor takes the raw materials and processes them in rolled sheets (like paper pulping to make paper towels or bath tissue) and creates a new, sheet material that is strong, lightweight, thin, and carbon-negative!

So, what can we do with these amazing sheets? We can manufacture virtually any molded car component from flooring to bumpers to exterior and interior panels. We know that composite materials offer extreme strength and flexibility in manufacturing. These composites offer something completely new and different because while they perform like other composites, they will negate more carbon than they produce!

The automotive industry won't be the only interested party here either, think building products, packaging, and electronics!

Links to the contributing companies the Greentown Labs' GoMove program:

www.greentownlabs.com

www.carbonova.com

www.fibrecoat.de

www.mitomaterials.com

www.endeavorcomposites.com

www.heartland.io

The Future of 5.0 Materials

The future of materials innovation, and really, innovation in general is limitless! Our past comes with the burden of negative effects, but we must frame progress in the time period it occurred in. We now know that carbon emissions into our atmosphere are rising and need to be reduced. However, when materials such as plastics and petroleum were in their infancy, we didn't know all (if any of) the negative effects. Plus, the positives were so clearly in focus – cheap abundant energy that the nation needed to advance, plus materials that were equally inexpensive and easy to mold and manipulate into various products from bottles to bumpers.

Remember, we have only had reliable measures for carbon emissions since the late 1950s, and research shows that carbon started rising in the late 18th century. A full 200 years before we really knew and understood these negative aspects of industrial progress.

So, where does that leave us today? Well, we are actually in a very good spot. Because we are more aware of emissions and the negative effects, materials innovation is centering not only on product advancements, but advancements that are not harmful to the environment and future citizens. In fact, material science is creating carbon-negative materials that not only alleviate any environmental sins of the future, but they can also atone for our sins of the past!

You see we are now advancing our materials in concert with saving the planet. The future of materials innovation will be shaped by how well we can utilize these two aspects in tandem. What is the best option for achieving both? We see it as the advancement of bio-based materials.

Biomaterials are not just an element of future innovation, but the epicenter of materials for some time to come. Biomaterials typically have carbon neutral, or carbon negative characteristics. Meaning the growing and processing of these materials usually comes with a carbon benefit, not a carbon penalty!

Of course, we could be a little biased as authors who run a material innovation company whose core business is engineering new biomaterials. We at Heartland see our campaign to use biomaterials to decarbonize plastics (and other materials), as a core part of the Industry 5.0 movement.

"Innovation is the ability to see change as an opportunity, not a threat." A great quote from Steve Jobs. He also stated that, "Innovation distinguishes between a leader and a follower."

The time to lead that change in our world is now. The decisions we make today will have a long-lasting impact on our future generations. We need to foster progress, nourish hope, and move toward a sustainable future.

We have the potential to turn imagination into reality, and many unheard-of companies are working on those dreams right now. Our actions should be guided by sustainability, and our legacy of innovation should be one of resilience and hope. This is the moment to shape our collective future, and we all play a role.

If we attack the issue of sustainability seriously, our grandchildren will not even know the meaning of the term "carbon footprint", because it won't exist!

In a few decades, the materials we buy could feature a whole new periodic table. Scientists are developing new synthetic materials that combine the strengths of different elements into one material. This is allowing for more durable, energy-efficient, and sustainable products to be created, and opening the door for new business ventures. Many of them are merely great ideas on paper today but will be thriving industries tomorrow!

As this sector is currently worth $2.1 trillion and is expected to grow to $4.5 trillion by 2030, this industry will have a major impact on the global economy. We will see huge growth of industries like aerospace, automotive, and construction; all of those will be dependent on the development of new, sustainable materials.

We see the future of materials and material science to be extremely optimistic. Past innovations had unintentional consequences with negative side-effects. The push for advancement led to the degradation of our environment, and the quest for progress has resulted in the depletion of our natural resources. However, devastating, they were all done in the spirit of human advancement.

Today, we see the same thirst for progress with a new barometer of kindness to the environment. To reference Shaw again, being "reasonable" might equate to being satisfied with the status quo and continuing down our precarious path. Maybe it's time to be unreasonable and take our planet and its resources a bit more seriously.

276

Part III

People - Planet – Potential

278

Chapter 17:

People - The New Sustainable Leadership Era

Why Leadership Matters

Leadership matters. We hear this all the time, but why? Because all organizations follow the mindset of the leaders in charge. We follow leaders for direction. We follow them for guidance in uncertain times. We also follow them for inspiration, and validation of beliefs. However, in an organizational structure, we also follow leaders for our own status and recognition.

It's human nature to emulate the people we see (and choose) as leaders, both good and bad. Sometimes, unknowingly we follow leaders who have less than desirable intentions, however, we believe that most leaders have beneficial goals and interests at heart.

History is dotted with examples of each. A look at the Roman Empire gives us illustrations of all points on the leader "continuum". From Nero, whose reign was peppered with corruption, cruel behavior and most famously setting Rome ablaze and blaming it on a religious group. He is considered one of the poorest leaders in history, and really walked on the edges of evil.

So why did the good people of Rome align with Nero? One reason was power. People in power sometimes resort to fear and intimidation to control their followers. Nero was an extreme example, but even today we can see authoritarian leaders who use threats and coercion to control employees. Bottom line is that human psychology is based on following a strong leader, and it goes back to prehistoric times when leaders essentially kept you safe and alive!

On the other hand, we have Julius Caesar. Not without faults, Caesar was considered one of the genuine statesmen of ancient Rome. Caesar was able to unite his people and transform the Roman Republic into what we know as the Roman Empire. He introduced political reforms and social programs designed to benefit the people of Rome, including land distribution and debt relief. He truly had a vision of what the empire would look like, and what it meant to be a citizen of Rome.

In the simplest terms, a leader is tasked with creating the corporate vision, painting that vision for all to see, then enrolling the stakeholders (internal and external) into that vision.

In the modern era, we think about leaders like Steve Jobs. He led one of the great movements of our age with his passion for the computer (and what it could contribute to society). Did he have a vision for Apple (and the entire home computer industry)? Yes. Was he able to paint that vision to employees, consumers, and investors? Oh yeah. Did he gain legions of followers from his almost "evangelical" efforts? You bet! His impact is still felt today, over 10 years since his untimely passing.

Will we see a leader cut from the cloth of someone like Steve Jobs, or Julius Caesar in sustainability? Will one company, or one county stand up and spur change in a monumental way? We hope so, because it will take an epic effort to meet the lofty environmental goals we have set. At the cornerstone of that country, company or local movement sits a leader destined to enroll and inspire us in this vision.

Corporate leadership plays such a crucial role in promoting sustainability because corporations have such a significant impact on the environment and society! Typically, the larger the organization, the bigger the impact. Because their decisions and actions can have far-reaching consequences for the environment and for future generations, large corporate leaders carry a large and unique burden.

If a sustainable business model incorporates environmental, social, and economic factors into its operations to minimize negative impacts and maximize positive ones, then it's paramount that the corporate leaders model that mindset for creating effective sustainability strategies that balance these circumstances.

Leaders need to drive sustainability efforts by setting clear goals, developing, and enforcing policies and procedures that support sustainable practices, and allocating resources to sustainability initiatives. They must also engage stakeholders, including employees, customers, and investors, to promote sustainability values and ensure that sustainability is integrated into the company's culture and values.

In short, corporate leadership plays the most crucial role in promoting sustainability. By setting the tone for the organization's commitment to sustainable practices and ensuring that sustainability is integrated into all aspects of the company's operations, tomorrow's sustainability champions will lead the way.

The Sustainable Board

For a company to become sustainable, the efforts must be clearly modeled by all corporate managers, but it starts at the top with the board of directors. Sustainability must be part of the corporate strategy, and while the board is not tasked with outlining or acting directly on strategy, it is their responsibility to equip the firm with the leadership team that will be responsible for these efforts and the most important choice the board will make is the CEO.

While the CEO sits at the top of an organization, and is most visible to the employees and staff, it's the Board of Directors that can ultimately set the tone for culture, success and driving change towards sustainability. Their actions and attitudes can influence the behavior and values of employees, customers, and especially the stakeholders. By showing a strong commitment to sustainability, board leaders can encourage and motivate the company's c-levels to direct and support the efforts.

However, here's where a huge gap exists between sustainability and board-level directors. Most board members are senior executives who are retired, semi-retired, or at least out of the day-to-day direction of their companies (otherwise, they'd probably not have the spare time to serve on the board). These leaders have decades of experience, and many times they ran companies that aligned with the boards that they serve on.

That multitude of experience of leading a firm was probably 10, 20, or 30 years ago. If we back up in time and look at the business landscape, there was little, or no attention paid to sustainability (at least not on the wide scale we see today). So, our typical board member, while very versed at funding, financing, and operations, probably did not serve in a direct leadership role in a time where sustainability was a C-level topic, let alone a board-level one.

It's of no fault, just timing and the fact that this revolution is just recently upon us. Compare that to the board members of the 1960s. Did many of them have experience with computers or the burgeoning digital world? Of course not. However, the sharpest boards did recognize the future, and while not directing any computerization efforts of the companies they served with, they did support the movement and find savvy leaders to fill those leadership seats within the organizations that did have direct experience.

Today is no different, current board members know that a company's ability to thrive will be directly impacted by their sustainability initiatives, and the efforts to market them to all stakeholders.

Going back to Mark Epstein's "Making Sustainability Work", he notes that, "Senior executives must be knowledgeable, support the organization, and effectively communicate the mission, vision, and strategy to the other members of the organization. The commitment of the board of directors and management encourages employees to act in ways that are compliant and consistent with company strategy. If leaders are not knowledgeable enough about sustainability to motivate their subordinates or institute the proper strategy, structure, or systems, then sustainability actions are unlikely to be successful."

Epstein, Marc J.; Rejc Buhovac, Adriana. Making Sustainability Work (p. 86). Berrett-Koehler Publishers.

We couldn't agree more with these authors. Without knowledgeable leaders in place at the board level, not only will the company's sustainability actions be unsuccessful, so will virtually any effort to stay in business in a 5.0 world!

The Sustainable CEO

Since the CEO is the highest-ranking company officer, they oversee all corporate activity, and are responsible for the organization's ultimate success. The toughest decisions lie at the feet of this individual. Former U.S. President, Harry S. Truman famously said, "The Buck Stops Here"! Meaning, that whatever happens within the organization, it's ultimately the person at the top's responsibility.

Typical CEO job descriptions include the following duties:

- Creating, communicating, and implementing the organization's vision, mission, and overall direction.
- Leading the development and implementation of the overall organization's strategy.
- Implementing the strategic plan that guides the direction of the business or organization.
- Overseeing the complete operation of an organization.
- Evaluating the success of the organization in reaching its goals.
- Looking at potential acquisitions or the sale of the company under circumstances that will enhance shareholder value.

- Representing the organization for civic and professional association responsibilities and activities in the local community, the state, and at the national level.
- Participating in industry-related events or associations will enhance the CEO's leadership skills, the organization's reputation, and the organization's potential for success.

So, outside of these *normal* day to day applications of strategy, what makes the Sustainable CEO unique? In Marc Epstein's book, "Making Sustainability Work", he points out that the new CEO must also govern these nine distinct elements of the business to ensure that sustainability is achieved.

They include:

1. Ethics
2. Governance
3. Transparency
4. Business Relationships
5. Financial Returns (Investors and Lenders)
6. Community Involvement/Service
7. Value of Products and Services
8. Employment Practices
9. Protection of the Environment

On the surface, these seem like elements of any business that wanted to survive would tend to, however look back just a few years and you can find hundreds of examples of companies that weren't ethical, had no transparency, forged lopsided business relationships, demonstrated little or no community involvement, practiced heavy handed employment tactics, and put protection of the environment last on their list!

Let's Start With Ethics

The new CEO must put ethics ahead of profits. I know it seems fundamental, but the recent uncovering of Ponzi schemes in the finance industry demonstrates that the almighty dollar was placed way ahead of doing business in a fair and honest manner. This type of fraud is most painful to those at a lower income stratum, because typically, the people who are the most vulnerable get hurt the worst.

The CEO must set high standards for ethical behavior, at the executive level and throughout the organization. All team members need to be held to high standards when it comes to doing business fairly. The CEO must also look to all partners and vendors, to ensure that they are acting responsibly too.

Governance

Governance covers financial and non-financial aspects of the organization. This means that the CEO must focus his/her management decisions based on all stakeholders' interests, both inside and outside the organization. Utilization of corporate assets must be done in a way that manages them effectively and in good consciousness, and it's typically referred to as the CEO's fiduciary duty. The CEO must make decisions that are aligned with the company's strategy and mission.

Transparency

While Governance is mostly tied to managerial issues, transparency is more about the disclosure of information. CEOs must ensure that they are fully disclosing information in a fair and balanced manner. Those affected can be potential customers and/or employees along with those living in the nearby communities. Anyone who could benefit from or be harmed by company activities.

Non-transparent companies are fairly easy to detect. If you hear a CEO saying things like, "It's our intention..., We firmly believe that..., We are confident..., etc." basically speaking like a politician, you can bet they have something to hide! Here again we go to a leader we admired, Steve Jobs. He spoke in absolutes. He told us what Apple was going to do, and then they did it. Not always with the desired results, but the actions always aligned with the talk.

Business Relationships

How many stories have you read about corporations taking advantage of their size, scope, and market dominance to take advantage of smaller, less powerful firms or worse, minority-owned companies? Suppliers being leveraged into tiny margin deals? Exclusivity and territorial mandates that limit competitiveness and/or growth? IP given away for pennies on the dollar? Today's CEOs need to recognize that vendors and partners are long-term, value-creating ventures. Not short-term battles to be won.

Not only do they need to operate in an ethical manner, but sustainable companies also need to seek out the traditionally underserved and minority partners to improve the public's perception of a firm's social consciousness.

Financial Returns

Financial Returns might seem like a counterintuitive aspect of a sustainable business, especially when we outlined companies that put profits ahead of ethics earlier but remember that what we're talking about here is responsible earnings and returns. The CEO is liable for compensation to employees, return for investors and what we'll see in the next section, value for products and services.

If a company does not earn a profit (with emphasis on the word - EARN) from the products they make and/or services rendered, then they cannot stay in business. Profit ensures the long-term value of the company.

Community Involvement

We've seen the devastating effects that mass industrialization can have on a community, especially during Industry 2.0! In the early 1900s, entire neighborhoods were destroyed, and natural areas were laid to waste by unchecked industrial expansion. In NYC, disease-ridden tenements sprouted up all over the city, to support the ever-expanding factories. Natural resources were pillaged (and still are) to provide for our appetite for over-consumption.

CEOs will need to temper corporate progress with community development. They will need to not only preserve communities and aid in their advancement, but proactively get involved with the health, education, and safety needs of their neighbors.

Value of Products and Services

Value for products is where the CEO satisfies the needs of the company's customers. I once had a sales trainer ask me what the purpose of a business was. I replied, "To make money". Wrong! The purpose of a business is to solve problems. In the process of solving problems, customers will exchange a fair value typically in currency for the solutions.

Does your car have a dirt problem? A car wash will make it go away, for a fair price. Does your house have a water leak problem? A reputable roofer can patch that up. Does your company have an electronic data encryption problem? A computer programming firm can decipher that for you.

All business is based around solving problems, and customers will pay for that. The sustainable CEO needs just to ensure the customers are receiving fair values for said solutions.

Employment

No CEO can do everything themselves, that's called sole proprietorship! And even those are rare these days. All companies need people, and often, teams of people to function.

Again, going back to Industry 2.0, there are tons of stories of unsafe working conditions, long hours, and no child labor laws. Most employees of the day had no guarantee of wages, hours let alone vacation or health care!

Today, employment practices need to focus on development, diversity and basically catering to the employee's rights. Gone are the days of simply satisfying the customer, today's employees must feel engaged and valued as well.

Protection of the Environment

Bring this topic up in a boardroom in 1920, and you would have been labeled a lunatic. If you brought it up in 2020, you'd most likely be called a hero. Sustainable companies must be attuned to engaging in commerce without destroying the planet.

Our CEOs must, according to Marc Epstein, "be committed to minimizing the use of energy and natural resources and decreasing waste and emissions. At a minimum, the company fully complies with all existing international, national, and local regulations and industry standards regarding emissions and waste."

Epstein, Marc J.; Rejc Buhovac, Adriana. Making Sustainability Work. Berrett-Koehler Publishers.

One powerful example of business advocacy in recent years is the annual letter to CEOs from Larry Fink, the founder and CEO of BlackRock, the world's largest institutional investor. These letters have been published since 2012 and have become increasingly urgent and insistent about the need for businesses to define their purpose and set long-term strategies that incorporate sustainability factors.

In recent years, the focus of Fink's letters has increasingly been on sustainability and the need for companies to have a long-term, socially responsible approach to business.

In his 2021 letter, Fink emphasized the importance of companies having a clear and credible sustainability strategy and acknowledged that the COVID-19 pandemic had accelerated the shift towards a more sustainable economy. He also encouraged companies to consider their impact on all stakeholders, including employees, customers, communities, and the environment, and to take steps to address the pressing social and environmental issues of our time.

You can read Mr. Fink's latest letter to CEOs here - https://www.blackrock.com/corporate/investor-relations/larry-fink-ceo-letter

The Role of CSOs

A little newer to the C-suite is the role of Chief Sustainability Officer or CSO. In some cases, the position has existed for over a decade. Case in point our advisor, Eric Austermann, who has been at the C-level with three different companies spanning 19 years. However, most CSOs we've spoken with have been in the position for less than five years.

In this next section, we interviewed many CSO's and other sustainability champions to get their take on the importance of their roles, strategies, and their overall view on how companies are taking notice of the need for creating a sustainable path for their respective organizations. Here's a look at what a typical CSO/Sustainability Director does.

A Chief Sustainability Officer is a senior executive responsible for overseeing and implementing a company's sustainability strategy and initiatives. Their role includes developing and implementing policies, programs and projects that promote environmental, social, and economic sustainability, as well as reporting on the company's sustainability performance and engaging stakeholders on sustainability issues, typically in the form of ESG reports.

The CSO works closely with other departments and business units to integrate sustainability into core business operations, and to ensure the company meets its sustainability goals and commitments. Those business sectors include:

1. **Environmental Health & Safety (EHS):** EHS is responsible for protecting employees, the general public and the environment. They work closely with CSOs and other sustainability leaders to assess risks to health and wellness and manage safety programs.
2. **Corporate Social Responsibility (CSR):** CSR, like EHS, is concerned with environmental safety and how that can affect the company's reputation. CSOs will work with CSR to

engage stakeholders in addressing social and environmental issues. CSOs also help CSR in forging partnerships with external entities such as non-profits, government agencies, and environmental organizations to help align the company with regional and global sustainability issues.

3. **Procurement:** CSOs work with procurement departments to help develop evaluation metrics for suppliers with respect to their environmental and social performance. The CSO can help to encourage suppliers to source eco-friendly materials and outline environmentally friendly activities such as recycling and waste reduction programs.

4. **Operations:** Since Operations is the department within a company responsible for the day-to-day management of the production and delivery of goods and services, they play a crucial role in a company's sustainability efforts. When it comes to specifying materials, supply chain efforts, energy usage and resource management, Operations is ground zero for the CSO's involvement. CSOs support operations by:

   a. Implementing energy-efficient processes and technologies, such as using renewable energy sources, reducing waste, and improving resource efficiency.

   b. Managing supply chains to reduce the environmental impact of transportation and logistics, such as using more environmentally friendly modes of transportation and optimizing supply chain routes.

   c. Incorporating sustainability considerations into product design and development, such as using eco-friendly materials and designing products for recyclability.

   d. Engaging employees in sustainability efforts, such as through training and education programs and promoting environmentally responsible behavior.

   e. Co-collaborating with other departments, such as sustainability, procurement, and EHS, to integrate sustainability considerations into operational processes and decisions.

5. **Supply Chain:** Typically, a direct offshoot of Operations, Supply Chain departments are responsible for managing the flow of goods, services, information, and finances from suppliers to customers. The CSO plays a critical role in the Supply Chain department's sustainability efforts by ensuring that the company's practices are suited to minimize their environmental impact. Some of the ways that the Supply Chain department can support sustainability include:

   a. Implementing environmentally friendly and sustainable practices in logistics, such as optimizing transportation routes, using environmentally friendly modes of transportation, and reducing emissions.

   b. Evaluating and selecting suppliers based on their sustainability performance, such as their environmental and social practices.

   c. Collaborating with suppliers to encourage the adoption of sustainable practices and improve their sustainability performance.

   d. Managing inventory and reducing waste through practices such as just-in-case resilience programs and reducing overproduction.

   e. Integrating sustainability considerations into supply chain processes and decisions, such as through life-cycle assessments of products and services.

6. **Marketing and Communications:** The focus of marketing is to create awareness for a company, then positively shape the attitudes of potential and current customers. Those customers can be external, or internal stakeholders. For the CSO, marketing and communications are vital to the success

of their sustainability mission. The CSO will lean on marketing to:

    a. Communicate the company's sustainability message and initiatives to customers, stakeholders, and the public.

    b. Promote sustainable products and services, such as those made with environmentally friendly materials and produced through sustainable processes.

    c. Incorporate sustainability into branding and marketing campaigns, such as by highlighting the environmental benefits of products and services.

    d. Conduct market research to understand customer attitudes towards sustainability and incorporate that information into marketing strategies.

7. **Human Resources:** This is where all responsibility for managing the company's employees and workplace culture. The CSO, in cooperation with HR, plays a crucial role in a company's sustainability efforts. By promoting sustainable practices and behaviors among employees and incorporating sustainability into HR policies and programs, the CSO can ensure the company and its employee partners are adhering to sustainability protocols. The CSO can help HR support those goals by:

    a. Developing and implementing sustainability training programs and initiatives to educate employees on sustainable practices and behaviors.

    b. Integrating sustainability considerations into recruitment and talent management processes, such as evaluating candidates based on their sustainability knowledge and values.

    c. Promoting workplace wellness programs and initiatives, such as encouraging the use of public transportation, carpooling, and active transportation.

    d. Developing and implementing employee engagement programs, such as green teams, to encourage employee involvement in sustainability initiatives, inside the company and outside working with the community.

Ultimately, the goal of a CSO is to increase the long-term value for the company and its stakeholders through adoption and adherence to all sustainable business practices.

Decentralized Leadership in 5.0

Just like we could "feel" the good vibes from leaders we respect, we can tell when leadership is less than stellar. The best leaders we've been exposed to, always pointed to their "teams" when good things happened. We know too that sustainability must be a total company effort. Everyone will play a part in hitting mandates and goals. No single actor will be able to accomplish this on their own.

However, we can point to individual leaders who have steered the ship in the wrong direction and tanked their firms. Moving away from pure autocratic, centralized leadership towards team-based efforts that get real results will be evident in the 5.0 movement.

We all know bad leadership stories when we hear (or experience) them. They make us cringe, sigh, and shake our heads in disbelief. How is it that a once successful business could be shrinking or even closing its doors for good? You would think that once that happened, every business leader would learn the telltale signs, and avoid them at all costs. However, there is one common link to many a sad story in business, and it starts at the top with marginal "Centralized Leadership".

Once the world's largest retailer, Sears Roebuck and Company, was dominant for a century. Starting with a small catalog in 1888, Sears grew to rule the retail industry, and by the 1960s boasted over 3500 stores! Not to mention the literal millions of catalogs sent to homes across the country (those catalogs were the pre-Internet, hard copy version of online shopping we enjoy today)!

However, how many Sears stores do you see today? As of the writing of this book, there are exactly 18 left - according to the ScrapeHero database. How is it humanly possible to deflate a business so completely? The answer? Bad leadership, and more precisely, bad centralized leadership!

Sears faced increasing challenges and competition in the retail industry in the late 20th and early 21st century. The rise of discount retailers like Walmart and Costco, the growth of e-commerce in the form of Amazon, and changing consumer preferences due to the ease of shopping online contributed to the company's decline.

Efforts to adapt were too little, too late. Sears' leadership team suffered from frequent turnover (once the ship starts sinking, it's tough to find good captains!). They also took the "checkbook" approach to save the company, cutting measures like renovations of their stores (many fell into disrepair), divesting higher quality goods for less expensive merchandise, laying off crucial staff members, and decreasing their marketing spending. All the while the retail landscape was changing underneath them.

Sears also made some questionable acquisitions, like Kmart. Nothing spells disaster like gluing two failing companies together to try to save both. In the end, you're left with one, bigger failing company! On top of that, to collect some quick cash, the company sold off some of its better assets like the credit card division, only pushing them over the edge faster.

Sears did make efforts to venture into online retailing. However, its online retailing initiatives were not as successful as those of many of its competitors. Sears struggled to keep pace and after many years of decay, ultimately filed for bankruptcy in October 2018.

How is it possible to make so many bad decisions over and over? The answer is the same centralized leadership structure. The people at the top might have been revolving, but the decision-making process was the same and they were typically out of touch with the rapidly changing retail environment going on outside of their office.

There are reports of many mid-level managers at Sears sounding warning signs to the executives about the strategic direction the company was going, but almost all of those voices fell victim to the systemic leadership style of top-down decision-making.

You might say "That was decades ago, today we don't see as much dysfunctional centralized leadership." Really? Think Theranos!

Industry 5.0 will dictate a new leadership style, and in our opinion, it's because of the structure of leadership and experience associated with sustainability. Let's explain.

Take a snapshot of the business landscape today and you'll see a higher attention to environmental stewardship. It's been gaining ground for decades, but until recently the momentum rarely reached the C-suite on a broad scale. Today we do see many if not most of the Fortune 500 will dedicate C-level executives with "Sustainability" or "ESG" attached to their roles. However, those experienced executives were most likely mid-to-high-level directors 10, 20, or more years ago.

They did not climb the corporate ladder during a boom in sustainability efforts. It might have been on the company radar, but 20 years ago, it was just a small blip.

Contrast that to today's entry-level managers, who have blossomed during a time when sustainability was a hot topic; they may even hold degrees in sustainability (something unheard of 20 years ago)! They have grown up and matured professionally during a time of eco-consciousness. So, what we are left with is a temporal gap when it comes to the Green Movement.

Regenerative business practices may seem somewhat elusive to those in the Boardroom, while younger generations have grown up with almost a "duty" towards environmental stewardship. We understand that this is a generalization, but our experience in this sector shows that we are certainly over the target here!

The solution? Decentralize leadership and decision-making.

Decentralized leadership (or flat organizations) refers to a management style where power and decision-making authority are distributed from a top central control structure (pyramid org chart) down to mid and lower-tier managers.

Good examples of decentralized leadership include:

1. **Flat organizations:** Some companies, particularly in the technology sector, have adopted a flat organizational structure with minimal hierarchy and a decentralized leadership approach. In these companies, decisions are often made through collaboration and consensus-building, rather than by a single leader or small group of executives.

2. **Cooperatives:** Cooperatives are businesses that are owned and controlled by their members, who elect leaders and make decisions together. This form of decentralized leadership allows for equal participation and decision-making power among all members, rather than having a single leader or small group of leaders making decisions on behalf of the group.

3. **Community-based organizations:** Many non-profit organizations and community groups operate on the principle of decentralized leadership, with power and decision-making shared among members of the community. This approach can help to ensure that the needs and perspectives of all members are taken into account and can help to build trust and participation within the community.

4. **Virtual teams:** In a virtual team, members may be located in different geographic locations, and may not have the opportunity to work together face-to-face regularly. In these teams, decentralized leadership can help to ensure that all members have the opportunity to contribute and make decisions, regardless of their physical location.

To be fully actualized (Ha! Maslow again!), the sustainability movement cannot be directed by a few empowered individuals at the top of a virtual pyramid. In fact, to date, it hasn't. Much of the activism towards a more sustainable planet has been carried out by the young amongst us.

It must become a working part of our day and engrained in all of us as participants in the global economy. In the same way that workplace safety has become commonplace, so will the need for sustainability awareness.

298

Chapter 18:

Planet - Engineering Earth

We mentioned it earlier, but it bears repeating...

Carbon itself is not the problem. The problem is that there's too much carbon in our atmosphere and not enough carbon in our soil.

A core factor of the 5.0 revolution will be carbon; how to get more back in our soil ecosystems and in concert, reduce the carbon emissions our planet is subjected to every day.

In the same types of conversations that spurred our idea of Industry 5.0, we also discussed the big ideas behind it. We simply asked ourselves, "What is the best way to reclaim our planet?"

These discussions continued over months, and they began to evolve into a concept that we believe could (and should) be adopted worldwide. The idea began taking shape when we started thinking about the planet as a whole, not as individual cities, countries, or continents. We began to look at the Earth as one big, living, breathing organism.

Our focus soon became like that of a doctor and their patient. What if someone were sick with multiple ailments? How would we diagnose them? How would we treat them? And how would we measure the patient's progress? The focus is on the Earth as an entity. It's not regional, it's not societal and it's not governmental. The solutions need to focus on the interconnectivity of the entire planet.

We know that we must sequester large amounts of carbon (the act of returning carbon to our ecosystem). When we say "large amounts" we mean returning enough carbon equal to the emissions we see currently - by the way, that's about 110 million tons every day! We quickly realized that there was no manmade machine big enough to tackle this challenge. The only mechanism capable of repairing our planet is the planet itself. You see, the Earth is already one big carbon-sequestering machine…it just needs some tweaks and adjustments to keep up.

We deemed the concept, "Engineering Earth". In a way, it is as simple as that, using the natural defense system built into the planet to heal itself. However, the implementation, control, and management of such a program is a huge undertaking, requiring unprecedented amounts of cooperation and coordination.

Engineering Earth does focus on regenerative agriculture at the core, but we go way beyond that to not only responsibly cultivate carbon-sequestering cover crops, but to utilize the biomass and grain for more sustainable products downstream. Essentially, using the carbon sequestered in the growing process to reclaim the soil, but also using the carbon contained in the biomass to multiply the carbon benefits throughout the materials supply chain.

By using our knowledge of human psychology, we turn our thirst for advancement and our need to solve problems (Maslow!) into a giant carbon sequestration mechanism. In a perfect Industry 5.0 scenario, the more we produce and consume, the better it is for the planet. Let's take a look.

How Do We Engineer an Entire Planet?

Start by Asking the Right Questions

So, we know that the Earth is an intelligently designed carbon sequestration engine. Our planet's rainforests act as its lungs, its soil acts as its skin, and our waterways act as the circulatory system. Reengineering these systems (or rethinking how we as humans interact with them) to optimize the carbon cycle is the most effective solution we must create a sustainable future.

Think about this, about 37% of the land on Earth could be used for farming, ranch, or pasture lands. That means of the 37 billion total acres of land on Earth, we could use up to 13.7 billion acres to rescue the planet in the form of regenerative agriculture. Estimates are that just 2% of America's farmland could sequester 1 Gigaton of CO2. That's a lot of opportunity.

We spoke in detail about regenerative agriculture earlier, and of course, there's no way that we can flip a switch to move all farming to regenerative practices, but we must start somewhere! Implementing regenerative farming practices will empower Earth to store more carbon in less time than any man-made technology ever could!

The core of Engineering Earth starts with the soil, but we go far beyond that to create an ecosystem that dovetails with our economy and societal needs. So, to outline our idea, let's start with some conceptual questions:

- What if there was a way to standardize climate-smart agriculture and provide farmers with the tools and knowledge to grow crops more sustainably?
- What if there was a way to grow climate-smart crops that are proven to not only sequester more carbon, but grow in shorter cycles, with less water, with fewer pesticides or herbicides, and will improve soil quality year over year?
- What if there were a more efficient and cost-effective way to accurately calculate the massive carbon tonnage being sequestered and the total reduction in GHGs?
- What if there was a way to offer underserved farm/landowners a level playing field with the large, corporate-owned mega-farms by teaching them to rotate crops that require no expensive planting tools, no special harvesting machinery, nor elaborate irrigation methods?

- What if these crops could grow in virtually every farming region of the planet?
- What if we could use these crops not to compete with food, but processed to provide new, bio-based raw materials for industrial and commercial use?
- What if that processing is purposely designed to be done with less energy, in less time, and at lower costs/energy to transport?
- What if these new materials can replace established products that are dangerous to humans, as well as destructive to the planet?
- What if these new materials can be engineered in a way to reduce the carbon footprint of today's synthetic materials by 50% or more?
- What if these new materials can not only reduce the carbon footprint of traditional materials but also reduce weight, and increase strength all while lowering end-use costs?
- What if these new materials could create a new commodity asset class on the scale of oil, corn, or steel?
- What if there were willing customers, ready to purchase these materials in large quantities and the only limitations were available acreage to grow, and operational space to process?
- And finally, what if there were experts in these new raw materials that could educate the masses on all of these benefits and more?
    - Experts that have established partnerships with research institutions, underserved farmers, manufacturers, distributors, and end users.
    - Experts have established a gap in the marketplace for this commodity and have scores of customers who have approved these products for use in their supply chains.

- Experts who can market, and partner with marketers to launch this product (and the ancillary products) to a mass audience.

The ideas above are not simply theory; they are proven entities of a new biomaterials industry and the guiding theory of the concept. Engineering Earth will require three essential areas of human engagement to ensure the program's success - Education, Innovation, and Collaboration.

Education

Nelson Mandela once said, "Education is the most powerful weapon which you can use to change the world." We agree, and the entire point of Engineering Earth is to do just that...change the world. Through education, we can communicate not only the dangers of our unsustainable path but also the many positive courses of action that will be required to counter it.

Education takes place on multiple levels within Engineering Earth, and at the agricultural level, we seek to assist farmers (especially those underserved) with the methods and protocols for successfully rotating in new "industrial-use" crops like industrial hemp or flax.

By combining highly carbon-negative crops and piloting large-scale regenerative agriculture practices, the program will ensure drastic increases in above/below ground sequestered carbon, reduced GHG emissions, and improved soil health. The synergies will carry over year to year, and gain ever-increasing yields of all rotated crops, more carbon sequestered, less GHG emissions, and ultimately increased ecosystem sustainability (e.g., better nutrient cycles, reduced soil erosion, increased water quality, etc.).

At the consumer level, the program looks to enlighten the public on the advances of carbon-negative technologies and their viability in the marketplace. Consumers will need to be comfortable with knowing a portion of the goods they buy today (cars, furniture, home appliances, toys, electronics) will contain a higher level of biomaterials in the future. They also must have confidence that these products will perform at parity, or better than what is available today.

At the commodity purchaser level, we will allow those who participate in "traditional" supply chains and established materials, to understand the benefits of these new commodities. Biomaterials can compete on the global stage as they are lighter, stronger, and less cost in use, than the materials they will replace and/or augment. Commodity purchasers look for as much "insurance" as possible, especially when you consider that the raw materials are essentially perishables! But today the futures markets are full of those types of crops in the forms of wheat, corn, soy, rice, and so on.

At the research level, crop science will guide agronomists and farmers in developing new, innovative ways to capture carbon and measure those results. Methods will include leading-edge technology such as Artificial Intelligence (AI) on satellite imagery and on-ground biomass and soil sampling (e.g., Haney Soil Test Methods).

Innovation

Innovation is an entire chapter in this book, so no need to rehash the elements of sustainability innovations on the horizon, but as innovation is at the core of the project, an idea of the scope and breadth of new technologies that will bolster the Engineering Earth program is warranted. New tech sectors will include:

- Seed genetics
- Farming inputs, or more likely the reduction of inputs (nutrients, herbicides, pesticides, water)
- Low or no-till harvesting/planting equipment
- Localized sourcing (leading to more circular economies)
- Logistics efficiencies

- Storage and distribution
- Futures markets
- Carbon markets
- Industrial processing
- Materials R&D (both raw materials and finished products)
- Recycling

This is a short list, but an idea of the scope across industries that is needed to put a project like Engineering Earth into action. Even the name suggests that we will be blazing new trails, reaching far beyond the traditional to use our planet's natural defenses, combined with industry to combat the negative effects of environmental damage.

Collaboration

One person can build a wall. Get 5 million of them working together and you'll build the Great Wall of China!

Collaboration is the key to the success of such a large-scale project. Individually, each member could make incremental contributions to reversing carbon emissions, but collectively we have the power to enact that change across farms and industries all over the globe.

A program like Engineering Earth will need partners such as research organizations, chemistry labs, farmers, landowners, raw materials suppliers, product engineers, manufacturers, OEMs, investors, and consumers. A circular, sustainable economy will have a lot of moving parts!

It will take collective efforts, but individual actions (adopted on a large scale) are also crucial in achieving sustainability. Small changes in our daily lives, such as reducing energy and water consumption, recycling, and using sustainable modes of transportation can contribute to a more sustainable future. Furthermore, individual actions can influence social norms, policies, and practices, creating a ripple effect that can lead to broader changes.

Yes, it's a big idea, and cooperation across boundaries is essential, but we feel the message and potential simply lay the perfect foundation for collaboration across global societies and economies.

The Approach to On-farm Processes

As the Engineering Earth concept begins with farming, the efforts will go beyond regenerative practices to include the measurement and validation of the reduction in carbon emissions and in concert, the sequestering of carbon back into the soil. New methods will require accurate and timely measurements of soil health, in fact we see real-time measurements in our future.

Calculating these figures can be challenging for farmers, especially in smaller operations where sophisticated technical tools are certainly not available. The Engineering Earth project needs to be dedicated to both reducing costs for these farmers with initial supplements for inputs, but also long-term carbon improvements.

The research teams will need to build these models, most likely beginning with existing technology in the form of computer simulation programs like DayCent, which tightly integrates crop growth and biogeochemical processes, by optimizing industrial crop production (which does not exist today) and by doing so, we will create a model where farm efficiencies can be measured, monitored, and quantified.

These future models will be used to identify innovative management practices that help enhance yield, maximize soil carbon sequestration, decrease inputs, lower GHG emissions, and improve overall farm profitability. Each of these pushes us closer to our sustainability goals.

Equipment is also a limitation/barrier for smaller and new producers. Partnering with equipment manufacturers, the program seeks to provide shared regional equipment and eventually a fractional ownership model that decreases, or even eliminates CapEx investments for smaller farms. The primary benefactors of a program like this will be underserved producers starting in the U.S, with plans to expand globally.

The research teams' GHGs/Carbon sequestration focuses are:

- On-farm GHG emission and carbon sequestration estimations through DayCent-type modeling, machine learning models using satellite, and drone-based remote sensing data for crop biomass estimation, and life cycle and techno-economic analyses of commoditization processes.
- Carbon sequestration at the product level, LCAs as a result of material replacements.
- Decarbonization of all agricultural practices.

Finally, the program will remove producer barriers by developing, piloting, and testing climate-smart practices with all producer partners, which includes instruction and direct training for farmers on the benefits of industrial crops as rotational covers, low-till or no-till practices, nutrient management, reduction of fertilizer, herbicides, and pesticides, planting for a high carbon sequestration rate and crop rotation/diversification.

Ultimately the project will enable farmers to take a leadership role in addressing climate change in a holistically integrated project. The data, tools, and knowledge from this project will help identify optimal ways to leverage agriculture by creating the most cost-effective, scalable, climate-smart solutions.

Commercialization of Biomaterials for Industrial Use

Teaching farmers to grow new crops destined for commercial markets is just part of the program. If we simply moved farmers into new crop rotations, and more regenerative methods to improve their soil without a viable offtake path for the crops and associated biomass, the program falls flat on its face.

There must be a clear path to commercialization downstream to guarantee farmers healthy profits, and a consistent offtake for their product. The Engineering Earth program will not only revamp farming, but it must also engineer the path to market and the lasting desire of consumers for the products.

We start this by creating a reliable supply chain for biomass offtake. Much easier said than done, we're talking about a supply chain that doesn't exist, few set-asides for industrial crop acreage, no large-scale processing, no established sales channel, and little pull-through economics (today) to monetize the product.

So, how do we get this off the ground? Fortunately, we have a team who has been working on this idea for a few years.

The Engineering Earth idea is spearheaded by a nucleus of members who are currently doing significant work in the area of mitigating GHG emissions and enhancing carbon sequestration, while many of the project partners also account for vast experience in USDA funding capacity building and management. That covers the supply side, the demand side will be fueled by Industry 5.0.

How? Businesses, and manufacturers, in particular, will be looking beyond energy savings and conservation to lower their carbon footprints. Remember we spoke of Scope 1, 2, and 3 emissions, with Scope 3 having the major potential for impact. Scope 3 includes raw materials and purchased goods (that come from those raw materials).

Those materials in many cases today are not carbon friendly - think plastics, metals, and as we mentioned even wood. Many of these materials can be replaced, or more likely, augmented with biomaterials. A perfect example of this is in plastics. A lot of research is going into bioplastics and bio-additives that blend with polymers. Carbon footprints can be reduced up to 100% (pure bioplastics) and 50% or more with bio-additives. The trick is to find the right biomaterials that can be compounded into a variety of polymers, rubbers, asphalts, types of cement, particle boards, etc., all while being viable to grow in a traditional farming environment. The good news is that we are discovering those "Goldilocks" crops today. From bamboo to hemp to cotton and flax, we are seeing a new breed of industrial crops that don't require completely new farming models to grow them, and on top of that, they don't compete with our food crops due to the rotational nature of regenerative farming.

Engineering Earth Outcomes

The primary outcomes of Engineering Earth are to

- Reduce GHG emissions and increase carbon sequestration via climate-smart on-farm activities/practices.
- Create more reliable, scalable methods to measure the GHG and carbon benefits of industrial crops that are repeatable, correlatable, precise, and error-free.
- Create a more reliable, scalable carbon tracking mechanism via remote sensing technologies (verified by certified ground truthing efforts and third-party oversight),
- "Seed to Ship" supply chain carbon credit ownership supported by formal LCAs.
- Increase the awareness of biomaterials as "sustainable", and "eco-friendly" commodities and create a clear competitive advantage for farmers in the sustainability arena.
- Ultimately, we can create a pathway for new products that are made from sustainable materials and sourced using climate-smart technologies.

It's shaping up to be a perfect blend of agriculture and manufacturing opportunity. However, there is still a big gap in collaborative efforts among the private sector, farmers, and public institutions when it comes to biomaterials as commodities. However, this gap represents an opportunity for our team.

In addition to the creation of a new reliable raw material, is the parallel emergence of sustainability mandates that have manufacturers scrambling for new methods to reverse the adverse effects of their carbon-intensive products.

The solutions lie in both the benefit from the new breed of raw materials, and the rethinking of traditional manufacturing methods that can be tough on the environment. The Engineering Earth team knows that the task at hand is monumental and will not be easy. It requires long hours, dedication and getting their hands dirty...literally!

311

312

Chapter 19:

Potential - Where Can We Go from Here?

"Opportunities do not come with their values stamped upon them. Everyone must be challenged. A day dawns, quite like other days; in it, a single hour comes, quite like other hours; but in that day and in that hour the chance of a lifetime faces us."

— Maltbie Davenport Babcock

On the cusp of a Net Zero world in 2030, human progress will resonate harmoniously with the rhythm of nature. As we stand poised on the brink of transformative change, the horizon reveals the promise of a sustainable world where the ideals of innovation, collaboration, and conscious stewardship have woven together a tapestry of unprecedented achievement.

In this new era of collective determination, the concept of net zero has become more than a mere aspiration—it has evolved into the guiding North Star, lighting our path towards a tomorrow where human advancement and the embracing our planet are in perfect balance.

As we move forward into this era of Industry 5.0, we envision a world of clean technologies, regenerative practices, and enlightened mindsets, resulting in a world where our prosperity thrives hand-in-hand with environmental consciousness.

A Focus on Saving Our Natural Resources

We know that natural resources are essential for the survival of life on our planet. They provide us with the raw materials to produce food, clothing, shelter, and other necessities of life. The most critical natural resources are water, forests, minerals, soil, and air.

Here on Earth, water is the key element essential for life. Our attention to prudent consumption patterns and efficient use of water in agriculture and industry will become the norm. As a result, many regions worldwide that were facing water scarcity, will now see an abundance as conservation efforts increase and lift millions of people and the environment into a new vision of prosperity.

Forests are critical for regulating the Earth's climate, maintaining biodiversity, and providing vital ecosystem services. They also contribute significantly to the global economy through timber, non-timber forest products, and ecotourism. In a net zero world, the trajectory of deforestation will be dramatically altered as we embrace a profound shift in its relationship with forests and natural ecosystems. Deforestation, once a byproduct of unsustainable exploitation, will transform into a narrative of preservation, restoration, and coexistence.

Governments, industries, and communities worldwide will rally around activities that promote the conservation of forests as vital carbon sinks and biodiversity reservoirs. More sustainable land use practices will encourage land conservation, ensuring that forests remain intact and thriving.

Minerals are essential to produce almost everything we use in our daily lives, from electronics to construction materials. In a net zero world, the mining industry will undergo a profound metamorphosis, aligning its practices with sustainability and environmental stewardship. The traditional image of resource extraction marked by ecological degradation and carbon-intensive processes will give way to new thinking that prioritizes responsible mining, circular economies, and clean technologies.

Our air is affected by all the above. The overriding output of Industries 1 and 2 was an extreme amount of pollution that we now measure as GHGs or carbon emissions, and we now know that fossil fuels play the largest role in these. Renewable energy, EVs, lower carbon materials, and regenerative agriculture will all contribute to a return to the pure air our ancestors once enjoyed and allow us to pass an unpolluted world on to our children and grandchildren.

Overall, overexploitation and unsustainable consumption patterns will give way to fully sustainable actions that will lead us to a reclamation of natural resources, creating balance in ecosystems worldwide, and promoting sustainable living on our planet.

Reversing Biodiversity Loss

Biodiversity is crucial for maintaining ecological balance and providing essential ecosystem balance that affects our natural resources - clean water, air, and soil. In a net zero world, the reversal of biodiversity loss will emerge as a testament to humanity's dedication to restoring the natural cycle of life that sustains our planet. This effort will involve a combination of conservation, restoration, sustainable land management, and collective action on a global scale.

The creation and expansion of protected areas will play a pivotal role. Vast swaths of land and ocean will be safeguarded, allowing ecosystems to recover and thrive. These areas will serve as havens for endangered species and as beacons for ecological research and restoration techniques.

Efforts will focus on restoring degraded habitats to their natural state. Reforestation initiatives, wetland rehabilitation, and the removal of invasive species will help rejuvenate ecosystems, creating spaces where biodiversity can flourish once more. These carefully managed reintroductions will help restore ecosystems to their natural balance.

Biodiversity conservation and climate resilience will intertwine with our need to expand areas for new communities - think of the "Line" in Saudi Arabia!

Public awareness campaigns and educational programs will inspire a sense of responsibility for the natural world. Future generations will be raised with an understanding of the importance of biodiversity will contribute to its sustained protection.

Nations, organizations, and individuals will collaborate on a global scale, sharing knowledge, resources, and best practices. International agreements and initiatives will provide a framework for coordinated action, recognizing that biodiversity is borderless.

Sustainable Development

Sustainable development seeks to balance economic growth with environmental protection and social well-being. It's the core of what Industry 5.0 stands for. We recognize that the three pillars of sustainability - economic, environmental, and social - are interconnected and interdependent and that sustainable development can only be achieved by addressing all three of these pillars simultaneously.

Sustainable development aims to meet the needs of the present generation without compromising the ability of future generations to meet their own needs (our definition of sustainability). It involves the efficient use of natural resources, the reduction of pollution and waste, but doesn't stop there. It includes the promotion of social equity and inclusion.

We already see the beginnings of this movement. In Bhutan, the government has adopted a Gross National Happiness index to measure progress, focusing on factors such as social well-being, cultural preservation, and environmental sustainability.

In Costa Rica, they have balanced their efforts to promote protection of the environment and social well-being by implementing policies to promote ecotourism. This has helped to conserve the country's natural resources while generating economic benefits for local communities.

In Kenya, the Maasai Mara Wildlife Conservancies Association has created community-based conservancies that protect wildlife habitats while providing economic opportunities for local people.

These practices offer many benefits to people, the environment, and the economy. They create new job opportunities, reduce poverty and inequality, improve health and well-being, protect natural resources, and reduce greenhouse gas emissions simultaneously.

Renewable Energy Everywhere

The future of energy is here. By 2030, the world will see an enormous increase in renewable sources such as solar, wind, and hydropower. With advancements in technology outlined in the innovation chapter, many countries have begun investing heavily in renewable energy sources to reduce carbon emissions and create a sustainable future.

Industry 5.0 will spur more to join the effort, and we see the cost of renewable energy falling rapidly, making it more accessible and cost-effective for everyone. This trend is expected to continue, making it a viable option for anyone looking for an affordable and reliable source of electricity.

In addition, nuclear fusion will also be considered as a viable option. While the technology is still in its infancy, it will offer clear advantages over today's fission techniques. Fusion offers reliable and clean energy with minimal environmental impact, and without the need for uranium or plutonium for fuel. Fission could extract the base feedstock from isotopes of hydrogen - the most abundant element in our Universe. Furthermore, nuclear fusion power plants will be safer than fission, as any interruption in the process will cause the nuclear reaction to stop, and not "run-away" as our current technology does.

In this new era, wind turbines collect power from the breeze, solar panels silently collect the sun's power atop rooftops, and hydroelectric generators create power from the flowing of our rivers.

Through our collective efforts, we have harnessed the very elements that sustain life on Earth to drive progress, power homes, and fuel industries. The legacy of Industry 5.0 will not only be one of technological advancement but also a testament to our capacity to shape a harmonious coexistence with our planet.

The air will be fresher, the skies clearer, and the carbon footprint lighter. As we bid farewell to the ills of fossil fuels, we embrace a future of limitless possibilities powered by nature's abundant and renewable sources.

Sustainable Cities Become the Norm

Cities will be designed to be more sustainable, with an emphasis on public transportation, energy-efficient buildings, and green spaces. Urban planning will focus on reducing the carbon footprint of cities and improving the quality Sustainable cities are becoming the norm as more and more people realize the importance of living in an environment that is both energy efficient and environmentally friendly.

We will begin to recognize the importance of living in an environment that is both energy efficient and environmentally friendly and our communities will reflect this. With advances in green technology, architects and urban planners will be able to design cities that are not only aesthetically pleasing but also contribute to the long-term health of the environment. Sustainable cities will focus on reducing waste, promoting renewable energy sources, improving air quality, and creating lush green spaces for residents.

Sustainable cities are the future of urban planning. By using renewable energy sources, green spaces, and efficient design, cities can reduce their energy consumption while promoting healthier lifestyles. The goal is to create an environment that not only works for today but also for years to come.

The culmination of sustainable city planning, and the pursuit of net zero emissions paints a breathtaking picture. A vision of interconnected communities that have flourished through thoughtful design, conscious choices, and the commitment to a greener future.

As the view descends on the cities of 2030, they will stand as living testaments to the potential of human ingenuity, where bustling streets thrive in harmony with green spaces, efficient transportation networks hum with clean energy, and resilient infrastructures weather the storms of change.

It is our duty to evolve, adapt, and coexist with the environment that nurtures us (our final Maslow reference!). From the smallest energy-efficient dwelling to the grandest urban masterplans, the legacy of sustainable city planning resounds not only in the structures we have erected but in the culture of stewardship we have woven into our daily lives.

As we look towards a net zero future, let's remember that every choice made today echoes through the world of tomorrow. We will build cities that are not just statements of progress, but symbols of harmony—proof that a balance between humanity and nature is not only attainable but indispensable for the world we share.

Circular Economies Prevail

Local economies will thrive in our Net Zero future. The model encourages the reuse and sharing of resources, which reduces waste and costs while promoting sustainability. We will incentivize businesses to create sustainable products, sourced with local materials, and all while giving them a competitive edge in the marketplace.

Circular economies will emerge and revolutionize the way businesses and communities use resources. Based on the idea that resources should be used efficiently, reused, and recycled whenever possible, this approach to resource management will reduce waste, conserve energy, and minimize environmental degradation.

The concept will be an effective way to reduce our reliance on finite resources. By encouraging reuse, recycling, and the sharing of resources, we will move away from the wasteful linear model of take-make-dispose and towards a more sustainable approach.

New Technology Leads the Way

Technology will play a significant role in creating a sustainable future. For example, the Internet of Things (IoT) can be used to optimize energy use in buildings and homes, and blockchain technology can be used to create transparent supply chains and reduce waste.

New technologies have the potential to drastically reduce our environmental impact by enabling us to use resources, create renewable energy sources, and drastically reduce waste more efficiently. As technology advances, it is becoming increasingly easier to access information that can help us make better decisions and live more sustainably. From smart buildings that monitor energy usage to AI-powered energy management systems, there are a variety of tools and solutions available to help us create a more sustainable future.

From blockchain and Artificial Intelligence (AI) to automation, new technologies are providing solutions that can reduce environmental impacts, increase efficiency, and improve the quality of life for all.

These solutions are helping to create a more sustainable future for our planet and generations to come.

Some of the exciting new projects that are paving the way for a 5.0 future include:

1. **Carbon Capture and Utilization (CCU):** This technology involves capturing carbon dioxide emissions from power plants and industrial processes and using it to create new products, such as building materials or biofuels. CCU can help reduce greenhouse gas emissions and create new economic opportunities.
2. **Vertical Farms:** Vertical farms use advanced technologies such as hydroponics and LED lighting to grow crops in stacked layers, without the need for soil or pesticides.
3. **Electric and Autonomous Vehicles:** The widespread adoption of electric and autonomous vehicles can reduce emissions and improve air quality.
4. **Green Buildings:** Green buildings use sustainable materials and design features to reduce energy consumption and promote indoor air quality.
5. **Ocean Cleanup:** The Ocean Cleanup is a project aimed at cleaning up plastic pollution from the world's oceans.
6. **Sustainable Aviation:** The aviation industry is exploring new technologies such as electric and hybrid aircraft, as well as using sustainable biofuels, to reduce emissions and become more environmentally friendly.
7. **Carbon-Neutral Cities:** Some cities are committed to becoming carbon-neutral by 2050 or sooner and are implementing strategies such as investing in renewable energy, improving public transportation, and promoting sustainable development.

These are just a few examples of the many exciting new projects on our horizon, and that are paving the way for a greener future.

Sustainable Agriculture Worldwide

Agriculture is one of the most essential parts of ensuring a sustainable future for our planet, and we dedicated a good deal of this book to the topic. It involves farming practices that prioritize the conservation of natural resources, minimizing damage to soil and water, preserving biodiversity, and promoting the efficient use of land and other resources.

Not only does it help protect the environment, but it also helps to ensure food security for future generations by reducing reliance on chemical fertilizers and pesticides. Sustainable agriculture has been proven to be beneficial in both economic and environmental terms, making it a crucial component of achieving a sustainable future.

By 2030, we will witness a new wave of sustainable agriculture, with an emphasis on reducing the use of pesticides and fertilizers, using crop rotation and regenerative farming techniques, and promoting local and organic food production.

Cover crops will be a core element of sustainable farming, and the practice will spread to small and large farms alike. They will replenish the soil, reduce erosion and runoff, suppress weeds, and provide habitat for beneficial insects. Cover crops will also contribute to water conservation and improve crop yields. By increasing organic matter in the soil, they will make farms more resilient against climate change, leading to an increase in sustainable food production for generations to come. They will reduce soil erosion, improve soil fertility, and sequester carbon from the atmosphere.

Additionally, new technologies such as precision agriculture may be used to optimize farming practices and reduce waste. With these changes, we can ensure that agriculture remains sustainable in the future while feeding our growing population.

The story of Industry 5.0 and regenerative farming will be told by the endless landscapes that have been revitalized but in the very essence of nourishment, connection, and responsibility. With renewed viewpoint on sustainability, we will continue to sow the seeds of change, cultivating a world where every harvest not only feeds the body but replenishes the Earth.

When we stand in tomorrow's fields, we will witness a new understanding that our relationship with the land is not one of dominion, but of stewardship; that in healing the soil, we heal ourselves. Where farming is not just a means of sustenance, but a testament to the resilience of the human spirit and the enduring power of partnership with nature.

Conservation Will Be Natural and Effortless

In a 5.0 world, protecting our natural habitats will become a priority. We will come to realize that our world relies on the resources provided by nature to survive and function, and if we do not take care of them, they will be gone - forever!

Without them, we would surely face dire consequences, and we might see a world as Robinson outlines in "Ministry for the Future". Protecting the habitats that make up our environment will be important for us, and second nature to our future generations.

Overall, sustainable society in 2030 will be characterized by a greater emphasis on environmental protection, social responsibility, and economic stability. It will lead us to achieve a sustainable world, with most of the benefits reserved for future generations.

Becoming a Fully Sustainable Planet

"Fully - Sustainable - Planet" ... it has a nice ring to it!

Becoming a sustainable planet by reducing our carbon footprint cannot be accomplished by one initiative. There is no one law, mandate, or corporate initiative that can save our planet. It's a collective effort of millions of companies and billions of people taking little steps every day. Those little steps all contribute to the collective march towards the Industry 5.0 era.

It's unrealistic to think we can use reductionistic methodologies to solve holistic problems. To say it in other words – it will take a revolution to accomplish all of these goals.

In this book we've discussed in detail:

- Why sustainability is paramount to not only our survival but also the entire planet.
- How we need to hone our focus on the end game.
- Where the biggest changes will take place.
- What methods will get us there.
- When the best time to begin is - immediately, if not sooner!

Industry 5.0 will be the first industrial revolution that begins to proactively cure the unintended ills of the first four. We will see regenerative farming come back into vogue, companies will value the emotional currency of their employees as much as their profits, and humanity may begin to put its self-centered goals aside for more altruistic values.

Sustainable decision-making throughout the value chain will be foundational to our planet's ability to thrive into the future. Avoiding the issues confronted in this next revolution could certainly lead to our extinction and the eventual destruction of our planet.

But let's be optimistic for a moment (if you've noticed, we've tried to keep the aim of this chapter pointed towards the optimistic) and envision what the future will look like if we meet our environmental goals, if we act on the mandates, and take the issue of sustainability seriously. What will the world look like by 2030 if we are successful? We are confident that it will look more like our vision of 5.0, and less like the current path we're on.

This is why we feel so strongly about our views on 5.0, and why we have ingrained it completely into our business model, our daily lives, and we aren't the only ones. Cultural norms are shifting, and we as people are fundamentally tackling the most important issues of our lifetimes. Individuals, communities, and now corporations are shifting their views and embracing sustainability.

Gone are the days of pushing the issue off as something to think about later, or someone else's problem. We now see sustainability front and center, where it belongs. And the collective "We" are doing something about it. What a revolutionary time to be alive!

326

Appendix A

Sustainable Business Glossary

BSR

Business for Social Responsibility

International business coalition and sustainability consultancy originally known as Business for Social Responsibility. Today, it's known as BSR. From their website, BSR is described as "...a sustainable business network and consultancy focused on creating a world in which all people can thrive on a healthy planet."

"Through our insights, advisory services, and collaborations, we enable business transformation to create long-term value for business and society."

BSR's focus areas include:

- Climate Change
- Equity, Inclusion, and Justice
- Human Rights
- Nature
- Supply Chain Sustainability
- Sustainability Management

https://www.bsr.org/

CDP

Formerly known as Climate Disclosure Project but now just CDP.

From their website, "CDP is a not-for-profit charity that runs the global disclosure system for investors, companies, cities, states and regions to manage their environmental impacts. Over the past 20 years we have created a system that has resulted in unparalleled engagement on environmental issues worldwide."

https://www.cdp.net/en

CDSB

The Climate Disclosure Standards Board

From their website, "CDSB is an international consortium of business and environmental NGOs. We are committed to advancing and aligning the global mainstream corporate reporting model to equate natural capital with financial capital."

"We do this by offering companies a framework for reporting environmental information with the same rigour as financial information. In turn this helps them to provide investors with decision-useful environmental information via the mainstream corporate report, enhancing the efficient allocation of capital. Regulators also benefit from compliance-ready materials."

"Recognising that information about natural capital and financial capital is equally essential for an understanding of corporate performance, our work builds the trust and transparency needed to foster resilient capital markets. Collectively, we aim to contribute to more sustainable economic, social and environmental systems."

https://www.cdsb.net/

CR&S - CSR

Corporate Responsibility and Sustainability - Corporate Social Responsibility

The two terms here are very similar, and typically cross-reference definitions when searching. According to Learning to Give.org, CR&S/CSR is, "... any action a corporation does to benefit the relationship between a corporation and the community, and to make a positive difference in the community with employee engagement, financial support, and volunteerism. Corporate social responsibility is a business trying to do well in the community through responsible actions."

https://www.learningtogive.org/resources/corporate-social-responsibility-and-sustainability

CSO

Chief Sustainability Officer – the most senior executive in the business responsible directly for sustainability

Most of us are very familiar with the C-suite positions. CEO, COO, CFO and such. However, newer to the scene is the CSO, or Chief Sustainability Officer. There are other CSOs - Chief Security Officer, Chief Sales Officer, etc., but for this discussion we're focusing on sustainability (obviously!).

The CSO will create, author and develop company strategies to address issues such as energy use, resource conservation, recycling, pollution reduction, waste elimination, transportation, education, and building efficiency. They also serve as the sustainability champion, often overseeing training efforts for all functions within the organization.

CSRD

Corporate Sustainability Reporting Directive – proposed EU replacement for NFRD

From the European Commission on Finance, "EU law requires all large companies and all listed companies (except listed micro-enterprises) to disclose information on their risks and opportunities arising from social and environmental issues, and on the impacts of their activities on people and the environment.

This helps investors, civil society organizations, consumers, and other stakeholders to evaluate the sustainability performance of companies, as part of the European green deal entered into force. This new directive modernizes and strengthens the rules about the social and environmental information that companies must report. A broader set of large companies, as well as listed SMEs, will now be required to report on sustainability – approximately 50 000 companies in total.

The new rules will ensure that investors and other stakeholders have access to the information they need to assess investment risks arising from climate change and other sustainability issues. They will also create a culture of transparency about the impact of companies on people and the environment. Finally, reporting costs will be reduced for companies over the medium to long term by harmonizing the information to be provided."

https://finance.ec.europa.eu/capital-markets-union-and-financial-markets/company-reporting-and-auditing/company-reporting/corporate-sustainability-reporting_en

DE&I

Diversity, Equity and Inclusion

DE&I is a conceptual framework that claims to promote the fair treatment and full participation of all people, especially in the workplace, including populations who have historically been under-represented or subject to discrimination because of their background, identity, disability, etc.

From Wikipedia "Diversity" describes a wide variety of differences that may exist amongst people in any community, including race, ethnicity, nationality, gender and sexual identity, disability, neurodiversity, and others.

"Equity" is the practice of providing fair opportunities via personalized approaches based on individual needs, thus aiming to "level the playing field" by taking into account the different starting points of different individuals. Therefore, "equity" aims to achieve fairness by considering each individual's trajectory and context, and should not be confused with the notion of "equality" which aims to treat everyone the same.

"Inclusion" specifies the desired outcome, namely, ensuring that individuals find opportunities and spaces to participate, regardless of their differences.

https://www.dictionary.com/browse/dei

https://en.wikipedia.org/wiki/Diversity,_equity,_and_inclusion#cite_note-1

EPR

Extended Producer Responsibility

Extended Producer Responsibility is a concept where manufacturers and importers of products should bear a significant degree of responsibility for the environmental impacts of their products throughout the product life-cycle, including upstream impacts inherent in the selection of materials for the products, impacts from manufacturers' production process itself, and downstream impacts from the use and disposal of the products.

A great example of this is a car with an internal combustion engine. The manufacturer is not responsible for the carbon emissions to build the vehicle, but the fossil fuel emissions of its anticipated lifetime on the road.

Producers accept their responsibility when designing their products to minimize life-cycle environmental impacts, and when accepting legal, physical, or socio-economic responsibility for environmental impacts that cannot be eliminated by design.

https://www.oecd.org/env/waste/factsheetextendedproducerresponsibility.htm

ESG

Environmental, Social and Corporate Governance

We see ESG mentioned a great deal in the finance and investment world. This is because it is becoming increasingly important to portfolio analysts and advisors as to stability and growth of firms, especially with the 5.0 revolution upon us. ESG as described earlier is essentially:

4. Environmental: The environmental aspect of ESG focuses on a company's impact on the natural environment. This includes factors such as carbon emissions, energy efficiency, waste management, pollution, resource consumption, and climate change adaptation. Assessing a company's environmental performance helps identify its efforts to mitigate environmental risks, promote sustainability, and contribute to the transition to a low-carbon economy.

5. Social: The social aspect of ESG refers to a company's impact on society, including its relationships with employees, customers, communities, and other stakeholders. It encompasses factors such as labor practices, human rights, diversity and inclusion, employee health and safety, product quality and safety, community engagement, and philanthropy. Evaluating a company's social performance helps determine its commitment to social responsibility, ethical practices, and positive social impact.

6. Governance: The governance aspect of ESG focuses on the systems and structures that govern a company's operations and decision-making processes. It includes factors such as board composition and independence, executive

compensation, shareholder rights, transparency, risk management, and corporate ethics. Evaluating a company's governance practices helps assess its accountability, integrity, and alignment of interests with shareholders and stakeholders.

As mentioned above, ESG factors are increasingly considered by investors, regulators, and other stakeholders as important indicators of a company's long-term value and sustainability. They provide a deeper look into a company's impact on the environment, society, and its overall governance framework. ESG analysis is increasingly important to investors to help make more informed decisions, and it enables companies to manage risks and thereby seize new opportunities in the pursuit of responsible business practices.

FASB

Financial Accounting Standards Board

Established in 1973, the Financial Accounting Standards Board (FASB) is the independent, private- sector, not-for-profit organization based in Norwalk, Connecticut, that establishes financial accounting and reporting standards for public and private companies and not-for-profit organizations that follow Generally Accepted Accounting Principles (GAAP).

The FASB is recognized by the U.S. Securities and Exchange Commission as the designated accounting standard setter for public companies. FASB standards are recognized as authoritative by many other organizations, including state Boards of Accountancy and the American Institute of CPAs (AICPA). The FASB develops and issues financial accounting standards through a transparent and inclusive process intended to promote financial reporting that provides useful information to investors and others who use financial reports.

The Financial Accounting Foundation (FAF) supports and oversees the FASB. Established in 1972, the FAF is the independent, private-sector, not-for- profit organization based in Norwalk, Connecticut, responsible for the oversight, administration, financing, and appointment of the FASB and the Governmental Accounting Standards Board (GASB).

https://www.fasb.org/facts

GRI & GSSB

Global Reporting Initiative

GRI was founded in Boston (USA) in 1997 following on from the public outcry over the environmental damage of the Exxon Valdez oil spill, eight years previously. Our roots lie in the non-profit organizations CERES and the Tellus Institute, with involvement of the UN Environment Programme. The aim was to create the first accountability mechanism to ensure companies adhere to responsible environmental conduct principles, which was then broadened to include social, economic and governance issues.

The first version of what was then the GRI Guidelines (G1) published in 2000 – providing the first global framework for sustainability reporting. The following year, GRI was established as an independent, non-profit institution. In 2002, the GRI's Secretariat relocated to Amsterdam (The Netherlands), and the first update to the Guidelines (G2) launched. As demand for GRI reporting and uptake from organizations steadily grew, the Guidelines were expanded and improved, leading to G3 (2006) and G4 (2013).

In 2016, GRI transitioned from providing guidelines to setting the first global standards for sustainability reporting – the GRI Standards. The Standards continue to be updated and added to, including new Standards on Tax (2019) and Waste (2020), a major update to the Universal Standards (2021) and the continued roll-out of Sector Standards (2021 onwards).

https://www.globalreporting.org/

Global Sustainability Standards Board

The GSSB has sole responsibility for setting the world's first globally accepted standards for sustainability reporting – the GRI Standards. Established as an independent operating entity under the auspices of GRI, GSSB members represent a range of expertise and multi-stakeholder perspectives on sustainability reporting.

The GSSB works exclusively in the public interest and according to the vision and mission of GRI.

https://www.globalreporting.org/standards/global-sustainability-standards-board/

IASB, IFRS, IIRC, ISSB, & SASB

International Accounting Standards Board

The International Accounting Standards Board (IASB) is an independent, private-sector body that develops and approves International Financial Reporting Standards (IFRSs). The IASB operates under the oversight of the IFRS Foundation. The IASB was formed in 2001 to replace the International Accounting Standards Committee (IASC). A full history of the IASB and the IASC going back to 1973 is available on the IASB website.

Under the IFRS Foundation Constitution, the IASB has complete responsibility for all financial reporting-related technical matters of the IFRS Foundation including:

- Full discretion in developing and pursuing its technical agenda, subject to certain consultation requirements with the Trustees and the public
- The preparation and issuing of IFRSs (other than Interpretations) and exposure drafts, following the due process stipulated in the Constitution

- The approval and issuing of Interpretations developed by the IFRS Interpretations Committee

https://www.iasplus.com/en/resources/ifrsf/iasb-ifrs-ic/iasb

International Financial Reporting Standards

The IFRS Foundation is a not-for-profit, public interest organisation established to develop high-quality, understandable, enforceable and

globally accepted accounting and sustainability disclosure standards.

Our Standards are developed by our two standard-setting boards, the International Accounting Standards Board (IASB) and International Sustainability Standards Board (ISSB).

https://www.ifrs.org/

IIRC International Integrated Reporting Council

The International Integrated Reporting Framework and Integrated Thinking Principles have been developed and are used around the world, in 75 countries, to advance communication about value creation, preservation and erosion.

The cycle of integrated reporting and thinking result in efficient and productive capital allocation, acting as a force for financial stability and sustainable development.

Integrated reporting aims to:

- Improve the quality of information available to providers of financial capital to enable a more efficient and productive allocation of capital
- Promote a more cohesive and efficient approach to corporate reporting that draws on different reporting strands and

communicates the full range of factors that materially affect the ability of an organization to create value over time

- Enhance accountability and stewardship for the broad base of capitals (financial, manufactured, intellectual, human, social and relationship, and natural) and promote understanding of their independencies
- Support integrated thinking, decision-making and actions that focus on the creation of value over the short, medium and long term

The Integrated Reporting Framework and Integrated Thinking Principles are maintained under the auspices of the IFRS Foundation, a global not-for-profit, public interest organisation established to develop high-quality, understandable, enforceable and globally accepted accounting and sustainability disclosure standards.

https://www.integratedreporting.org/the-iirc-2/

International Sustainability Standards Board

A proposed new body under IFRS. The International Sustainability Standards Board (ISSB), established at COP26 to develop a comprehensive global baseline of sustainability disclosures for the capital markets, today launched a consultation on its first two proposed standards. One sets out general sustainability-related disclosure requirements and the other specifies climate-related disclosure requirements.

https://www.ifrs.org/news-and-events/news/2022/03/issb-delivers-proposals-that-create-comprehensive-global-baseline-of-sustainability-disclosures/

Sustainability Accounting Standards Board

SASB Standards guide the disclosure of financially material sustainability information by companies to their investors. Available for 77 industries, the Standards identify the subset of environmental, social, and governance issues most relevant to financial performance in each industry.

Effective August 1, 2022, the Value Reporting Foundation–home to the SASB Standards–consolidated into the IFRS Foundation, which established the first International Sustainability Standards Board (ISSB). SASB Standards are now under the oversight of the ISSB. The ISSB will build upon the SASB Standards and embed SASB's industry-based standards development approach into the ISSB's standards development process. The ISSB actively encourages preparers and investors to continue to provide full support for and to use the SASB Standards until the SASB Standards become the IFRS Sustainability Disclosure Standards.

https://www.sasb.org/

IBE

Institute of Business Ethics

The IBE is an important partner to any business wanting to preserve its long-term reputation by doing business in the right way.

All organisations need to demonstrate they are trustworthy in order to operate effectively and sustainably. Reputations are not based solely on the delivery of products and services, but on how an organisation values its stakeholders. Having a reputation for acting with honesty and integrity not only differentiates an organisation, it makes it more successful.

Since 1986, the IBE has advised organisations on how to strengthen their ethical culture by sharing knowledge and good practice, resulting in relationships with employees and stakeholders that are based on trust.

We achieve this by:

- Acting as a critical friend to organisations we work with

- Advising senior business leaders and those with responsibility for developing and embedding corporate ethics policies
- Supporting the development of these policies through networking events, regular publications, research and benchmarking as well as training
- Providing guidance to staff through bespoke training and decision-making tools
- Educating the next generation of business leaders in schools and universities.

The IBE is a registered charity funded by corporate and individual donations. https://www.ibe.org.uk/

IPCC

Inter-Governmental Panel on Climate Change

Created in 1988 by the World Meteorological Organization (WMO) and the

United Nations Environment Programme (UNEP), the objective of the IPCC is to provide governments at all levels with scientific information that they can use to develop climate policies. IPCC reports are also a key input into international climate change negotiations. The IPCC is an organization of governments that are members of the United Nations or WMO. The IPCC currently has 195 members. Thousands of people from all over the world contribute to the work of the IPCC. For the assessment reports, experts volunteer their time as IPCC authors to assess the thousands of scientific papers published each year to provide a comprehensive summary of what is known about the drivers of climate change, its impacts and future risks, and how adaptation and mitigation can reduce those risks. An open and transparent review by experts and governments around the world is an essential part of the IPCC process, to ensure an objective and complete assessment and to reflect a diverse range of views and expertise. Through its assessments, the IPCC identifies the strength of scientific agreement in different areas and indicates where further research is needed.

https://www.ipcc.ch/about/

NGOs

Non-governmental organizations.

An NGO, or Non-Governmental Organization, refers to a non-profit, voluntary organization that operates independently from government entities and is typically driven by a specific mission or cause. NGOs are often created by individuals or groups to address societal, environmental, or humanitarian issues and work towards the betterment of communities and the world at large.

The world is full of non-governmental organizations (NGOs) that are dedicated to improving the lives of people, animals, and the environment. From Amnesty International to Greenpeace, from Médecins Sans Frontières to World Wildlife Fund and Oxfam, these renowned NGOs have made it their mission to make a positive difference in the world. But there are many other lesser-known NGOs that strive every day to do their part in making this planet a better place.

Non-governmental organizations (NGOs) play a critical role in tackling some of the most pressing social and environmental issues of our time. They strive to stand up for those who have been neglected or overlooked, advocate for human rights, and work to create a more sustainable future. From providing food aid to developing countries to advocating for the rights of women and children, NGOs are essential players in creating positive change in our world.

SDGs

Sustainable Development Goals of the United Nations

The 2030 Agenda for Sustainable Development, adopted by all United Nations Member States in 2015, provides a shared blueprint for peace and prosperity for people and the planet, now and into the future. At its heart are the 17 Sustainable Development Goals (SDGs), which are an urgent call for action by all countries - developed and developing - in a global partnership. They recognize that ending poverty and other deprivations must go hand-in-hand with strategies that improve health and education, reduce inequality, and spur economic growth – all while tackling climate change and working to preserve our oceans and forests.

The SDGs build on decades of work by countries and the UN, including the UN Department of Economic and Social Affairs

https://sdgs.un.org/goals

TCFD & TNFD

Taskforce Climate Financial Disclosures - How companies should report on their climate impacts

One of the essential functions of financial markets is to price risk to support informed, efficient capital-allocation decisions. To carry out this function, financial markets need accurate and timely disclosure from companies. Without the right information, investors and others may incorrectly price or value assets, leading to a misallocation of capital.

The Financial Stability Board (FSB) created the TCFD to develop recommendations on the types of information that companies should disclose to support investors, lenders, and insurance underwriters in appropriately assessing and pricing a specific set of risks—risks related to climate change.

https://www.fsb-tcfd.org/about/

Taskforce on Nature-related Financial Disclosures – how companies should report on their nature impacts

The mission of the Taskforce on Nature-related Financial Disclosures is to develop and deliver a risk management and disclosure framework for organisations to report and act on evolving nature-related risks, with the ultimate aim of supporting a shift in global financial flows away from nature-negative outcomes and toward nature-positive outcomes.

https://tnfd.global/

UNGC

United Nations Global Compact

The United Nations Global Compact is a voluntary initiative launched by the United Nations in 2000. It encourages businesses and organizations to adopt sustainable and socially responsible policies and practices. Participants commit to ten principles in areas such as human rights, labor, environment, and anti-corruption. The UNGC serves as a platform for companies to engage in dialogue, share best practices, and collaborate on sustainability issues.

https://unglobalcompact.org/about

VRF

Value Reporting Foundation – (merger of SASB and IIRC)

The Value Reporting Foundation (formerly the International Integrated Reporting Council - IIRC) is an organization that promotes integrated reporting as a means for companies to communicate their broader value creation story, including financial and non-financial information, to stakeholders. Integrated reporting provides a holistic view of an organization's strategy, governance, performance, and prospects, integrating financial, environmental, social, and governance (ESG) information in a single report.

https://www.valuereportingfoundation.org/

344

About the Author

John Ely is the current Chief Marketing Officer at Heartland Industries. He is responsible for evaluating, developing, and implementing strategic marketing and corporate growth plans and directing all business development initiatives. Heartland is a material science company that engineers natural fiber additives to lower the carbon footprint of plastics and other high-carbon materials.

Along with the marketing duties, John publishes articles on sustainability, regenerative agriculture, the future of polymers, and material science - to name a few. He has won four Bronze Quill awards for his business writing along the way.

John's sustainability journey started long before it was fashionable. His career included product management on solar/photovoltaic electronics in the 1990s and as a business partner in a Northern California solar business in the early 2000s. From there he worked with plastics manufacturers and contributed to BASF's Zero Energy Home in 2005. In the 2010s, he worked on AMETEK's Solar Products Team.

John is an accomplished executive, developing and managing marketing departments for companies such as A Solar, UNIPOWER, AMETEK, and Crane Plastics. He holds undergraduate degrees in Engineering, Business Management and a Master's Degree in Marketing and Communications.

John also served as an adjunct professor at Franklin University where he taught business, marketing, and advertising courses, and currently serves as an instructor at the University of Akron's Polymer Training Center. He is a former corporate mentor at The Ohio State University's Fisher College of Business and serves on the Board of Directors at the Ohio Energy Project.

346

Made in the USA
Monee, IL
19 September 2024

65997086R00207